CATHY PORTER was bo.... .... 1947 and grew up there. She spent a year in Poland before studying Russian and Czech at London University. Since then she has written extensively on the political, cultural and intellectual life of nineteenth- and twentieth-century Russia. She is the author of *Fathers and Daughters: Russian Women in the Revolution*, *Alexandra Kollontai: A Biography*, and books on the 1905 revolution, Moscow in the Second World War and the Civil War. She has also translated Kollontai's fiction and Tsvetayeva's diaries. Cathy Porter lives in London.

VIRAGO PIONEERS are important reassessments of the lives and ideas of women from every walk of life and all periods of history, re-evaluating their contribution in the light of work done over the past twenty years or more – work that has led to important changes of perspective on women's place in history and contemporary life.

LARISSA REISNER

CATHY PORTER

Published by VIRAGO PRESS Limited 1988
41 William IV Street, London WC2N 4DB

British Library Cataloguing in Publication Data

Porter, Cathy
  Larissa Reisner.
  1. Reisner, Larissa—Biography
  2. Authors, Russian—20th century
  —Biography
  I. Title
  947.084′092′4   PG3476.R4Z/

  ISBN 0-86068-857-7

Typeset by Florencetype Ltd. of Kewstoke, Avon
Printed in Great Britain by Cox & Wyman Ltd. of Reading, Berkshire

CONTENTS

TRANSLITERATION, DATES AND ACKNOWLEDGEMENTS

There are several approved systems of Russian transliteration. Mine follows one popular with British historians, rather than any standard convention, so that in the text the common Russian surname ending is rendered 'y' (as in Dzherzhinsky), the Russian name 'Larisa' is rendered 'Larissa' for easier pronunciation, and other names already familiar in English (like Sofia, Lydia, Alexander) will also be given in their anglicised versions. In the notes, names and the translations of Russian book titles and their authors will be given in a modified version of the Library of Congress transliteration system.

Until January 1918, dates are given according to the old Russian calendar, thirteen days behind that of the west. The new calendar was actually adopted at the end of February 1918, but to avoid confusion I have followed those who use New Style dates from the beginning of January 1918, and have indicated them with the abbreviation NS in brackets.

I would like to thank Andrew Rothstein for speaking about his friendship with Reisner, giving me books, searching for sources and ensuring that the book was written, as well as for his numerous constructive comments on the manuscript.

CHRONOLOGY

1894   Tsar Nicholas II comes to the throne. Rapid expansion of Russian industry. Disastrous harvests, followed by famine. Mikhail Reisner and Ekaterina Khitrova meet and marry in Lublin, Poland.

1895   *1 May*: The Reisners' daughter, Larissa, is born.

1896   Thirteen hundred people are crushed to death during celebrations of Nicholas II's coronation. A wave of strikes hits St Petersburg.

1897   More disastrous harvests, followed by famine.

1898   Founding of the Marxist Social Democratic Labour Party, and of the Second, Socialist, International. The Reisners move to Tomsk, in Siberia, where Reisner teaches law at the university.

1899   Igor Reisner is born.

1901   The new Socialist Revolutionary Party carries out numerous terrorist assassinations of government ministers and officials.

1902   Throughout Russia, peasants riot, workers strike and students demonstrate for reforms; Reisner supports the students' cause.

1903   The Reisners leave Russia to avoid arrest, and move to Berlin.

1904   Russia declares war on Japan. In Russia, defeats unleash demonstrations, riots and strikes. In Berlin, Reisner defends German socialists tried in Berlin for crimes against the Russian Tsar.

1905   *9 January*: 'Bloody Sunday' is the start of Russia's first revolution. Reisner becomes a Bolshevik.

1907 The revolution is defeated. Terrorists carry out over two thousand assassinations. The Reisners return to St Petersburg. Larissa is enrolled at a girls' *gimnazium*.

1908 Reaction is triumphant in Russia.

1911 More student riots. The Tsar's court comes under the influence of the 'holy man' Rasputin. Russia promotes the first of a series of wars in the Balkans for control of the Ottoman Empire. More terrorist assassinations.

1912 The strike movement grows. Larissa starts writing poetry.

1913 Tsar Nicholas is urged on by his foreign minister to aim for world domination, via the Black Sea and the Dardanelles. The Bolsheviks sponsor anti-war Women's Day demonstrations in Moscow, St Petersburg and elsewhere. Larissa enters the University of St Petersburg.

1914 *28 July*: Austria declares war on Serbia; *2 August*: Russia enters the war to protect Serbia; *4 August*: England declares war on Germany.

1915 Russia driven out of Serbia. At the front, whole regiments surrender. At home, living costs soar and wages decline. There is open talk of revolution. The Bolsheviks' popularity grows. Larissa launches *Rudin*, a satirical anti-war magazine.

1916 A massive mobilisation for a new offensive against Germany, in which two million Russian lives are lost. Russia's industry, agriculture and government are in chaos. *Rudin* is closed by the censors. Larissa writes articles for Gorky's socialist journal *Chronicle*.

1917 *23 February*: Women demonstrate in their thousands on the streets of the newly renamed Petrograd. The Tsar abdicates, in favour of the new Provisional Government. Bolshevik leaders – Lenin, Trotsky, Kollontai and others – return from exile. Larissa teaches literacy and literature at workers' clubs, meets a number of leading Bolsheviks, including Fyodor Raskolnikov, and is drawn into the Revolution. A new offensive against Germany brings yet more defeats and sufferings at the front. *25 October*: The Bolsheviks take power at the Second All-Russian

Congress of Soviets, and declare an end to the war. Larissa works for the new government, cataloguing the art treasures of the old régime.

1918   Tsarist officers and ministers form the new White Guard army to defeat the Revolution, and Britain, France, Japan and the US plan to invade. *February*: The first Allied landings in North Russia. *March*: The Germans resume their invasion. The Bolsheviks sign the Brest–Litovsk treaty with Germany. *May*: Czech prisoners of war rise up against the Bolsheviks, and the Civil War starts in earnest. *Summer*: Larissa joins the Bolshevik party, marries Fyodor Raskolnikov and leaves Moscow, with sailors of the Volga Naval Flotilla, to fight the Czechs and Whites. She starts writing her 'Letters From The Front'. *December*: She becomes the Red Army's first woman political commissar.

1919   *Summer*: The Whites are in the Crimea and the British are at Tsaritsyn. Larissa Reisner fights at Tsaritsyn, until it falls to the Whites, then she leaves for Astrakhan. *Autumn*: Bolshevik fortunes start to improve, and the Whites are driven from Petrograd and south Russia.

1920   *April*: The Poles attack Russia from the west, but the Bolsheviks gain the Northern Caucasus. Larissa takes part in the campaign to drive the British out of neighbouring Persia, where she contracts malaria. *Late summer*: The Poles drive the Red Army back from Lvov and Warsaw. *October*: Larissa visits Riga, to cover for *Izvestiya* the signing of a peace treaty with Poland.

1921   The Whites are in tatters and the Allies are forced to withdraw. *March*: With the war over, the New Economic Policy is introduced, to restart the economy. *Late March*: Raskolnikov is appointed first Soviet ambassador in Afghanistan. *May*: Larissa accompanies him to Kabul, to work with the women of the Afghan Emir's harem and persuade them to support the Bolsheviks. She writes a series of articles there, which are later turned into a book, *Afghanistan*.

1923 Larissa returns to Moscow, where she attends writers' meetings and works as a journalist. *September*: she visits Berlin and Hamburg as a clandestine Comintern officer and journalist, taking part in the aborted revolution there, and describing it in *Hamburg at the Barricades*. She embarks on a relationship with Karl Radek.

1924 Larissa ends her marriage to Raskolnikov. Her 'Letters From The Front' are published as a book, *The Front*. *Late summer*: She travels around the Urals, Northern Siberia, Byelorussia and the textile regions near Moscow as a special *Izvestiya* correspondent, and adopts twelve-year-old Alyosha Markarov, an orphan. These travels throughout industrial Russia are the subject of her book, *Coal, Iron and Living People*. *Winter*: she visits Germany again, and writes more articles, for *Izvestiya* and *Red Paper*.

1925 Although weakened by exhaustion and frequent malaria attacks, Larissa continues work as a journalist, and she writes a jubilee monograph about the Decembrist uprising of 1825.

1926 Larissa contracts typhus, and on 9 February, she dies.

INTRODUCTION

'Nature gave her everything, intelligence, talent and beauty,' wrote the poet Lev Nikulin.[1] Fighter, writer, first Bolshevik woman commissar, Larissa Reisner, the 'Revolutionary Pallas', had an almost magnetic fame in the 1920s. To many Communists in Europe and Soviet Russia who knew her, she seemed to embody all the heroic newness of the Revolution – a model for the future, and of the 'new Soviet woman'.

She was a larger-than-life figure, and her short life was such a full one, even in those revolutionary times, that it is often hard to see her clearly through the halo of legends and hyperboles surrounding her, or to detach ourselves from the rich, sometimes overpowering language of her writings. These writings span only a decade, but they evoke a whole epoch, and they will be the focus for this short account of her life.

Thrown from poetry into revolution, she joined the Bolshevik Party in 1918, at the age of twenty-two. For the next two years she sailed on the great warships of the new Red Navy, fighting on the front line of the Civil War from Kazan to the Caspian Sea. And there she found her own style to describe the horror and the heroism of those years.

Those early heady days of the Revolution produced a whole new generation of women. Thousands of them, most also in their teens or early twenties (and most, like Reisner, without children), left home to fight with the Reds and set about creating for themselves a new life, no longer bound by family and marriage. Strong, proud, liberated and idealistic, the 'new Soviet woman' inspired generations of Soviet women to come.

Western feminists may find it easier to identify with Alexandra Kollontai and the first generation of women Bolsheviks, who articulated the old dilemmas facing women in the revolutionary movement since its origins in the 1860s – the choice between working to free themselves, or sacrificing their own interests to the general struggle. Kollontai struggled throughout her life for a synthesis between the two, campaigning within Russian socialism for women's rights, and appealing directly to women themselves to make their own demands of the Revolution.

As the daughter of this generation of socialist feminists (and of cultured socialist parents who supported women's rights), Larissa Reisner was able to take for granted much of what they had struggled for. Unlike Kollontai, she was reticent about the personal and specific aspects of women's liberation in revolution, and was never primarily involved in addressing the inequalities which women continued to suffer after the Bolsheviks took power. Nor (unlike Kollontai) would she have had the prestige or experience in the Party to do so had she wanted.

Larissa Reisner came of age at a time when it finally seemed possible for women to overstep the conventional female ethic of submission, renunciation and domesticity. Her writings vibrate with the power and challenge of women's life in the Revolution, and of the limitless possibilities, uncertainties and dangers opening up for them. Like most who fought and suffered at the front line in those years, she talked (we may feel to her cost) more of the sacrifices and the heroism than of her own needs and feelings. Yet beneath the surface of her writings can be detected many of the inner conflicts and insecurities she faced as a woman.

Denied for centuries any access to knowledge, dignity or power, women were being told overnight to take for granted their ability to decide their own lives, take paths women had never travelled before, and live at the cutting edge of the male world. Yet thousands of women working in the factories to support themselves and their children had their energy sapped by the double burden of work and housework. And the confidence of those at the front was frequently obstructed by men desperate to cling to their old power. Larissa Reisner makes light in her writings of the difficulties she experienced as a woman at the front. But several men who fought with her recall the trials and tests to which they subjected her, and her fight to win their trust. They describe her reckless courage in battle, and the wit, warmth and sincerity of the talks she delivered to them on board ship.

Only by fighting for the Revolution as equal partners of men, Reisner believed, could women make a new place for themselves in the reorganisation of power. Only through partnership with men could women's traditionally despised strengths be inscribed into the new culture. Many Soviet women then, and now, consider her to have served the cause of their liberation in Bolshevik Russia from where she was, fighting on the front line of the Revolution and writing about it.

She was one of the first, if not the first, to write of the Civil War. From 1921 to 1923 she lived in Kabul, and was one of the first to write of post-1917 Afghanistan. After that she visited Berlin, Hamburg and the Ruhr, as *Izvestiya* correspondent and Comintern officer, and described Germany's aborted revolution. In the years before her death, she travelled widely throughout Russia, also for *Izvestiya*, and recreated the life of the people she met there.

A recent Soviet bibliography of works by and about Larissa Reisner covers nearly twenty pages. Yet she is better known in the Soviet Union now as a precursor of writers like Dmitrii Furmanov and Alexander Fadeev, whose novels about the Civil War are now Soviet classics. In the 1920s, however, she was considered one of the finest writers of the Revolution. Now at last Reisner is being rediscovered in the west, and her major works have been excellently translated into English.[2]

After her death in 1926, just three months before her thirty-first birthday, Karl Radek wrote:

In her died a Communist deeply attached to the Russian working class, but who also, thanks to her great culture, became associated with the revolutionary movements in East and West. In her died a profoundly revolutionary woman, a precursor of the new type of person, born in the throes of revolution.[3]

Scores of friends, fellow-writers and fighters brought her vividly
to life, with her endless wanderings, her thirst for experience, her
courage in battle and her poetic, some said 'virile' mind. Popular
Bolshevik writers like Vsevolod Vishnevsky and Boris Lavryonov
wrote plays about her, and poets like Boris Pasternak evoked the
extraordinary appeal of her life:

> Larissa, now I start to feel regret
> That I'm not death, or nought compared with it.
> I'd like to know how to these scraps of days
> Life's chapters without glue so firmly stick.
>
> Oh, how I had that raw material weighed!
> Winters slumped back in heaps, then downpours swept,
> And with a blanket blizzards tightly swathed
> Young suckling cities close against their breasts.
>
> People on foot flashed past in wind and rain,
> Trucks crawled round the first turn in the road,
> Plunged to the neck in water were those years,
> In floods across the shallows new ones flowed.
>
> Yet ever more did stubborn life persist
> In simmering in its still, while nests were built:
> Ringed round with street-lamps lay the building sites,
> With starlight, words and reason they were filled.
>
> Just look around, which one of us was not
> From flakes and hazy reservations made?
> For we were reared by some exquisite ruins
> While you alone stand far above all praise.
>
> And you alone, so well dislodged by strife,
> Burst through in one clenched salvo to enthrall.
> Had fascination not been known to life,
> To answer it you'd be right on the ball.
>
> You billowed up like some tempestuous Grace
> Though scarcely lingering in its living fire.
> At once lost mediocrity her face,
> While imperfection too brought forth your ire.
>
> In depths of legend, heroine, you'll walk,
> Along that path your steps will not fade.

Tower like a mighty peak above my thoughts;
For they are at home in your great shade.

(Boris Pasternak, 'In Memory of Reisner'[4])

In her lifetime she was much published in Soviet Russia, and there has been a steady interest in her there since her death. In 1928, her two-volume *Complete Works* appeared, followed in 1958 by the first edition of her *Selected Works*. In 1963, the journal *Novy Mir* [New World] published a selection of her letters. Two years later, a second, annotated edition of her *Selected Works* appeared, including these and other letters, plus some of her articles, and 1980 saw the publication of a third edition of her *Selected Works*. Many of her friends' numerous articles about her were collected in 1969 into a book of memoirs.[5]

Sometimes these articles and obituaries seem filled with too much grief and praise. In writing of her, it has sometimes been difficult for me to distance myself from this – in terms, anyway, of providing the sort of criticisms and counter-arguments appropriate to a more 'balanced' account of her life in the Revolution. This kind of 'balance' can so often end in a patronising, facile jokiness. People *were* heroes and heroines then. What I have tried to do is to let Larissa and those who knew her explain for themselves the nature and the causes of the worship she inspired in her lifetime, as well as some of the resistance she encountered. For as a woman, born of Russia's educated élite, she had to struggle for many years against the distrust of more proletarian men like the journalist Lev Sosnovsky; for many older Bolsheviks like him, who had suffered exploitation at work, or lived in prison, exile and the political underground, she simply hadn't *suffered* enough:

In our Party circles, which had come through the underground organisation frayed, ragged and unversed in the elementary conventions of civilised life, the figure of a thoroughly beautiful person, refined from head to foot, in appearance, words and deeds, was alien to us. We had so often been deceived by those who came over to us that it was hard to risk disappointment yet again. So a silent, endlessly repeated trial was held on Larissa Reisner that strangely transformed itself . . .[6]

Pasternak's poem about her mourns the passing with her death of the old era. Reisner too was a sensitive product of that élite St Petersburg culture, and she remained loyal throughout her life to her parents' values. Unlike Pasternak, however, and most of her poet friends, she rejoiced immediately in the new culture born of 1917. She described the Russian Revolution, said Radek (with whom she had a relationship in her last years), 'in such a way that it could only be described by one in whom the soul of a great poet was joined with the soul of a great warrior':

Her one theme is the October Revolution. But as long as people fight, think and feel, and as long as they are drawn to find out 'what it was like', they will read her books and will not put them down until they have reached the last page, for they have the smell of revolution about their breath.[7]

Her writings, with their dramatic juxtapositions, heightened clarity and vivid scholarship, give fresh meaning to the contradictory interraction of the old world with the young Revolution. They contain both the rich individuality of the old culture, and the new flourishing, collective that supersedes it. And in the new collective writing of the Revolution, Larissa Reisner's has a resonance of its own.

Chapter One

CHILDHOOD

Tsarist Russia entered the twentieth century poor and ignorant, a vast country ruled by an outdated autocracy, and populated mainly by illiterate peasants only recently freed from serfdom. The Orthodox Church, from which the tsars derived their divine authority to rule, sanctified the baiting of Jews and religious dissidents, and enforced the patriarchal virtues of women's submission by associating them with every conceivable vice and sin. The peasant woman was regarded as barely human, and even the noblewoman's life was generally an exhausting process of continuous childbearing, drunken husbands and household drudgery.

The 1890s saw a spectacular growth in Russian industry. Yet for all the technical innovations and improved communications, most Russians lacked even the most elementary political rights, including the right to vote, and the peasants continued to live in poverty, crippled by taxes and famine.

When Nicholas II came to the throne in 1894, the peasants were still suffering the results of a series of disastrous harvests and famines, in which thousands died. A law was passed further restricting their right to leave their villages. But more and more of them were being driven by poverty off the land and into the towns, where they worked, in appalling conditions, in the new factories now appearing all over Russia. Women were slower to leave the villages for the factories, and there, as at home, they were underfed, sexually harassed by their employers, and exhausted by endless toil and pregnancies. Women were slower too to protest. But once their anger was aroused, they protested with courage and often violence, often outdoing the men in militancy.

By the mid-1890s, it seemed to many in Russia as though tsarism might at last be in its death throes. In the factories a new strike movement was stirring, disconnected, undirected but potentially revolutionary. At the universities, students were rioting for reforms. And in underground revolutionary circles, socialists were discovering in the works of Marx a new philosophy and strategy of revolution. Many women Marxists, like Alexandra Kollontai and Elena Stasova, who had previously felt very unsure of themselves in the revolutionary movement, derived new confidence from their striking sisters. And they worked with men to give practical support to the strike movement, which was spreading throughout Russia to the kingdom of Poland.

The major part of Poland, through repeated partitions, lay under tsarist domination, and was one of the most industrially thriving areas of the Russian empire. In the Austrian sector near the Ukrainian border, in an unspoiled area of rolling hills and endless forests, lay West Galicia and its capital, the picturesque town of Lublin. Lublin was the birthplace of Rosa Luxemburg, and was one of the less developed parts of the country, but it lay on the intersection of two important trade routes, connecting Kiev to the Baltic, and Lithuania to Cracow, the Czech lands and Austria. There, as in the Russian sector, native Polish language and culture was heavily repressed in favour of German, and native intellectuals were replaced by autocratic Austrian administrators, under whom Galicia's old landowners, driven by famine off the land, were given minor jobs. As the unrest in the factories turned into political strikes against the administration itself, a dynamic new Polish nationalist movement arose, inspiring every political grouping and workers' organisation, and providing the impetus for Poland's new Marxist party, the Social Democratic Party.

The Khitrovs, of Russian origin, were one of Lublin's wealthiest, noblest and most cultured families, descended from the seventeenth-century diarist and poet Alexei Khrapovitsky, Catherine the Great's editor, and related to the then Russian Minister of War, General Sukhomlynov. But even the Khitrovs were swept up against their will in the heady climate of the 1890s, when their daughter, Ekaterina Alexandrovna, defied them to attend socialist meetings. It was probably at one of these that she met Mikhail Andreevich Reisner, a socialist lecturer at Lublin's Pulawa Agricultural Academy, whom she was to marry.

Reisner was born near Vilna (Vilnius), in Lithuania, into an equally wealthy and cultured East Elbian landowning family, descended from Nicolas von Reusner, a seventeenth-century authority on Roman law. Reisner had attended school in St Petersburg, then studied law at Warsaw and Kiev universities, before arriving in the 1880s at St Petersburg University, where he wrote a doctoral thesis in constitutional law, under the supervision of Alexander Blok (father of the famous Symbolist poet of the same name). In St Petersburg he attended socialist meetings and read Marx, and by the time he had finished his thesis he was a Marxist.[1]

The Reisners' marriage was a very happy one, according to all who met them, and on 1 May 1895, their daughter, Larissa ('Lyalya'), was born. A formal photograph of the three a year or so later shows Larissa in her starched and spotless baby clothes; Ekaterina Alexandrovna, eager and indomitable, and Mikhail Andreevich, proud of his family and retiring into it. A large, heavy, peaceful man, with a surprisingly sweet voice, he was by now a lawyer of some repute, as well as a popular teacher and supporter of student causes. But at home, he was only superficially head of the family. Its real leader, wrote the Reisners' young friend Vadim Andreev, was Ekaterina Alexandrovna, and 'woe to anyone who tried to contradict her'. A slight, sharp, freckled woman, 'with the mind of a mathematician and a small body filled with willpower . . . she lived with her whole being, constantly excited about something, proving something, making some point.'[2] Passionate, witty and obstinate, she had learnt at socialist meetings to argue with fire, passion and a sharp sense of her opponent's weakness. She had a quick ear, a gift for argument and story-telling, and a deep love of literature, and her family and friends were constantly urging her to write. In a tram or on a train ride recalled Andreev, she would intervene in arguments between passengers and win everyone round with a witty joke. At home, she followed Reisner's successes with pride, and celebrated them with parties. Both were demanding, adoring parents: 'There was never conceivably any talk of punishment,' wrote Andreev. 'One word, just the name of Ekaterina Alexandrovna, was enough to make it a pleasure to do what she wanted.'

Both were proud in the memory of their ancestors and their culture, and those who disagreed with them often found them stand-offish. This pride, their response to the prevailing vulgarity and reaction, went with them, according to Andreev, 'like the sword and dagger to the Three Musketeers'. Reisner was a demanding teacher, intolerant of lateness or laziness, and he would brace himself for work with daily exercises and cold baths. Inherited money and plenty of domestic help enabled them to live a comfortable, cultured life, and they both attached enormous importance to domestic order and routine: 'It was a sin to use the wrong fork at the dinner-table, a great sin to put one's elbows on the table, and a mortal sin, never forgiven by anybody, to eat with an open mouth.'[3]

Those considered vulgar or reactionary found the Reisners disdainful and élitist, and Andreev later described evenings when an offending guest came to drink tea. Mikhail Andreevich, carefully holding a silver saucer under his glass of tea, would murmur encouragingly, the guest would pluck up the courage to speak, then Ekaterina Alexandrovna would put in a few dry, witty words, and the guest would lapse into silence. Within the family, however, there was much warmth, and friends found them hospitable, and prone, like all families of the old Russian intelligentsia, to long discussions over the tea-table. People wrote of their comradeship, their uncompromising integrity, and their deep faith in socialism, 'which they preached like a religion,' said Andreev.

For behind the neat and conscientious Reisner *ménage* lay a powerful united vision of the world, based on their shared early experiences in the socialist movement. Reisner began to apply his theoretical legal studies to a more practical support for the revolution in the factories. He made contacts with Marxist revolutionaries in Russia, and with socialists in Germany and

Paris, where he often travelled on business. And in 1895, when rioting students in Moscow, St Petersburg and Kiev were arrested for refusing to take the oath of allegiance to the new Tsar, Nicholas II, Reisner became their champion.

Throughout Larissa's earliest years, the turmoil in Russia was driving her parents further to the left, and away from their past. There were more disastrous harvests, followed by more famines. In 1896, hundreds were arrested, after a wave of textile-workers' strikes in St Petersburg spread to some two hundred and sixty factories throughout Russia. Students, revolutionaries and religious dissidents were rounded up and sent off to Siberia, and the newly formed Siberian Rail Company promoted the adventurous and the politically dissident to emigrate there and populate its barren wastes. In 1897, Reisner delighted his students and attracted the censors' pen by writing about the political alliance between the autocracy and the Orthodox Church. And the following year he was appointed Professor of Law at the ancient city of Tomsk, the Siberian capital, home of the first university in Asiatic Russia.

The family travelled the two thousand miles from Lublin to Eastern Siberia on the largely completed Trans-Siberian line, and on to Tomsk, where for the next five years Reisner lectured in law and comparative religion. And there, on 8 January 1899, their son Igor ('Goga') was born.

In 1896, a special branch line had opened up the town to visitors, and it had become an important cultural and economic centre, employing mainly rail- and print-workers. But Tomsk was better known as the historic dumping-ground for political exiles, and these had a great influence on the ferment in the factories and the university. With art, science, literature and law all pointing to inescapable new revolutionary conclusions, student riots became an everyday event, and Reisner began to attend meetings of the new Marxist Siberian Union of the Russian Social Democratic Party. He also became increasingly active in workers' strike support groups, where his aristocratic manners earned him the nickname '*barin*' ['the gentleman'].

In 1901 the new Socialist Revolutionary Party was formed, to foment the revolution in the countryside, and to assassinate prominent members of the government. As the new century opened, peasants rioted, estates were looted, terrorists launched a wave of political assassinations of ministers and officials, and the universities of Russia were convulsed by student riots which spread to Latvia and Poland. In retaliation, whole villages and Jewish communities were massacred, all universities in Russia were closed, and students were expelled and drafted into the army. Reisner again took up the students' cause, and supported the protest demonstrations that followed. And in 1903, as peasant riots and retaliatory pogroms reached their height, he was expelled from the university.

Fearing further reprisals, the family packed up and left Tomsk for Berlin, where Reisner had friends. It was probably then that the Reisners finally severed connections with their families, for apart from a sister of Ekaterina Alexandrovna's in Lublin, Larissa seems to have had no contact with them. At any rate, family money stopped coming in, and for the next four years, when Reisner found it almost impossible to get work, they suffered comparative, but nonetheless painful, poverty.

In Berlin, the environment in which Larissa had lived for her first eight years changed abruptly. The family settled in shabby lodgings, drawing on their dwindling fortunes, augmented by whatever translation jobs Reisner could get. Food was often short and new clothes were few, and although frayed collars and cuffs were always starched (and the Reisners, despite their poverty, still managed to employ a servant), Larissa would suffer for the rest of her life from the damage to her feet from wearing Igor's boots.

But from those years in exile grew her lifelong attachment to Germany. She attended a primary school in the working-class district of Zehlendorf, where the children became her closest friends, and German became her first language. She became especially close to Thérèse Benz, the woman who helped her mother around the house, and remembered her stories for the rest of her life.

The Reisners' reduced circumstances in Berlin freed them

from much of the constraint and formality of their old life. Mikhail Andreevich had already made contact with socialists in Berlin during previous visits there. And in those four years in Germany, when wages fell, and the Kaiser launched a rocketing new arms programme, they made new, more radical friends. Now their flat was filled not with Russian professors but with German socialists and exiled Russian revolutionaries, Bolsheviks, some of them, living illegally in Berlin, who came and went with mysterious haste. And as Reisner widened his legal expertise to construct defences for them, he made friends with many leaders of the German Socialist Party, including the veteran August Bebel and Karl Liebknecht, the radical Reichstag deputy.

In January 1904, Russia declared war on Japan. Six months later, after a series of disastrous Russian defeats, the country was again swept by demonstrations, strikes, riots and terrorist attacks. That summer, Socialist Revolutionaries assassinated the Russian Governor of Poland, and blew up the Minister of the Interior. This was followed by a horrifying wave of pogroms, arrests and deportations, and Russian exiles in Germany now came under increased police surveillance. That autumn, a number of German Social Democrats were arrested and charged with crimes against the Russian Tsar. Reisner was asked by Liebknecht to help prepare their defence, and when their trial opened in Konigsberg, he acted as legal consultant to the defence.[4] The Reisners became especially close in those days to Liebknecht and his Russian wife, and Larissa would always recall her visits with Igor and her parents to their house, where 'Auntie Sofia' would give them coffee and shortbread.

On 9 January 1905 hundreds of workers in St Petersburg were killed by government troops as they stood outside the Tsar's palace to present their petition for a constitution. 'Bloody Sunday' was the signal for Russia's first revolution. Month after month, as war brought fresh agonies of defeat and suffering, the countryside was ablaze with riots, the cities were convulsed with strikes and the universities became public forums for endless protest meetings. While new extreme right-wing groups organised yet more pogroms and massacres in retaliation, the Tsar issued a manifesto rallying his citizens to the throne, and promising elections for a new, 'consultative', Duma [parliament]. In May, most of the Russian fleet went to the bottom of the Tsushima Straits, and that summer there was a general strike in Odessa, supported by the crew of the Battleship *Potemkin*. Women were being drawn into the revolutionary movement now in vast numbers, as street-fighters and speakers, and were laying down their tools to give the strike movement an unprecedented strength.

In September, workers in Moscow organised a general strike which lasted into the following month. And finally, on 17 October, the Tsar capitulated, with a manifesto offering amnesty for political exiles, and promising universal manhood suffrage in elections to a new State Duma. In those 'days of freedom' new workers' clubs and theatres opened, and workers' Soviets [councils] were formed to direct the strike movement in St Petersburg and elsewhere. A month later, delegates to the St Petersburg Soviet were arrested. Moscow's Soviet retaliated by organising an armed rising, and several hundred people were killed when troops were sent in to crush it. The 'days of freedom' were over.

The Reisners and their friends watched the upheavals of 1905 with delight and horror. Since they did not rush back to Russia after the promised amnesty, they cannot have had much faith in it from the start. But they longed to return, and in that year Reisner joined the Bolsheviks. He wrote several articles for their new paper *Proletarii* [The Proletarian], which involved him in a brief correspondence with Lenin. He started work on his book *Russian Absolutism and European Reaction*, published the following year. And in late November he made a brief trip to Tammerfors, in Finland, for the Bolsheviks' First All-Russian Conference, attended by most of the party's future leaders.[5]

Strikes and riots continued in Russia to the end of that year, but with less intensity than before. By the spring of 1906, hundreds of strikers, peasants and revolutionaries had been arrested, all the reforms proposed by the new Duma were rejected, the Duma itself was dissolved, and the revolution crushed. That year, the Reisners left Berlin for Paris. There Reisner helped his socialist friends to set up the First International Socialist University, as well as writing anti-tsarist articles for the French socialist press. But with reaction again triumphant in Russia, the revolution smashed and Bolshevik fortunes at their lowest ebb, these articles were now of a more conciliatory character.

The Reisners' move to revolutionary politics had been a hard one, fraught with uncertainties for them and their children, and although they would always consider themselves to be Marxists, Marxism itself was then in crisis. For them, like thousands of others in 1905, the Bolsheviks had seemed the only party to lead the working class to overthrow tsarism. The defeat of the revolution destroyed that faith, and many socialists now felt that the only real alternative to autocracy lay with the parties of bourgeois liberalism. In the years following the 1905 revolution, the Bolsheviks were driven underground by repression, and into a particularly hard-line political style. In opposition to this appeared a new 'creative' Marxism, influenced by Freud and the individualist philosophers of the west, which asserted the importance of personal creativity, a more individualistic interpretation of human behaviour, and a new enlightened sexual psychology, which combined with the new technology of contraception to challenge all previous assumptions about sexuality. In those years Reisner too became a 'seeking' Marxist, and was greatly influenced by the 'psychological', 'intuitive' legal theories of L. Petrazhitsky, which he attempted to integrate with Marxist notions of class.[6]

With revolution receding into the distant background, Reisner gradually abandoned his links with the Bolsheviks. By 1907, his rehabilitation in Russia was apparently complete, and he was offered an assistant professorship in constitutional law at St Petersburg University. Bolshevik friends would later criticise his conversion to academic life. But on the Reisners' return to St Petersburg, they continued to support protesting students and sacked strikers (for whom they helped to organise hardship funds). For this they were put under police surveillance, and as the revolutionary movement again gathered momentum, they embarked on a more active support for it.

In St Petersburg, they rented a modest flat on a small side-street on the St Petersburg Side, down which horse-trams travel-led on to the Sympatia Park, and the Bolshoi Prospect, and overlooking at the back a large dismal courtyard. There, at 25 Bolshaya Zelenina, Larissa Reisner grew up, and from there she left, in 1918, to join the Revolution.

With more money and a more leisured life, the Reisners could now afford to take holidays on the Black Sea. Ekaterina Alex-androvna organised literary soirées at the flat, and finally, at the age of forty, she took her family's advice and started writing short stories, several of which were published. For Igor and Larissa there were riding, skating and skiing lessons, visits to the opera, the ballet and the theatre, and everything a cultured bourgeois family could give their children. Nine-year-old Igor, sharp and freckled as his mother, was sent to a good private boys' *gimna-zium*, Larissa was enrolled in D.T. Prokofieva's private *gimna-zium* for girls, and both were encouraged to think independently, raid the library for literature, science and history books, and express themselves freely at the dinner-table.

At the age of twelve, Larissa was a tall, active child, with dimpled cheeks, regular features and auburn plaits wound round her head like a crown. Despite the damage to her feet during the family's years in exile, she loved dancing and sports, and at the first signs of frost she would dash out with her skates to the rink, for she excelled at figure-skating. After her working-class school in Berlin, she found the conservatism and gentility of her St Petersburg school 'a real agony', and was frequently reprimanded for expressing revolutionary views in class. But she did her homework and worked hard, especially at literature. Both she and Igor regularly earned the title of *otlichnik*, or top of the class, and their school successes were regularly celebrated with family parties.

People who knew the Reisners at this time observed the protective, even exclusive, love between them, and a special order evolved over their years in exile. Since they tended not to discuss the heart of their politics at the dinner-table, many outside their closest circle, while appreciating their great honesty, felt they showed a somewhat abstract kindness towards humanity. But this was because socialist principles were too dangerous to be discussed freely. These principles, which had capsized their life in the past, were to cause them much grief in the years to come.

People suffered in various terrible ways from the failed revolution and its reactionary aftermath. Tsar Nicholas, a prey to fears and superstitions, locked himself up with a mass of charlatans offering magic cures. The strike movement slumped. There was an epidemic of suicides and murders, and child prostitution, sex-clubs and pornography did a thriving trade. In this climate of fear and despair, terrorism flourished. In 1907, the Socialist Revolutionaries' assassinations of government officials leapt to a staggering total of two and a half thousand, and members of the Tsar's security police started infiltrating the Socialist Revolutionary Party, from which they assassinated two liberal Duma deputies. In that year, the terrorist campaign reached its climax, then collapsed, with the arrest of hundreds of terrorists and suspects.

Many professors at St Petersburg University had disliked Reisner's socialism from the start and almost immediately after he had taken up his post there a number of them started spreading the rumour that he was working with the government and its secret police. This rumour was picked up by L.V. Burtsev, a populist liberal of the old school, and repeated as fact in the historical journal *Byloe* [The Past], of which he was editor. Since Burtsev had always seemed to people like the Reisners such a firm socialist, his slander was a particularly damaging one. But as Radek said,

the great world of learning is essentially a tiny world of learned men. Therefore there is no muck, pettiness or meanness that great scholars won't use against an enemy . . . So the old gossip-monger latched on to this bit of slander, and added his own private grudges . . .[7]

Torn impossibly between teaching and politics, Reisner withdrew into teaching, and limited politics to discreet support for student causes.

For years he struggled for his political honour, against the 'one-eyed monster' from Peer Gynt, against slander, myths, whispering campaigns and insinuations that couldn't be challenged or brought to legal proceedings. . . .

In the home, need, worry and finally bitterness and despair took over. Larissa understood well why their home became emptier, why her father's voice was heard less often, why he paced up and down for hours, and why he built a wall between the family and both the university and the revolutionary movement.[8]

By 1911, the Tsar and his hysterical wife Alexandra had put their country's fate in the hands of the 'holy man' Rasputin, who claimed to relieve the symptoms of their haemophiliac son and heir and was now deciding on virtually all matters of state, too. That summer, Russia promoted the first of a series of disastrous wars in the Balkans for control of the Ottoman Empire. There was a fresh wave of student riots, followed by mass arrests, dismissals and deportations. Universities came under police control, and a hundred and twenty-five professors resigned in protest.

That autumn, P.A. Stolypin, President of the Tsar's Council of Ministers, was assassinated by secret police agents in the Socialist Revolutionary Party. And it was Burtsev who unmasked one of the Party's most active terrorists, Evno Azef, as the agent responsible. This revelation (in this case true) gave new weight to his slander against Reisner, who in desperation published a personal appeal, 'To Public Opinion', to defend his political honour. But the mud stuck, as it was intended to, and although Reisner remained one of Russia's most authoritative constitutional lawyers, the Reisners were increasingly isolated and avoided.

Later, in an unpublished autobiographical essay, Larissa described the way in which her earliest years were shaped by the 1905 revolution and its defeat:

Two children, born in terrible danger, were reared on the easy, destructive genius of analysis which reigned in the family. At the age of ten, they knew life, and could accurately assess each new hurricane, as it threw their shaky nest from place to place. They were accustomed to seeing their father and mother as an eternal defence against the eternal loneliness demanded by the implacable criteria set to their lives.[9]

The Reisners closed in on themselves, and against the outside world, and there was a new severity, reserve and even stiffness in their dealings with it. For Larissa, those years were to guard her forever against idolatry and idle talk, and to arm her with the strong sense of satirical mockery that would later be so characteristic of her as a writer. And it was then that she began, through writing, to create her own world, independent of her parents, and to grapple with the conflicts and insecurities of growing into a woman in revolutionary Russia.

The cultural upheavals changing the face of Russian culture in the 1890s found expression in the Symbolists, poets like Konstantin Balmont and Valerii Bryusov, who saw the universe as a system of correspondences, poets as priests of an estoteric art, and poetry as a religious activity, twinned to music. The revolution of 1905 produced a ferment of experimental writing. More openly radical writers, like Maxim Gorky and Leonid Andreev, founded a new revolutionary school of fiction, and Symbolists became 'mystical anarchists'.

Seventeen-year-old Larissa lived under the influence of Symbolism, and immersed herself in the works of Bryusov, Anna Akhmatova and Alexander Blok, the greatest Symbolist of all, whose musical, mystical evocation of St Petersburg's misty mirages had a lifelong influence on her. But she was also hearing at home of new literary and philosophical circles, in which new poets renounced and replaced the old idols. Symbolism was disintegrating in headlong collision with the verbal perfectionists of Acmeism and the 'poet artisans' of Futurism. And the realist school of fiction was being superseded by the 'metaphysical', or 'pessimistic', school of writing, typified by the nihilistic philosophical dramas of Leonid Andreev.

Andreev was regarded by many then as the successor to Tolstoy. His rough, realistic plays and stories were preoccupied, like Tolstoy's, with the elemental realities of sex and death, and filled with defeat, despair and an all-round total negation of culture. His work evidently struck a responsive chord in the Reisners,[10] and was to have a great influence on Larissa. They first met him, with his wife and son, Vadim, in the summer of

1911, while on holiday at the Black Sea, and for the next three years he was a close family friend. He also became Larissa's literary mentor, and encouraged her to write for the philosophical literary journal *Shipovnik* [Sweetbriar], of which he was editor, and which published many of the best-known satirical artists and poets of the 1905 Revolution.

Despite the Reisners' friendship with Andreev, their enthusiasm for pessimism was not wholehearted, and as the revolution began once again to stir, they slowly emerged from their isolation. The year 1912 saw the publication of Reisner's two-volume work *The State*, a compilation of his earlier writings and lectures.[11] In the same year, he put himself at the service of the socialist educational Samsonievsky Society, which ran workers' clubs in St Petersburg. He was soon travelling regularly by horse-tram to factories and workers' clubs in the city's dingy suburbs, where he would lecture on literature and politics to factory-workers. These talks, delivered with great emotion and without notes, were always carefully prepared and calculated for his audience, and Reisner soon felt quite at home there, meeting factory militants and revolutionaries, and learning about the latest strike or protest meeting. He was an extremely popular teacher, and Vadim Andreev, who visited one of his lectures the following year, recalled the shock of recognition amongst the audience as he spelt out the revolutionary conclusions of H.G. Wells's *The Time Machine*.[12]

Meanwhile Larissa, with Andreev's encouragement, was pouring out a mass of poems. Many of her first efforts were inspired by the scientific metaphors of the then fashionable 'biological' poetry. Solemn, symbolic and heavy, few were ever completed. Torn from the old culture by a hatred of its injustices, she was struggling to discover a new way of writing, a style to imitate, and a voice of her own with which to enter a literature dominated by men. She read voraciously, and sat up until late at night grappling with Marx, Engels and the classics of western and Russian literature and socialism. In Poehlman's *History of Ancient Socialism and Communism* she found the inspiration for her first play, *Atlantida*, about a young man who by his death saves the continent of Atlantis from destruction. And in the heroines of Shakespeare she discovered new possibilities of female strength and identity, and the inspiration for her first literary studies, of Ophelia and Cleopatra.

Chapter Two

POETRY AND REVOLUTION

In the summer of 1912, seventeen-year-old Larissa passed her final school examinations with a gold medal, and longed to go to university. Women were banned as full-time students then, and could enrol only with the special permission of the authorities, and only as external students, unable to take the final qualifying exams. But with her mother's encouragement, and her father's contacts, she was eventually admitted to attend St Petersburg University the following year.

Meanwhile she was wrestling with her Shakespeare articles and *Atlantida*, her 'play for reading'. By early 1913 it was finished, five acts and eight scenes long, an awkward mix of socialism and symbolism, talent and inexperience. When she sent it to Andreev to publish in *Sweetbriar*, he demanded cuts and she reworked it according to his suggestions. In the summer, she visited her aunt in Lublin, and from there she wrote to her mother:

You know all the joy and grief with which I'm publishing it. But what's so terrible is that I just cannot cut as much as Andreev wants. Every line I discard seems essential, as though the whole were carved from one block . . . I polish and I grind – God alone knows what it costs me. I'll soon be able to return 'Atlantida' to you, all covered in cuts and blood. If Kopel [man] demands more changes I shall refuse, for I feel with my whole being that it would go against both my artistic feelings and my conscience as a writer . . . It's some consolation that Andreev himself has found nothing to criticise in the first two acts . . . For heaven's sake, write and tell me how 'Atlantida' will appear – will it really be in pieces, in anthologies?[1]

That autumn, she returned to St Petersburg for the start of the university term. Earlier that year, women in the capital had celebrated the new socialist International Women's Day by taking over the Stock Exchange and demanding their right to vote. Even then women students were still very rare at the university. She enrolled nonetheless in an extremely ambitious series of courses at the faculties of Law and Philology, and at the Institute of Psychoneurology. Twenty-year-old Vsevolod Rozhdestvensky (later a well-known Soviet poet) described her rite of passage that September into the male world of the university, and the impact on the students of her first appearance at the lecture hall of the Philological Faculty.

They were waiting for Professor Zelinsky to arrive for their classical philology and literature lecture, he wrote, when instead there walked in a tall, elegant young woman in a well-cut grey English suit, white blouse and man's tie. Her appearance was so startling, he recalled, 'there was something so un-Russian in her proud manner and sharp, laughing eyes', that the students gasped and catcalled. Blushing with embarrassment, she made for the only free place, next to Rozhdestvensky, and took out her exercise book and pencil. Zelinsky came in, and pretending not to notice her, started on his lecture, during which Larissa took notes so furiously that her pencil broke, and she asked Rozhdestvensky rather peremptorily for a knife. She continued to cover her embarrassment in haughty silence until one day she strode up to Rozhdestvensky at the student notice-board, smiled at him with her mocking smile, stretched out her hand in salutation, and proceeded to question him earnestly about his poems.[2]

Rozhdestvensky became one of her closest friends at the University. In this male society, the only possible one in which her talents could flourish and assert themselves, almost all her friends were inevitably men. But in taking on the rights and privileges of men, she was also developing her weapons against them, and her university experiences sharpened her talent for mockery in the face of male power and arrogance. It was this talent that partly explains her ability later to deal so confidently with men's authority over her.

Another student, Igor Ilinsky, recalled a sociology lecture at the Psychoneurological Institute. An ambitious young professor read a lecture loaded with terms like 'cumulative collective aggregates' and, in the discussion afterwards, he 'sought the opinion of Larissa Mikhailovna'. She replied gravely, with modestly lowered eyes that the lecture had 'shone with rare scholarship', but had 'omitted to mention the work of Stoll and Schmidt on demographic complexes'. Pride forced the professor to reply that, although he was familiar with their work, they 'provided little of value in comparison with the American school'. The secret was, wrote Ilinsky, that 'Stoll & Schmidt' were manufacturers of pharmaceutical goods, and he imagined the lecturer for ever after searching for them in the libraries of Berlin.[3]

Gradually her awkwardness melted. She began to mix with other students, most of them radical young poets, like Rozhdestvensky and Ilinsky, who burned with loathing for the sons of the nobility. Poetry played the most important part in her life then, and as she struggled to finish her *Atlantida*, she poured out her feelings in a mass of verses, most of them unfinished and unpublished, and all heavily influenced by the new Acmeist poets, Andrei Bely, Sergei Gorodetsky and Lev Gumilyov, then all the rage in St Petersburg. The young poets clustering round the Acmeists entranced her with their visual and verbal vividness and their complex word associations. But she was also repelled by the disdainful distance they put between their poetry and the events now hurtling Russia towards war.

In 1913, as the Tsar moved Russia closer to a war for the Dardanelles and Constantinople, there were strikes and demonstrations throughout Russia. But none of this was visible from the heights of the Acmeists' journal, *Apollon*. Here, far from the surrounding chaos, were images of a world derived from art, literature and architecture, and sanctified by the ancient traditions of 'Heleno-Christian culture', whose end, said the Apollonians, was near. According to the Soviet poet Vera Inber:

Life was suffocatingly hard, reality was repulsive, and all hopes were projected on to the fall of tsarism. Beauty lay nowhere, and instead

appeared its surrogate – aestheticism – which enabled a whole generation of the Russian intelligentsia to drag reality through a straw and thus
find it bearable.[4]

With her student friends, Larissa was ironic about her romantic attraction to the Acmeists and the aesthetic perfectionism of
the past. She was a part of the old culture, and would never
abandon it, though she struggled for the rest of her life against its
influence and for a new aesthetic to replace it. These conflicts,
vested in irony, expressed themselves, according to Rozhdestvensky, in a tendency to pose unanswerable riddles and surprise
people. 'This offended some, especially as her conclusions often
went with an ironic smile.'

Vadim Andreev later described how guests coming to drink tea
with the Reisners would often find her aloof, sitting stern,
straight and silent, with lowered eyes, while fifteen-year-old Igor,
the star of the evening, talked like a grown man about art, music,
theatre and politics. Ekaterina Alexandrovna, disliking his waving arms and flushed face, would quieten him with a few dry,
witty words. Professor Reisner would make the occasional quiet
observation. 'And Larissa, suddenly raising her eyelashes, would
come out with a clever, rather mannered aphorism, then fall back
into enigmatic silence.'[5]

Something of this haughtiness and irony is conveyed in the
portrait painted of her by the artist V.I. Shukhaev. But her
friends found it stiff and unlifelike, and behind the haughty
manner, they found her not so complicated after all, with a
passion for dancing, skating, riding, long walks and reading, both
serious and frivolous.

She was especially close to Rozhdestvensky. The two would
take long walks around St Petersburg and its islands, and their
friendship, according to him developed into a 'student romance'.
In the spring they went rowing on the river Neva, and during the
long white nights of the northern summer, they would wander
along the city's canals, sitting on the steps to admire their granite
reflection in the motionless waters. They loved their town, and
Blok's evocation of its cold, misty beauty. But it was Larissa,

recalled Rozhdestvensky, who, long before their other poet friends, was talking too of the factories and working-class districts far from the centre, and insisting that Blok had grasped the revolutionary instinct there far more directly than Valerii Bryusov, then at the height of his popularity.[6]

Since she now led a fairly independent life in the city with her friends, she also visited the Stray Dog Café, the fashionable meeting-place of St Petersburg's bohemian élite and their patrons (contemptuously called the 'pharmacists'). There, in a vaulted cellar in the depths of a courtyard on Mikhailovskaya Square, Symbolists and Acmeists like Blok and Akhmatova would read their poems and manifestoes. And there she met the new generation of poet revolutionaries, the Futurists, who came to the Stray Dog to declare war on aestheticism, declaim their poems and subvert the idea of poet as priest. In the front line of the Futurists' war against poetic respectability was Vladimir Mayakovsky, a Bolshevik since the age of fourteen, who had just published his first poems. With his outrageous dress and brilliant, aggressive, vernacular poetry, Mayakovsky became the Stray Dog's most dazzling and shocking performer, and Larissa was deeply impressed by him.

This war between the poets was the prelude to many of the literary battles in which she was so deeply involved after the Revolution. But even in 1913, literary meetings at the University were increasingly ending in fierce arguments, even fights. And as new student literary circles sprang up, Larissa was caught up in a turmoil of debates on the purpose and meaning of poetry.

Her closest friends were the members of the University 'Poetry Circle', a tight-knit group of young men and women of St Petersburg's intellectual *jeunesse dorée*, including Viktor Trivus, Dmitr Maizels, Vladimir Zlobin, Anna Regat and Rozhdestvensky. The Circle was small, wrote Rozhdestvensky, but ambitious in its goals:

Symbolism, which had so recently enslaved us, we now boldly dreamed of destroying . . . and aimed to reveal to the world new examples of a fresh expressive, freely intonated poetic language. Our programme was rather proud, and we would not settle for less, for in the naïveté of our youthful enthusiasm we considered ourselves the arbiters of taste. . .[7]

The Circle did indeed have some influence at the University in forming literary tastes. They put out a scruffy, badly printed magazine, *Bohème*, and Larissa, as its editor, sought out new contributors. They met not in the University, but in each other's homes – shabby student rooms alternating with comfortable bourgeois apartments, like the Reisners'. To these meetings new poets would bring the manuscripts of their latest works, and Larissa, in an even but elated voice, would read her verses about the French Revolution, about the Decembrists, Russia's first revolutionaries, and about St Petersburg, the tsarist capital:

> Peter's granite
> Barely covered the peat
> And Benkendorf rules
> Where once ruled the Graces . . .

Other poems were written in the fashionable 'artistic' manner. 'The Hermitage', for example, uses the morbid, frenzied images of Mikhail Vrubel's paintings to describe the artist, in tragic conflict with reality, and unable to escape through aestheticism:

> The palette, gilded by thick, clear lacquer,
> Cannot assuage the new thirst.
> An endless succession of dreams run on,
> And the hand clenches in frenzy to a fist.
>
> Fearing to squander the April warmth,
> The exhausted day subsides.
> And on the wall a dead Vrubel
> Breaks the curdled seal of horror.
>
> But there is a limit to toil and desire
> The head of the Gorgon on the canvas laughs,
> Laughs grotesquely, overcoming groans
> Like the thunder of beaten ore.[8]

The Reisners warmly encouraged Larissa's first awkward poetic efforts, and on the day her first poem was published in the

Poetry Circle magazine, they threw a party and the celebrations lasted a week. But friendly student criticism was a good antidote to too much praise. And her poems, with their various and unusual themes, and their decadent wealth of images, came in for a great deal of criticism from her fellow-poets, who liked to needle her by finding fault with them.

One writer she recruited to the magazine was Lev Olkonitsky, a twenty-two-year-old student at Moscow's Commercial Institute (now the Marx Institute of Economics), who wrote poetry under the name of Lev Nikulin. They communicated through letters, and it wasn't until three years later that they met. Nikulin, who was to be a lifelong friend, wrote years later that she didn't always take criticism easily – 'Who does?'. But she did enjoy the sharp and often heated discussions which followed the readings, in which the young poets defended, tore apart and praised each other's works. She had been well prepared, by family discussions and her mother's talent for argument, to defend her views and parry opponents. Her talk was bright, romantic and full of para-doxes, according to Rozhdestvensky, and in arguments she was decisive, resourceful, witty and able to keep her patience, even at moments of greatest excitement. 'She was proud of her "male mind",' wrote Nikulin, 'though she wasn't without flirtatious-ness either.'[9]

She was still heavily influenced by the writings of Andreev, despite his now ebbing popularity. Andreev had by then moved to a pretentious modern villa in Finland, where he lived all year round with his second wife, drinking heavily. The Reisners saw less of him after that. But when he decided to find a family in St Petersburg to look after his fifteen-year-old son, Vadim, it was his friends the Reisners whom he eventually chose.

When Vadim came to live with the Reisners in the autumn of 1913, the neat, conscientious tenor of their life at first seemed strange to him after the anarchic, happy-go-lucky atmosphere of his father's house. But 'it was with them', he recalled, 'that I felt for the first time a recognition of my own childish self, and started to be someone people talked to seriously, as an equal.'[10]

He at once loved Ekaterina Alexandrovna, with her attentiveness to all that was important to him, above all his love for his father, which she tried always to sustain in him. Professor Reisner took him off one evening to a workers' meeting, in a shabby hall in a suburb whose existence he had never dreamt of, and there for the first time he learnt about the strike movement in the factories. Igor, with whom he went to school, showed him the authority that came from school success: 'No one could toss their head like him, destroy with one glance an over-excited classmate, or emerge with dignity from a difficult situation. . . .'

Vadim soon got used to the Reisners' insistence on starched collars and hard work. Encouraged to make sense independently of the books in their library, he started for the first time in his life to read, and to join in conversations at the family dinner-table. 'Being a "Reisner" filled me with new pride,' he wrote. 'Breathing the stern and tender air around me, I started living with the Reisners' interests, loves and dislikes, and I learnt more from them than from anyone else in my life . . .'

By the time Vadim came to write of Larissa, he found it hard to see her clearly through the fame that surrounded her. He remembered her as:

a young girl, who'd recently finished at the *gimnazium*, writing decadent verses and dreaming of revolution because in the Reisner family it was impossible not to . . ., but enjoying even more the radiance of youth surrounding her, and her unusual beauty – her huge green eyes and her pale hands, like white butterflies, flying to adjust her hair, which was wound like shells on her ears.

When she walked along the street, she seemed to bear her beauty like a torch, and even the coarsest objects gained from her presence a new tenderness and gentleness. I remember the pride I felt when we walked together through the narrow streets of the St Petersburg Side. Not one man passed her without observing her – and according to the author's own statistical observation, every third would stand rooted to the spot watching her as we passed into the crowd . . .

Few men escaped the common fate of falling desperately in love with her then. But the moment any of them tried to speak of their overwhelming feelings for her, they would be banished from the house, like a heretic from church.

Although three years younger than she, Vadim clearly included himself amongst them. And it was from Larissa that Vadim learnt the most important thing of all – his need to write poems. Sometimes, returning from school, he would find her, in a light white shirt, her hair over her face, struggling with her latest poem. He remembered her, pacing like a mirage around the twilit room, shadowed by the lantern in the courtyard below, then sitting down quickly at a table and scribbling with a stump of pencil, then standing up, gazing through the hoar-frosted windows, and pacing and murmuring again:

> 'Putting his hand on his sensitive sword
> The youth, in love with the ringing dawn,
> Thus spoke . . .'

Her murmuring and the rhythm of her steps were sweet music to me, and seized by this creative atmosphere, I too started writing poetry, not casually, or coincidentally, but as a matter of sheer necessity.

*

In 1913, Larissa's articles on Shakespeare's heroines were published in the Latvian capital of Riga, under the male pseudonym Leo Rinus. And that winter, when *Atlantida* finally appeared in *Sweetbriar*, there were family celebrations that lasted into the spring.[11] But by then she had lost interest in her play, and when it was discussed at meetings of the Poetry Circle she would dismiss it with a frown. *Atlantida* had been inspired by an older generation of poets, who had taught her the clarity and sharpness to describe the world at its cutting edges. For this she would always be grateful to them, and her writings remained filled with their influence long after Russia had plunged into revolution. But now she put aside *Atlantida* and its naïve dreams of individual heroism and sacrifice. She was ready to write in a different, more angry, polemical way.

By June 1914, strikes and demonstrations in Russia reached their highest point since 1905. On 28 July, Austria declared war on Serbia, Tsar Nicholas ordered mobilisation, and on 2 August,

Russia entered the First World War. The strike movement collapsed amidst a surge of anti-German feelings. Men were mobilised, women took over their jobs, and in St Petersburg (renamed Petrograd the moment war was declared), large groups of soldiers marched down the streets, shouting patriotic songs. On 17 August, Russian troops were hurled into East Prussia, and the British press raised high hopes of the invincible 'Russian steamroller'. Three weeks later, the 'steamroller' had been crushed, with the loss of some fifty thousand Russian lives.

It was the outbreak of war, when Larissa's old poet idols degenerated en masse into patriotism, that the asethetic detachment of *Apollon* finally lost its charm for her. And as repression mounted, and hundreds of journals (including *Apollon* itself) were forced to close, Petrograd's poets roused themselves to new heights of patriotic intensity, matching even that of the starkly reactionary official press. Some, like Gumilyov, enlisted, while Andreev, by now a ghost of his former self, was awoken by war to write patriotic propaganda. Even the poets at the Stray Dog Café were now declaiming patriotic poems, and Mayakovsky's anti-war tirades were shouted off the stage.

The Reisners were acutely distressed by the intelligentsia's wholesale conversion to patriotism, and the war spelt the end of many old friendships. With Andreev they parted company for ever (although Larissa would always keep her admiration for his earlier writings), and poor Vadim had to leave.

The Poetry Circle continued to argue, debate and publish their poems through the ever-tightening censors' net. But in those first months of the war, when it was still so hard to see the features of the future, they were adrift. In the sadness of war, Larissa found a new, cruel, satirical wit to mock her old idols, with their treacherous eloquence, their snobbery and their convenient patriotism. And in mocking them, she was partly also mocking her own past.

Rozhdestvensky once recalled her complaining to him that she'd lost the ability to understand simple, natural things, but always wanted to sharpen and to complicate.

'But how's that?' I asked. 'You write verses about sunsets and Finnish lakes. Don't you love our simple Finnish pines and dunes?'

'I don't know,' she said. 'No, I don't love them. It's just a trick of the heart. I try to convince myself I do, but I'm actually indifferent to nature.'

'And people?'

'People are different, but again I want something complicated, extraordinary – not people as they are now, but as they should be in the future, which I love and don't yet know. But I don't want to talk of people now. I'm afraid of getting carried away – and there'd be no stopping me. It's better to listen to them, and read poetry.'[12]

By the end of 1914, Russia's defeat in the war seemed beyond question. At the front, the tsarist army, ill-led and ill-equipped, had been cut to pieces by the Germans. Whole regiments were surrendering, and there was open talk of revolution. At home, soaring living costs, declining wages and rampant speculation brought new waves of strikes, demonstrations and riots. In the poor suburbs of Petrograd, women toiled all day while their children roamed the streets. Desperate and hungry, women started to loot and smash the food shops. As meetings and strikes were violently broken up by the police, there were more demonstrations against the police themselves. The voice of the poor became harder to ignore; and St Petersburg University, though still remote from the ferment outside, became the forum that summer for an endless series of student meetings. One evening after classes, in a cooling auditorium lit by the northern summer light, Larissa gave a talk entitled 'Towards which goal and by what route must mankind travel?' 'Her talk, bold, picturesque and original, frothed and foamed like unfermented juices,' wrote the poet Vera Inber. 'But it was material for real wine.'[13]

In the first months of the war, as the old magazines were closed, a mass of new magazines and journals appeared, most of them vulgar patriotic rags. And that winter, casting around for some serious, direct activity, and tormented by her inability to find it, Larissa began to consider the idea of publishing an anti-war literary magazine. She discussed the idea with her parents, and they obligingly agreed to sell furniture and pawn jewels to raise funds. Then she enlisted her student friends' support, and a name was chosen, *Rudin*, after the dubious hero of Turgenev's novel of the same name. Turgenev's Rudin, the elegant, inconsequential philosopher-revolutionary of the 1860s, who died a hysterical death on foreign barricades, summarised the whole history of the Russian pre-revolutionary intelligentsia. And in this name lay the journal's purpose – to expose patriotic platitudes, and to conduct a struggle of ideas, through satire and poetry, against war, obscurantism and the poetry of abstract mystical symbolism.

Larissa invited her friends home to discuss the scheme, an experience which E. Solovei, for one, found both exacting and exciting:

An apparently peaceful conversation over the tea-table was in fact a real test of a new person. But having endured it, one would be automatically dedicated to the memory of the 'Rudinists', and forever in the Reisners' favour.[14]

The first 'dedicatees' were mainly students from the Poetry Circle, but they were joined by a number of established poets, including Boris Sadovskoi, Vladimir Zlobin and the magnificent, majestic Osip Mandelstam, who had recently published his first anthology. That winter, Larissa wrote again to Lev Nikulin, inviting him to send more poems to the journal, and saying that she would soon be coming to Moscow on business. He sent his poems, and, as Moscow's literary world was so separate from that of Petrograd, he forgot about it until the following year, when he became one of *Rudin*'s most active contributors.

Rudin first appeared in the late summer of 1915. Published and edited by Larissa Reisner, with help from her father, it was just one magazine amongst a chaos of others, and all too clearly betrayed its editors' inexperience. But *Rudin* was exceptional, in those days of rigid press censorship, as a voice of opposition. In satirical articles and poems (most of them Larissa's) it branded government figures by name, attacked the priests of decadent literature, and cruelly caricatured Peter Struve, Burtsev and those who had abandoned socialism for 'legal Marxism' and religious orthodoxy. No other journal could have got such barbs past the censors, and it was probably because of Reisner's political isolation, and his interest to the security police, that *Rudin* was allowed to appear in the first place.

Its first issue appeared moderate enough at first glance, with its soft, large-format cover bearing the striking but apparently innocuous silhouette of the fashionable hero, with waving hair and flowing tie. But within the small number of pages that followed, his fashionable heroics were thrown back at him. *Rudin*'s aim, announced the front page, was 'to brand with the scourge of satire, caricature and polemic all the hideousness of Russian life'. Most of the poems and articles that followed were written by Larissa Reisner, under the pseudonyms 'E. Nitzman', 'I. Khrapovitsky' and 'Riki-Tiki-Tavi'.

As chief editor, she was responsible for the magazine's complicated finances, and for the even more complicated process of ensuring that page 4 carried the routine 'Passed by the Military Censors'. She also wrote poems, articles and *feuilletons* (many of them illustrated by caricatures), satirising tsarist bankruptcy and obscurantism, lampooning the political metamorphoses of Russia's liberals, and passing judgement on their most popular writers.

But it was poetry which had pride of place, and Larissa dealt very seriously with the magazine's poetry section. For this she wrote a number of poems, as did her old friends Rozhdestvensky, Maizels, Trivus and Zlobin, and they were joined by Mandelstam, Sadovskoi, Nikulin and others. Readers started sending in unsolicited verses, and she read them all with great attention, sometimes passing them on to other writers for a second opinion. But most material was discussed collectively, at friendly meetings like those of the Poetry Circle. There was always a great deal of laughter and argument there, and many students who had seen the stern young woman in the University corridor couldn't believe their eyes when they saw her showering an opponent with questions, and sighing comically as she read the shy letters of readers submitting their first poems.[15]

Her own verses for *Rudin*, mainly sonnets and revolutionary hymns, were on large, historical, revolutionary themes,

developed in an atmosphere of heroism and struggle. In her poem
'The Bronze Horseman', for instance, the poet challenges the
autocracy to vindicate the fate of Pushkin, punished by Tsar
Alexander I with exile:

> Divine Arab!
> Today the rising slave
> Counts all your losses
> And reads again
> The epic Decree
> Banning you to the Caucasus . . .

And, in 'Sonnet to Rudin', she ends:

> Ludicrous, reckless and alone,
> Rudin died on the barricades.
> Now an impartial court
> Will finish that unwritten chapter . . .[16]

Many of her poems were on the French Revolution, about
Camille Desmoulins, the revolutionary journalist, and about
Paris ('where haughty Gorat, after a duel, crowned the victorious
Marat'). Others, like 'The Song of the Red Blood Corpuscles',
reflected her interest in the new 'scientific', or 'biological' poetry:

> Eternally driven by the auricles' beat
> Our untroubled people
> Drinks from the ocean of inhaled strength
> And the oxygen of the sun . . .
>
> There where the fibres tire of work
> We throw in one winged leap,
> Like wind through an open window,
> The frenzy of its heat . . .[17]

But her subjects were often too ambitious, and her tone too
bombastic. Though their rawness was sometimes appealing, her
poems for *Rudin*, wrote Nikulin, 'frankly didn't correspond to
the needs of the situation'. She was much more independent and
interesting as a critic of others' works, and here she began to
abandon exotic images borrowed from books and to find a more

truthful, realistic prose style. In these bold, accurate judgements on the contemporary literary scene, there was a powerful, poetic, polemical style in the making.

In 'Valerii Bryusov and the Eternal Female', she scrutinises Bryusov's decline since 1905 into mystical sensuality. 'The Russian Jungle' is a more forthright attack on the fashionably pornographic writings of Mikhail Artsybashev and the brutish version of 'free love' glorified in his play, *The Law of the Wild*. There are other sharply critical articles on Evgeny Zamyatin and Konstantin Balmont. In 'From the Frying Pan into the Fire' she writes of Andreev: 'that great nihilist, who became a patriot, and broke the promise he had given in a moment of pathetic self-mockery.' And in 'Zarathustra and Rudin' she ends: 'Live, struggle, act! Or are we just Rudins?'[18]

One of her best articles is 'From Blok to Severyanin and Mayakovsky'. Here Blok is the starting-point, and from his verse she derives the evolution of Futurism, and identifies Mayakovsky's appeal for her generation of poets, his 'thirst for life and creativity'. Against them she puts the St Petersburg aesthetes, 'who dreamed of a crystal grave, and the fantastic funeral of their soul', and now 'show their soul for money, and aren't too well paid for their public execration'.[9]

By the autumn of 1915, the Germans had advanced far within Russia's borders, making some two and a half million Russians refugees. Soldiers were deserting, strikes were spreading, and Tsar Nicholas, now Supreme Commander of the army, was universally loathed. Shaken by war and rotten from within, the tsarist régime slipped into chaos. There were yet more women's 'food riots'. Revolution was stirring.

As *Rudin*'s subscribers increased, and its mailbag bulged with new contributions, the censors became more vigilant. In the spring of 1916, *Rudin* was banned from the capital's working-class Vasilevsky Island district, on the personal orders of the Governor-General of Petrograd. The journal continued to appear elsewhere, but as more and more articles fell under the censors' blue pencil, Larissa had to struggle daily with them for its survival. Finances became more complicated, too. Most of its sales were made at station kiosks, and A.S. Suvorin's newspaper agency in Moscow, which owned the monopoly on the revenue, was withholding payment. In the summer of 1916, when there was nothing left for the Reisners to pawn, Larissa went to Moscow herself to plead with the agency for an advance on the money owed.

In Moscow she stayed at the old merchants' Loskutnaya Hotel, in a large room draped in velvet, with a samovar and spice cakes on an oval redwood table. It was there that Lev Nikulin first met her. Since he had imagined her as a 'literary lady', with 'pince-nez, mannish clothes and a cigarette in her mouth', he was surprised, when she telephoned him, by the youthful voice that summoned him to her hotel without delay. And stepping through the door of her room, he was 'literally deprived of the gift of speech' at seeing at the writing-desk 'a young, smiling woman with two plaits wound like a crown around her high forehead'.

They were soon discussing the poetry of Mandelstam and Mayakovsky, Gumilyov and Akhmatova, and passing judgement on Moscow's literary parnassus. Nikulin was surprised by the sharp and independent judgements of this twenty-year-old woman, which he found in such contrast to her harmonious voice and laughter. 'My God, what a supremely bad writer!' 'Is that old pot-belly still churning out verses?' 'How can you like that rubbish!' They went on to discuss *Rudin*, and Larissa explained to Nikulin some of the journal's more difficult allusions. He had long been bewildered by its attacks on Burtsev, who was portrayed as a rat crawling from a naturalistically drawn skull (representing the defeated 1905 revolution). Since the Reisners had special scores to settle with Burtsev, Larissa defended this caricature to him with special vehemence. (And three years later, he saw her proved right, when Burtsev emigrated and became a fierce counter-revolutionary.)

Then it was business, and Nikulin accompanied her to the offices of Suvorin's agency to meet the taciturn Efremov, its director and Suvorin's trustee. Ignoring the stacks of unsold *Rudins*, withered by the sun and stamped 'Return', she adroitly persuaded Efremov to give her, against the odds, all the money she was owed. That evening they visited together the house of a well-known virtuoso violinist, whom Larissa had heard at concerts. But she irritated him by talking more boldly about music than she ought to have done, and they were shown the door.

Nikulin became one of Larissa Reisner's severest critics, for he, like others, could find her writing mannered and her self-confidence irksome. But he was also one of her dearest friends, and that autumn he visited Petrograd and was welcomed into the Reisners' family circle.

He recalled setting off late one night with Larissa to the Stray Dog Café. A number of Acmeists and Symbolists read their verses ('mincing, powdered and howling slightly when they came to the rhythm'). They sat there till the early hours, and heard Mayakovsky declaim an anti-war poem 'with the effect of an exploding bomb'. Then they took a cab home. As they drove in sleeting rain through the sleeping town, Larissa exploded with anger at the supra-aesthetic young Stray Dog *habitués*, 'with their beauty-spots on their cheeks, publicly taking on their shoulders all the sins of the world, while privately trying to advance themselves and live in comfort'. 'All those verses about hussars, lawyers and estates are *passé*,' she said. 'I want to write poems about biology and scientific problems, from a feeling of protest.'

That night the Troitsky Bridge had been opened to let ships through, and they had to join the waiting crowd of cabs, carriages and taxis filled with revellers making for the gypsies and taverns of the suburbs. While Larissa and Nikulin talked of poetry, of formal perfection and experiments, streetwalkers outside went from carriage to carriage in search of customers, and a crowd of pedestrians – homeless people and seasonal bricklayers and woodcutters – watched sullenly as the bridge came down. When at last the queue started to move, a top-hatted gentleman in a smart cab was first to dash across, and Nikulin would always remember her saying, as they came even with the workers: 'Here are the *real* people! The time will come when they won't have to make way for gentlemen in starched shirts!'[20]

That summer a new offensive had been launched along the Austrian front, in which a million Russian lives were lost. That autumn there was a massive new conscription drive. Seventeen-year-old Igor had just finished at his *gimnazium* and was exempt, but all first-, second- and third-year university students were drafted into the army, and Larissa lost touch for several years with a number of her old friends and 'Rudinists', including Rozhdestvensky and Ilinsky.

Rudin's existence became more precarious. The money from Efremov had brought its small readership their next issue, but his agency now stopped paying altogether. Debts mounted, and clashes with the censors became more frequent. A facsimile of Liebknecht's autograph on a precious note was censored from Professor Reisner's article 'The Liebknechts' ('Wilhelm and Karl, that heroic dynasty of fighters and national leaders'). Larissa argued with the censors, who finally agreed to restore the autograph, but cut from the same issue a broadside against the Tsar's fourth and highly reactionary State Duma. From the eighth issue the blue pencil struck out the article 'The Shakers and the Feelers', about 'provocateur exposures and exposing provocations'. Both Larissa and her father protested, but without success. Number 9 was the last, and late that autumn, when there was nothing left to pawn, *Rudin* was finally forced to close.

Shortly afterwards, Larissa (evidently against her mother's wishes) set off with a group of university friends, including the former 'Rudinist' poet Vladimir Zlobin, on a steamer-trip up the Volga. Even in the dull ferment of 1916, she saw the signs of the approaching revolution. 'My darlings,' she wrote to her parents from Kostroma:

It's impossible to describe it all. But my whole being is filled with the dark nights, the will-o'-the-wisps, the rustling waters beneath the oars, the endless saffron yellow shores, the tall undergrowth, and the forever pacified snow-white churches, arched by rainbows.

And another thing: we needn't fear for Russia. In the little sentry-boxes and market villages – along all the moorings of this vast river – everything is irrevocably decided. Here they know everything, forgive nobody and forget nothing. And when the time comes, they will pass sentence and exact punishments such as have never before been seen. . . .

I am sometimes exhausted by hopeless presentiments; if only the string doesn't snap too soon, if only these calm and terrible deeds don't remain mere words. But it's everywhere – beyond the yellowing forest edges, beyond the islands and rapids. And the elements are never mistaken. . . .

Mother, I left with an unforgiven guilt. Darling poppy, my soul has brightened this morning with the weather, and I beg you again to forgive me. . . . Please write, because you belong here with these people, and your words are their longings and griefs.[21]

Larissa does not reveal what was behind this argument with her mother. There may have been a sexual involvement with one of the men in the party, of whom her mother disapproved. But this trip away from St Petersburg and her family evidently spelt a deeper personal crisis – a need to get away for a while from her privileged life and separate herself from her parents, in order to see more clearly the new life stirring around her.

At the age of twenty-one, as she gathered her strength and resources for the years ahead, she had far surpassed the limited sphere of her mother's ambitions. Ekaterina Alexandrovna had encouraged her daughter to pursue an independent life of work, and through her had achieved everything she herself had yearned for. Perhaps the sense of guilt in Larissa's letter was for the opportunities she had grasped with such comparative ease, and for her mother's generation of women, with their sacrifices, confinement and sense of inadequacy. 'Rudin' was to be the title of an autobiographical work she started in 1919, about her university experiences and her family in those years before the Revolution; perhaps she scrutinised her past with a too uncomfortably critical eye, for her parents didn't like the work, and it was never published.

When she returned to Petrograd, letters were still pouring in to *Rudin*'s editor. Young authors continued to submit their first literary attempts. One reader suggested increasing the number of pages. Another asked why his copy had been held up. '*Rudin* is dead,' Larissa would say when readers telephoned the Reisners' flat, asking what had happened to it. The Poetry Circle survived a little longer, and even published a collective anthology entitled

Arion, but Larissa didn't contribute to it. Instead she started writing for Maxim Gorky's monthly literary political journal *Letopis* [Chronicle]. To this she contributed a series of articles on poetry and literature, as well as several translations of Rilke. But it wasn't until after the Bolshevik Revolution that she returned to her fascination with poetry, and the fate of poets old and new. In the days before it, only the Futurists actually supported the Bolsheviks. But now all art, literature and poetry were being hurled into the new world, because the old was collapsing.

As 1917 opened, soldiers in ragged uniforms were deserting from the front in their thousands, and pouring over the borders into the villages and towns. In the cities, strikes, demonstrations and women's food riots swelled to a new intensity. International Women's Day, 23 February, was celebrated in Petrograd that year by thousands of hungry women, wrecking, looting and demonstrating in an event of civil disorder unparalleled in Russia. The riots and strikes swelled and spread throughout the country. Tsarism tottered. And on 3 March, Nicholas II was finally forced to abdicate in favour of a new 'Provisional Government', formed mainly of landowners and headed by Prince Lvov.

In fact it was Petrograd's newly resurrected Soviet that now held the balance of power. And throughout the spring and summer, as exiled revolutionaries (including Lenin) flocked back to the capital, thousands of people rallied to the Bolsheviks' slogan of 'Peace, Bread and Land'. Increasingly restless now with her isolation at home, Larissa Reisner longed to play a more active part in the Revolution. In April, she attended a meeting to launch a new socialist daily paper, *Novaya Zhizn* [New Life], edited by Gorky, to which she contributed a number of articles over the next seven months. Although its contributors were all opposed outright to the Provisional Government, most of them, unlike her, were equally opposed to the Bolsheviks. The literary critic Victor Shklovsky recalled that first meeting: 'Reisner was saying something or other. Steklov was horrified, and kept asking people: "Is she a Marxist?" ' And the poet Gumilyov, equally horrified to hear of her new revolutionary sympathies, wrote to her: 'Enjoy yourself, but don't get involved in politics!'[22] She ignored Gumilyov's advice, and one of *New Life*'s first issues carried her stinging broadside against the decaying Provisional Government, which provoked a counter-attack from the official press and made Gorky's group fear for its life.

But all this was merely postponing the more active political involvement she now longed for. That spring, vast numbers of women, drawn for the first time into political life, were joining the Bolshevik Party as some of its bravest and most militant members. Bolshevik women of longer standing, like Alexandra Kollontai, Konkordia Samoilova and Klavdia Nikolaeva, were amongst the Bolsheviks' most popular speakers in the capital. And women soon represented such a powerful force in the party that Kollontai and others urged the formation of separate women's bureaux, to inform it of women's needs. Most women party members rejected the idea, though. What the Bolsheviks offered to Larissa, and a whole new generation of socialist women, was the dream of working as equal partners with men for the Revolution and their own liberation.

It was Larissa's first experiences of meeting Petrograd's masses which formed her as a revolutionary and changed her life. That spring, she took part in the Provisional Government's spelling reform programme, teaching literacy and literature classes at the workers' and sailors' clubs and theatres which had sprung up in the capital during the heady days of 1905. Driven underground in the aftermath of the Revolution, these clubs had now resurfaced, and there she discovered a new kind of writing, clumsy, popular and powerful. Many intellectuals sneered at the workers' first attempts to describe their life in plays and poems, but for Larissa they represented the creative pulse of the Revolution. And in a number of terse jottings and sketches for *New Life*, she celebrated the birth of this new proletarian culture – 'for only through revolution can art become the property of the masses, the true genuine inheritors of the cultural treasures of the past'.[23]

It was at the sailors' clubs of the Kronstadt naval base, on the Gulf of Finland, that Larissa made some of her firmest friends and met the Bolsheviks' fiercest supporters. There she saw again Semyon Roshal, an old friend from the Psychoneurological Faculty, now a talented young Bolshevik militant. She met Nikolai Markin, head of the Bolshevik Central Committee of the All-Russian Navy. And she met Fyodor Raskolnikov (the underground name of F.F. Ilin), whom she later married.

Born into a poor Petrograd family, Raskolnikov had become a revolutionary in 1905, when as a thirteen-year-old schoolboy he had rioted with his friends for school reforms. At seventeen, he had entered the Economics department of the St Petersburg Polytechnic, where he studied Marx's *Capital* and became an atheist. When he left he joined the Bolsheviks, and contributed a number of articles to their newspapers *Pravda* and *Zvezda* [Star] on revolution and literature – for he had a passion for Gorky and Andreev (and, to judge by his pseudonym, for Dostoevsky). By 1914, while Larissa was still agonising over Acmeism, Raskolnikov had been arrested twice, had lived in exile and prison, and had sailed as a naval conscript to Japan, Korea and Kamchatka. February 1917 had reunited him with the St Petersburg Bolsheviks, who had sent him to Kronstadt. And when Larissa met him he was vice-chair of the Kronstadt Soviet, editor of the local Bolshevik newspaper, and Bolshevik leader of the entire garrison.

His friend Nikolai Sukhanov, a Menshevik, described him then as 'an agreeable man, upright and well thought of. A convinced socialist and extreme Bolshevik, he is, unlike many others, completing his socialist education.' And an Asian communist leader who met him later recalled him as:

a handsome man, with blue eyes and close-cropped hair, more like an English student than a Russian Bolshevik . . . A natural man of action, quick, direct, incisive . . . with no interest in theoretical problems, but with a sharp and active mind . . .[24]

Larissa had been brought up to be an independent woman, and had always gone her own way. She had been romantically, perhaps sexually, involved with Rozhdestvensky, Nikulin and possibly other old student friends. But Raskolnikov was completely unlike any other man she had known, a model of Bolshevik daring and integrity, a fighting, self-educated man who shared her passion for literature and proletarian culture and writing. That spring she was swept from the orderly world of her parents into a new life with him in the Revolution, and a new kind of sexual partnership in struggle.

As the Provisional Government continued to urge the troops on against the Germans, strikes, peasant riots and anti-war demonstrations swelled to massive proportions. In May 1917, the government frantically opened negotiations with moderates in the Petrograd Soviet, from whom they chose their new Minister of War, the ambitious young Alexander Kerensky, and a new rhetoric of victory with which to launch a new offensive against Germany.

By July, the offensive had collapsed. In the countryside, the peasants' war was past the point of no return. In the cities, bread rations were further reduced, rail-workers struck and thousands of Petrograd's citizens thronged the streets day and night, demonstrating for bread, peace and Soviet power. On 3 July, workers from the Putilov arms factory came out on strike, supported by an entire machine-gun regiment. Men from several other factories, armed by the Bolsheviks and formed into Red Guard units, appeared on the streets, supported by armoured cars. Women became nurses, runners and support troops. The next day, twenty thousand sailors sailed into the capital from the Helsingfors and Kronstadt garrisons and marched on the Soviet building to demand that the Bolsheviks take power. Raskolnikov urged his sailors to return to their garrison, and most of them eventually did, but he and hundreds of other Bolsheviks were thrown into prison for their part in the premature July uprising.

At the end of July, more ministerial shuffles in the Provisional Government brought Kerensky to power as prime minister. But his power was disintegrating even as he took office. That August, in the wake of the summer offensive, a State Conference in Moscow appointed General Kornilov, commander of the Petrograd garrison, as Supreme Commander of the Russian army, to bring victory at the front and restore order at home. On 21 August, the Russian army fought its last battle when the Latvian city of Riga fell to the Germans. And on 9 September Kornilov staged a coup in Petrograd, supported by Kerensky and Boris Savinkov, the veteran Socialist Revolutionary terrorist. Kerensky withdrew his support at the last minute, and the coup collapsed. The masses again took over the streets, revolutionaries were released from prison, and Raskolnikov was sent south to Luga and Novgorod to organise the Revolution there.

By the second week of October, the Revolution could no longer be delayed. Red Guards were on the streets, joined now by women. Soldiers and sailors were clamouring for the Bolsheviks to take power. And at 9.30 p.m. on 25 October, while the Second All-Russian Congress of Soviets was meeting at the Smolny Institute, Kerensky's government was finally overthrown amidst muffled blanks from the battleship *Aurora*. The Bolsheviks took power.

It is not clear where Larissa Reisner was on that night, although there are several, probably romanticised, accounts of her activities. According to Shklovsky, she was among those who stormed the St Peter and Paul Fortress. ('Not a difficult assault. But the fortress had to be approached. To have the faith that the gates would open.') According to Vadim Andreev, she was on the Battleship *Aurora*, and it was on her instructions that shots were fired at the Winter Palace. At any rate, she was part of the elemental struggle for the new Russia, ready to defend to the death the Bolsheviks' dream of peace, bread and land. And immediately after the new government had seized power, she visited its central committee, huddled in a side-room at the Smolny, and offered her services to them: 'I can ride, shoot, reconnoitre, write, send correspondence from the front, and if necessary die . . .'[25]

All the Reisners were swept up in the historic events of that October. Nineteen-year-old Igor worked for the new Commissariat of Justice, and Professor Reisner was appointed by Lenin to draft one of its first decrees, on the separation of Church and State. He worked too for the Commissariat of Education, drawing up plans for the reform of the higher schools, and for a new 'Communist Academy' of Marxist social science. And Larissa herself started working in the Smolny with Anatolii Lunacharsky,

Commissar for Education, cataloguing the art treasures of the old régime in order to pass them on intact to the new.

Amidst a formidably creative agenda of legislative reform, the Bolsheviks had stopped the war but refused Germany's terms for peace. Now the war was at home, as they entered the first skirmishes with the old ruling classes. Tsarist officers, officials, gendarmes and members of the secret police joined forces with young cadets, hypnotised by talk of loyalty, honour and the oath, to defeat the mutinous rabble. And Kerensky, now 'Supreme Commander of the Armies of the Republic', prepared to march on the capital.

On 27 October, Kerensky's anti-Bolshevik forces, led by General Krasnov and his Cossack troops, marched on Petrograd from their outpost at Gatchina, twenty miles away, On the 28th, tens of thousands of men, women and children, with rifles, picks and spades in their hands, poured through the streets of the city to dig trenches and build barricades in its encircled suburbs. Raskolnikov played a leading part in the Battle of Petrograd two days later, in which the Whites were forced back by lack of reinforcements, and the capital was saved. Kerensky escaped Bolshevik capture and fled to Paris, and Krasnov was arrested, then released, having given his word of honour not to take up arms against the Bolsheviks. Thereupon he hurried off south, to mobilise the Cossacks of the Don and Kuban regions against the Revolution. He was soon joined there by a number of other tsarist officers, including Admiral Kolchak, and Generals Denikin and Yudenich, and with Allied support, they set about recruiting volunteers to their new counter-revolutionary army of White Guards.

Now the Bolsheviks had to deal with the chaos from within. Businesses, schools, railways, the army – everything was wracked and paralysed by sabotage. And as office-workers struck, premises were wrecked and files and funds removed, the huge wine cellars of the Tsar's Winter Palace, guarded by one small, sober Bolshevik soldier, threatened to drown the Revolution in a haze of alcohol.

Larissa Reisner was one of the first journalists after the Revolution to enter the Winter Palace, where the Provisional Government had held court. When the crowd had come there looking for Kerensky in October, they had found instead bronze, porcelain, paintings and statues, and they had smashed them in their fury. Now she talked to some of Tsar Nicholas's old servants, who had bravely stayed on to defend the royal treasures, and she discovered that despite everything many of them preferred the Bolsheviks, with their boots, guns and alien ways, to their old masters. They didn't insult them as Kerensky had done, one told her, and they smelt more real than the Tsar: 'The masters liked to smother themselves in scent, for they had no smell of their own.'

Her eerie experiences in the Winter Palace that November were the subject of her last article for *New Life*:

In the evening, covered with the first November snow, the Winter Palace looks as serene and untouched as the white square . . . Inside, nothing disturbs the elegant proportions and the flowing course of the galleries. The magnificent windows reveal the perspectives of the Neva, the pale sky, the Stock Exchange and the fortress, and the chandeliers, stoves and furniture are positioned to complement them. At the heart of the building lie the concert halls and ballrooms, of gold and malachite, round, domed, closed in on themselves. Here mirrors replace windows, and the city, with its factory hooters and church bells, is unspeakably distant. The pearl rotunda lies, as in the sleepy salty waters of the ocean depths, in an illusory realm of stairs, corridors and mirrors, which shatter the artifical light.

It's most unpleasant and oppressive to be here, where the Tsars lived for the past fifty years. Some tasteless water-colours, some portraits daubed god knows by whom, some furniture in the fashionably 'modern' style – all very hard to credit in a dwelling built for demi-gods! What sideboards, writing desks and wardrobes! My God, it's the taste of a stockbroker with 'five comfy rooms', nice furniture and a family snapshot album! One longs to shove all these knick-knacks in the fire, in honour of the taste and beauty of one nice old Florentine candelabra.

Even in the Alexander II period there are smudges of bad taste. Along a secret stairway leading from his dressing-room there's a little room which the maids of honour had to pass with shawls over their faces to get to their quarters. For it's a harem of nude females – of Dianas and Venuses, muses and shepherdesses, dancers and marquesses. The Hermitage Gallery will be proud of this collection, with its Watteaus,

Fragonards and Bouchets. But all the frames are double, and behind the chaste magnificent goddesses are obscene little playthings. And in the most prominent place of all are two French paintings, crude, worthless botch-ups, with the 'nudes' displayed as in a butcher's shop. Simple obscenity. And the remnants of this ancient barbarity are visible everywhere. . . .

The February Revolution caused little damage. Then Kerensky arrived . . ., assumed Nicholas's throne and made his offices in the best rooms – even in Alexander III's elegant Hermitage and Tretyakov Galleries. . . . Now everything is broken, ink-stained, covered in dust and cigarettes. Kerensky's carelessness with the Romanovs' property, now the property of the people, smells bad. Why did he take the Tsar's palace, sleep in his bed and wipe his feet on luxuries which are the people's? Why, after the Tsar had left for Tobolsk, did Kerensky order his billiard table and balls to be laid out for his own private game?[26]

The article appeared on 11 November to a heartwarming chorus of protests at its accusations of Kerensky's moral and political corruption, and Larissa left Petrograd with a special journalist's pass for Gatchina, from where Kerensky had just been driven back in panic. She returned on 15 November to find that *New Life*'s editors had publicly apologised to him for her article. The next day, she was given the right of reply:

The editors have apologised for having allowed, through an oversight, several references to Kerensky not as a politician but as a private individual . . . I simply set out my impressions of a visit to the Winter Palace. I care nothing for A.F. Kerensky, as a politician or an individual, and wrote about him only because his occupation of the palace was an essential part of the picture . . .[27]

The episode clearly soured her relationship with the editors of *New Life*, and spelt the end of her collaboration with them. Now she entered the Revolution as into her native element, and her writings overflowed with the drama and emotion of October. But she was searching too for a new simplicity and rigour in her writing, and for a 'new materialistic world-view', wrote Vera Inber, 'which with people like her, is cut with difficulty, like wisdom teeth, but remains forever'.[28]

The old order had ended, and the new life being born from its ruins had not to uproot the past but to transcend it. In her unpublished autobiographical work, 'Requiem' (later titled 'Rudin') she touches on some of the contradictions of her class, which she would struggle throughout her life as a revolutionary to overcome.

There is a secret tragedy hidden in the life of people crossing from the right to the left shores, especially if they leave without repentance and shame for their birth, their roots, their name, and the cruel dominance of the class to which they were born. Only war and hard labour can level and purge this: behind shared bars, and under shared bullets, private dislikes are forgotten, and people become brothers.[29]

For feminists now, her talk of 'brotherhood' may reveal other suppressed contradictions she faced as a woman entering the world in 1917. The Bolsheviks had declared war on the old family, in which women were treated little better than slaves, and had pledged to put something better in its place. Their new marriage law, of 20 December, razed the existing tsarist law to the ground by allowing any man over eighteen and any woman over fifteen to marry, and to choose which surname they took afterwards. The stigma of illegitimacy was removed, and women could now initiate divorce and receive alimony.

But despite many such progressive laws then and in the years to come, the changing of family life was a deeply painful process, especially for women. Some 88 per cent of women in Russia were still illiterate. Women widowed by war or abandoned by husbands had been forced to leave their babies in derelict orphanages, and by 1917, thousands of abandoned children roamed the streets of the cities, hungry and often armed. Drained and exhausted, many women longed more than anything else for some peace of mind and the chance to rebuild their shattered families. But women had also derived an extraordinary strength from the past three years of war. This new female strength was celebrated in the writings of Kollontai, and for many women then Larissa Reisner was its symbol and inspiration.

Chapter Three

CIVIL WAR

On 18 November 1917, Adolf Ioffe, former Chair of the Petrograd Military Revolutionary Committee, left the capital with a nine-strong Soviet delegation for Brest-Litovsk, on the Soviet–Polish border, to confront the German High Command with their demands for a negotiated armistice. The armistice was finally signed on 2 December, and peace negotiations began a week later.

By the end of December, Germany had presented the Bolsheviks with their punishing demands for some 110,000 square miles of Russian territory. The terms were rejected, and the negotiations broken off. Meanwhile British and French negotiators meeting in Paris concluded a secret accord, assigning to Britain the Baltic provinces and the oil-rich Caucasus, and to France the Crimea and the Don Basin, with its iron and coal. A few weeks later, Lord Balfour, the British Foreign Secretary, informed the House of Commons that his government did not recognise the Petrograd administration.

In early January 1918, the Bolsheviks resumed their peace talks with Germany, and a new Soviet delegation left for Brest-Litovsk, led now by Lev Trotsky, the new Commissar for Foreign Affairs. On 18 February 1918 (NS), with the negotiations deadlocked, Germany announced the resumption of its offensive on the Ukraine, to wipe out the 'oriental pestilence of Bolshevism' and 'restore order in Russia'. The next day, the Bolsheviks agreed to resume the peace negotiations, and four days later, after bitter arguments, they accepted Germany's final predatory conditions, while Germany prepared to overthrow the government by force if the treaty wasn't ratified.

Even as the Brest-Litovsk Treaty was being signed, on 3 March, the enemies of the Revolution were preparing to invade. Britain and France were secretly backing the counter-revolutionary White Guards assembling in the Don region and near the Finnish border. Japan, with French and British approval, was planning to seize Vladivostok and invade Siberia. On 6 March, one hundred and thirty Royal Marines disembarked at the northern port of Murmansk, followed on the 7th by another British cruiser and twelve days later by a French destroyer. Germany had occupied the Ukraine, and was threatening Petrograd itself. The rich left the capital for the south, hoping to sit things out until the spring and the start of a new German offensive. And on 12 March, in anticipation of an invasion, the Bolsheviks evacuated the capital eastwards, to Moscow, and the government moved into the Kremlin.

The Reisners too left for the new capital, emptying now as the enemies of the Revolution departed. Thousands of new arrivals were moved into the bourgeoisie's old houses, and the Reisners were crowded with several other families into a large mansion formerly belonging to Count Sheremetev, where they were generously allotted three small but comparatively luxurious rooms, and the shared use of kitchen and bathroom (without gas or geyser). Most were not so well housed, everyone was hungry, and all were thinking of the cold hungry days that loomed ahead.

On 16 March, the Bolsheviks eventually ratified the Brest-Litovsk peace treaty, which granted Germany a huge share of Russia's oilfields, industrial centres and farming land. The French and British governments were meanwhile placing their hopes in some fifty thousand Czech soldiers scattered along the Siberian and Eastern railways, who were waiting to be allowed home. These soldiers consisted partly of divisions formed since 1914 from Czechs living in Russia, and from Austrian prisoners-of-war whom the tsarist government had been intending to send to the French front. The Czechs had long regarded tsarist Russia as the future liberator of their people from Austria. It was Winston Churchill who first saw the possibilities of using them as an anti-Bolshevik, rather than an anti-German, force. And in the summer of 1917, the French government had lent 2,100,000 francs to the Czecho-Slovak National Council to recruit the Czech legions to the counter-revolutionary cause. In March 1918, after lengthy negotiations with the Allies and the Czech National Council, the Bolsheviks finally agreed that they should travel home via the eastern port of Vladivostok, on condition that they surrendered their arms. They did not do so.[1]

On 5 May, Japanese troops landed at Vladivostok. Two weeks later, encouraged by Bolshevik weakness, the Czechs revolted, occupying key points in the east and cutting off central and northern Russia from the corn-producing areas. The Czech uprising signalled a wave of White Guard revolts, financed by France, Britain and America. The Whites and the invaders, six hundred thousand strong, were opposed by some three hundred thousand men and women Bolshevik volunteers, untrained and exhausted. With the Allied intervention striking into the very heart of the country, conscription was introduced into the Red Army, industry was put on a war footing, and bread rations were cut to two ounces a day. Trotsky, now Commissar for War, boarded the special train in which he lived virtually throughout the Civil War, travelling thousands of miles to thousands of fronts, recruiting, exhorting and mobilising people against the Whites.

As the Civil War turned into a people's war of total social mobilisation, thousands of women set off to fight and die for the Bolsheviks. In the front-line towns, they learned to shoot, fight and bandage the wounded. On the home front they were everywhere – feeding, cleaning and hacking at the earth to build trenches and fortifications. They marched to the battle fronts to fight in men's regiments or in special Communist women's detachments. At women's meetings, they called on their sisters to fight for the Revolution. Women like Konkordia Samoilova and Alexandra Kollontai became some of the Bolsheviks' most popular front-line agitators. Others were recruited for propaganda, espionage and police work, gave talks to soldiers on the battlefield, and worked at the front for the Party's Political Departments, which were centrally co-ordinated in Moscow by a woman named Varya Kasparova.

For Larissa Reisner, that summer was the turning-point of her life. Swept from her old educational work, she joined the Bolshevik Party to fight the Whites. It is evident that Raskolnikov had been an important part of her life for some time. After the defeat of Krasnov outside Petrograd, he was sent at the head of a detachment of sailors to support the Revolution in Moscow. In January, he had read out Lenin's declaration of withdrawal from the Constituent Assembly, by now the centre of opposition to the Revolution. His rise to power after that was fast, first as a commissar of the Naval General Staff, then as a member of the Collegium of the Naval Commissariat. In the summer of 1918, he and Larissa registered their marriage under the new Bolshevik marriage law. And finally, at the age of twenty-three, Larissa left home and moved with Raskolnikov into the same room at the Loskutnaya Hotel where she had stayed in the summer of 1916. But now a Maxim machine-gun lay on the hall table, the main staircase was lined with armed sailor guards, and the Loskutnaya was called the 'Red Fleet', and was the hostel for the Naval Commissariat.

Larissa's writings tell us little about how her marriage to Raskolnikov weathered the storms and separations of war and revolution, and like most women fighting for the new Bolsheviks then, she tells us less than we might want about the details of her personal life. 'We can laugh now at those women who rejected love, reckoning that it would get in the way of their work,' wrote Adelaida Prokhorova, a single mother from Moscow who left her three-year-old son to go to the front. 'Possibly in those days we did err too far in that direction. Yet I know now that the reason we won in those unbelievably difficult days was because we were able to transcend our personal cares and attachments . . .'

For women like Larissa Reisner, who had no children, Revolution replaced the domestic and emotional burdens of marriage with a looser, more impermanent kind of tie. 'Those weren't the times for growing rubber plants or doing satin-stitch embroidery,' wrote Asmik Papyan, leader of a women's espionage group. The women of the Civil War idealised a new kind of partnership with men, and argued for a sexual comradeship that would transcend traditional family dramas and jealousies. 'Happiness then wasn't a pretty dress, a successful marriage and a cosy flat with a gramophone,' wrote Alexandra Bulygina, a nurse at the Urals front, 'Happiness was working amongst the wounded, and those stricken and dying of typhus.'[2]

As Larissa left home for the Revolution, she faced a new and uncertain future, and a marriage of constant separations, without home, security, the chance to have children, or even a room of her own for creative endeavour. And amongst the intense and entangled passions of revolution, patriarchy survived. Raskolnikov worshipped his 'warrior Diana', as he called Larissa once in a letter when they were apart. According to one western writer, he was also a 'morbidly jealous husband, who treated her roughly'.[3] If this was the case, her writings contain little evidence of it. She wrote not of the lingering forms of the old patriarchal family, but of the anguish and excitement of women's lives, of a new kind of family life in the revolutionary movement, and of the birth, from scratch and under fire, of a new morality. And despite the dangers, difficulties and separations, she lived, worked and fought with Raskolnikov for the next five years.

Shortly after joining the Party, she started working at the headquarters of the Naval Commissariat, housed on Vozdvizhenka (now Kalinin Street), in the house that had belonged to Shamsi Assadulaev, the former oil magnate. Raskolnikov and the sailors she had already met were some of the Bolsheviks' firmest supporters, most of them anxious to support women's right to work with men on equal terms. But now she was also meeting the masses – sailors reared by the tsarist navy, exhausted by years of war and disinclined to follow any orders, let alone those given by a woman. Now she had to face men who felt judged by her presence, and to force them to challenge the old degraded attitudes to women.

The naval headquarters seethed with activity, for several other institutions, including the *Peasant Paper*, had their offices there. Outside Raskolnikov's office, the passage resounded with the heavy footsteps of sailors. Inside, in Assadulaev's old ballroom, with its gilded chairs and white grand piano, Larissa would look out of the large windows at the Moscow river and the grim, vigilant capital, and dream of action. One night, in a silence broken by gunshots, Lev Nikulin accompanied her through the street patrols of the Arbat back to Vozdvizhenka. He had once seen at a chemist's laboratory a phial of cyanide, he told her, sealed with a skull and crossbones. ' "Then get it for me if you can," she said. "I'll need it if I fall into the White Guards' hands and they disarm me. I'm a woman, and they're animals." ' Nikulin refused. When he visited her at her hotel, there was no samovar and no spice cakes on the table, 'just a crust of stale black ration bread with straw, the yellow wooden box of a field telephone, a small polished Browning pistol, and piles of paper telegraph ribbons, announcing the latest Czech advances on the Volga'.[4]

By June, Czech forces had captured the central Volga town of Samara (now Kuybyshev), and brought to power Socialist Revolutionary members of the new Constitutional Assembly Committee, supported by the Allies, as the embryo of Russia's future national government. All nationalised or municipalised enterprises were restored to the landowners, Bolsheviks were massacred on the streets, and there was an epidemic of lynchings. By July, French advisers, encouraged by the Whites' successes on the Volga, were urging an immediate Czech offensive on Saratov, Simbirsk (now Ulyanovsk) and Kazan.

It was to Kazan that Reisner and Raskolnikov were to set off to fight the Czechs. But first, Raskolnikov was sent south on a secret mission to the Black Sea port of Novorossiisk, near the Crimea, to scuttle the Bolsheviks' fleet so as to prevent it from falling into the hands of the occupying German army. Larissa's room at the Red Fleet hostel was always crowded with friends and journalists, poring over the telegraph ribbons telling of the tragedy in Novorossiisk. Viktor Shklovsky recalled:

I remember Larissa Mikhailovna at the Loskutnaya. She was then Raskolnikov's wife. The fleet was lying almost in the Moscow River. It was embarrassingly crowded. I was in the enemy camp. When I'd reconsidered things and come back, she greeted me as the finest comrade. With her benign northern bearing, that was somehow good.[5]

With her friends, however, she spoke with a new fierceness and conviction. 'The Revolution can't fail!' she told Nikulin:

'The Left Socialist Revolutionaries are just coquettes – and you're no better!' And taking an issue of the paper *Evening Hour* from her desk, she read, sighing comically: ' "I met my sweetheart on the stairs . . ." Well I hope you met her for the last time! British submarines are attacking our torpedoes, military actions have started on the Volga – you should be ashamed! We must shoot counter-revolutionaries! It's unavoidable, it's civil war – hunger's worse . . .'

Then the sailor Andrei Zheleznyakov came in, 'to be neighbourly', and was introduced to Nikulin as the same sailor who that January had dismissed the Constituent Assembly with the words: 'The guards are tired!' He sat down, leafed through *Evening Hour*, shaking his head disapprovingly, then stood up and left.[6]

Just two years before, Larissa and Nikulin had been discussing poetry and literature late into the night at their student meetings. Now the 'Rudinists', who had renounced the old world in their poems, were experiencing its bloody end in war and revolution, and wrestling with the limitless visions now opening up of the origins and purposes of their work. Many of these visions took shape in the new Proletarian Cultural and Educational Organisation (or Proletkult), which aimed to train a new generation of working-class cadres in poetic composition and technique. A number of older Symbolists, such as Blok and Bryusov, lectured in Proletkult's studios to young proletarian poets, and much of the poetry that emerged from these studios celebrated the cosmic sweep of the Revolution in the rhythms and images of Symbolism.

Larissa Reisner always retained a special fondness for Blok, the guardian of so much that was precious to her in the old culture, now struggling to make way for the new. After 1917, Blok had shut himself away to write 'The Twelve', a verse account, part satire, part celebration, in startling, staccato rhythms reminiscent of Mayakovsky, of the events on Petrograd's streets. And that summer, Reisner would sit at the restaurant in the Hermitage

Park with her friends, drinking pink saccharine-sweetened water, and arguing into the night about Blok's 'Twelve' – 'and who wasn't arguing about Blok's "Twelve" in those days!' said Nikulin.

But now the days for discussions were drawing to an end. By July, Constituent Assembly Committees had assumed power in a series of Volga towns, each of which became the scene of protracted massacres. But the high point of the anti-Bolshevik campaign on the Volga was at Kazan, for four hundred years the Mongol stronghold in Europe. The key to the entire lower Volga, and thus to the whole of central Russia, Kazan was now the financial base for the counter-revolution: it was there that the Whites had hidden Russia's currency reserves (amounting to some £10,000 million), plus hoards of securities, stocks, platinum and gold. As the Bishop summoned the faithful to defend the Church, the University placed itself at the patriotic disposal of the new government, and the resurrected bourgeois press predicted the Allies' irresistible progress. The Bolsheviks' position there seemed hopeless. Yet it was at Kazan that they set up their Eastern Front headquarters.

In July, Raskolnikov returned from Novorossiisk to Moscow, now as Deputy Commissar for Naval Affairs and member of the Revolutionary War Council of the Eastern Front. From Moscow he was ordered to sail immediately, under the Eastern Front's operational command, to Kazan, via Nizhnii Novgorod (now Gorky), where his old Kronstadt comrade Nikolai Markin was in charge of organising a flotilla for him. 'Larissa too went off to the Volga with her flotilla,' wrote Shklovsky, 'eagerly packing up her life, as though strapping it all up to go off to another planet.'[7] Leaving Moscow by train with Raskolnikov and his sailors, she travelled two hundred miles east, along railway lines wrecked by sabotage, to Nizhnii Novgorod, where Markin had hastily created a flotilla of sorts from a number of river vessels and Baltic Fleet destroyers transferred there. Boarding their boats, they sailed another two hundred miles east.

So began her life on the Volga, the longest river in Europe, whose upper reaches had bred two legendary peasant rebellions in the seventeenth and eighteenth centuries, and whose lower reaches had long been a refuge for runaway serfs and religious sectarians. The peaceful spots on the Volga which she had visited with her friends in 1916 were now the scenes of some of the fiercest battles of the Civil War. For the next two years she fought on all the fronts there, as fighter and scout for the Volga Flotilla and the Fifth Army. In those early days of war, women's recruitment was still tentative and sporadic, and even later, relatively few women joined the navy. Larissa already knew most of the Baltic sailors who formed the core of the new flotilla, and they accepted her without too much difficulty on their ships. But for many sailors women on board simply meant bad luck, and her first appearance on the flotilla's battleships was often greeted with volleys of obscenities and abuse. To many sailors she seemed too young for the job, and too cultured to understand them, and they were aggressive, contemptuous or defensive with her. Others would try to exploit her vulnerability by demanding sexual favours of her, or insisting that she discuss the 'marriage question' with them. This first trip down the Volga was her first taste of things to come: now she had to prove and defend herself, learn to give as good as she got, and defend herself if need be with her fists.

Two hundred miles east of Nizhnii Novgorod the Volga broadens into a series of flowing lakes, and three days later they reached Kazan, with its Tartar and Mongol architecture, its watermelons and dust. Arriving in the town, they found complete chaos and the Bolsheviks in headlong retreat, as combined Czech–White Guard forces attacked from land and the Volga. The flotilla set itself up at the headquarters of the Eastern Front, on Bolshaya Prolomnaya Street. And from there they planned the retreat – or rather helplessly witnessed as the front disintegrated and a number of recently formed Red regiments, betrayed by their officers, collapsed and fled.

Yet even in the exhaustion and danger of the retreat Larissa was writing, from the Siberian Guesthouse, where she was staying. For her piece on Kazan, later included in her 'Letters from the Front', bears all the immediacy of an eye-witness account:

The town isn't taken yet, but its defeat is certain. The doors of abandoned rooms are slammed. The floors are littered with papers and scattered possessions. . . .

Nothing is worse than retreat. From all sides appear faces of neighbours not seen for many months . . . Before the porch appear the dim outlines of batteries, and dusty, tense, angry faces. . . . The streets are loud with cries, the thunder of heels, the clatter of cavalry . . . . Lorries pass, rattling the windows – and their noisy flight kills our last hope, and fills us with dread. In doorways still hung with useless signs like 'Operations' and 'Secretariat', women say goodbye to their loved ones, and behind them the servants sweep out the rubbish of the revolution. And in this sweeping away of our warm traces lies all the grief and dirt of failure. . . .

It's strange passing these unfamiliar houses with their locked doors, and knowing that . . . inside, people will be killed or captured. One forgets all the words and formulae meant to help preserve one's presence of mind in such moments. There remains only a sharp, cutting grief – and flickering beneath it, something 'in the name of which' we flee or stay. Choking with tears, the heart repeats: leave calmly, without panic, without humiliating haste. . . .[8]

Party members were the core of the new army and navy, and as such, Larissa had all the same rights as other sailors, but many more duties and she was expected to be tough, tireless and able to inspire confidence in the retreat. But when the first shells hit Kazan's Kremlin and the Front Headquarters, where the last remaining Red troops were stationed, all restraint was abandoned and desperate preparations were made to leave. Vatsetis, Commander of the Eastern Front, had escaped capture by steering a path with the help of a handful of fighters through the fugitives and pursuers, and had joined what remained of Soviet forces at the little village station of Svyazhsk, forty miles from Kazan on the banks of the Volga. It was there that the fugitives made for.

On 5 August, Larissa concealed the Bolsheviks' printing press and several important documents under her heavy army coat, with instructions from Raskolnikov to hand them over to the first Red detachment she met. Then at six in the evening, she said goodbye to her comrades (Raskolnikov was to leave at the last moment), and under a drizzle of rain and a crescendo of approaching gunshots, she joined the crowds of families and children streaming out of the town, with their chickens, blankets and samovars.

As far as the eye can see, pouring along the golden autumn fields, is a stream of poverty, of soldiers and carts loaded with precious household goods. What a relief it is to be with this living stream. Who are these refugees? Communists? Hardly. That woman in the front, carrying a baby in one arm and dragging a frightened goat with the other, certainly doesn't have a Party card. At each shot, each spasm of panic shaking the crowd, she crosses herself to all the spires. She is simply the people, the masses, escaping the ancient enemies. She is the whole of Russia, hoisting its bundle on to its shoulders, and walking along this boggy road to escape the Czech liberators . . .

Stumbling, falling and getting up again, they continued straight ahead across the muddy fields, driven in the night by exhaustion and the wind towards Svyazhsk. By midnight the drizzle had turned to a downpour, the darkened fields had become endless and boggy, and a swollen blue cloud hung over Kazan, now already taken. Raskolnikov, who had escaped just in time, had already broken through to the highway.

Beyond the town the noise of shellfire quietened, the sky was lit with the glow of fires and distant summer lightning, and a desolate flock of rooks made for the outskirts. The channel of fleeing women, children and carts started to thin, and Larissa bothered by her foot and weighed down by the documents and printing press under her coat, struggled to keep ahead. As dawn broke, they stumbled into a village and knocked on the door of a schoolteacher's cottage, and after a meal of warm bread and milk they took off their wet boots and fell asleep exhausted on the floor.

They walked on for two days, barefoot, their boots slung on sticks over their shoulders. Occasionally they would stop at the cottages of religious sectarians, who were generally sympathetic and fed them on creamy milk and fresh honey cakes. 'Civil war reigns on the main roads. You just have to turn into a country lane, or a path running through warm fragrant hedges, and again there's peace, and the transparent silence of late summer . . .'

On the third day, they were sitting exhausted outside the cottage of a friendly religious sectarian, eating boiled eggs and cucumbers, when there appeared a man in a blue jacket and red sash, looking suspiciously like a retired policeman. Their leader, a bow-legged, one-eyed sailor, calmly explained that they were there on holiday, looking for a cottage 'with all conveniences and a nice view of the river'. At this the visitor guffawed, and with one leap the holiday-makers were up and over the fields before he could catch them.

They spent the rest of that day dozing under wet haystacks, then stumbled off in the wet night straight into a detachment of Reds, where Reisner handed over her press and documents, and checked for news of Raskolnikov. After another day of snatched sleep in a field, they crossed the Volga, then walked for another hour and finally, on the morning of 9 August, they staggered into Svyazhsk, where Reisner again tried to find out about Raskolnikov. 'Don't worry, yours is all right – he's probably escaped to Paris,' a dashing commander said spitefully to her. 'A minute later, red and angry, he stood covered in hot tea – but it didn't change anything.'

Eventually a telegram arrived with the news that Raskolnikov had been captured by the Whites, and Larissa and her sailor friend Misha Kalinin prepared immediately to retrace their forty-mile journey to Kazan to find him. They were given new trousers, boots and greatcoats, a pass through Red lines was scribbled out for them on a cigarette paper, and the Commander of the Red Latvian regiment gave them two horses, after Larissa had persuaded him that Raskolnikov was Latvian too ('on his mother's side'). She mounted easily, for she was a good rider, and she was soon in agony, for the journey was a long one. But her chestnut mare, Beauty, was to be her friend for the next three years.

The two rode off along the silent paths of the warm forest, 'smelling of tar and wild strawberries'. Before long they met up with a detachment of Reds, who gave them soup, and a little further on they came across the headquarters of another Red detachment, this time of Cossacks, led by Commander Yudin. The Whites were just a few miles off and were expected at any moment to attack, 'and in those last hours of Yudin's life, strained and pulsing like a bursting vein, we spent several sharp, oath-filled minutes'.

After they had eaten and rested, a Cossack brought from the attic a smart man's suit and a dark Parisian ladies' costume, for which they gladly exchanged their boots and greatcoats. As they set off, in their new, convincingly bourgeois, disguise, Yudin said, 'Till we meet again!': 'And death, standing behind his back, smiled cynically in the darkness.'

They were riding on in the dark, avoiding the railway tracks, when suddenly the silence of the forest was pierced by the sounds of a woman in agony. Following the shrieks to a cottage bathhouse in a nearby peasant settlement, they found a young Kirghiz woman, labouring in an agony of childbirth on the floor. Reisner clutched the woman, who muttered to her through sweat-soaked hair. Then, in one terrible convulsion, she gave birth and fell asleep, her hot fingers still clenched. Next day, after attending the christening, the grateful father drove them in his cart through the forest, past the White checkpoints, towards the distant thunder of heavy artillery, and finally back into White Kazan itself.

It's as though ten years have passed since our retreat. The streets and buildings are familiar, yet they're hard to recognise. Everything is different: the officers, the schoolboys and the young ladies from educated families with their nurses' scarves, the open shops, the rollicking, hysterical brightness of their cafés – and all the tawdry, transient rash erupting on the body of the defeated revolution.

Now men with weapons and white armbands roamed the town searching houses for suspects, and cutting every Bolshevik throat on the spot. Commissars had their eyes poked out. Red prisoners walking in the streets were delivered to the mob to be killed and trampled on. The streets were littered with naked, mutilated corpses, with their eyes gouged out and their Party cards pinned to their chests.

Announcing that he was taking them 'somewhere quiet', their driver deposited them at the house of Kazan's chief of police. There, posing as a White officer and his wife, they drank tea with the police chief, his shrill wife and bored daughter. And after they had all cursed the Jews and Communists together, the police chief welcomed them into his neat house, with its potted geraniums, waxed floors, icons and portraits of tsarist officials.

Next day, Kalinin took the money and papers, and set off for the town for news of their comrades. And while the police chief's daughter leaned over the window sill spitting sunflower seeds at passers-by, Larissa scanned the newspaper for lists of Bolshevik prisoners. That evening, the town was shelled by the Reds, and everyone hurtled down to the basement, where Larissa found a number of workers' families living huddled in a corner, and she managed to exchange discreet glances with them.

When after two days Misha still had not returned, the police chief, assuming that he had been mobilised, advised her to go off herself to look for him, and she left without papers, passport or money, for the town centre. On the way, her tram stopped to let pass a cart plastered with the slogan: 'All Power to the Constituent Assembly!', and loaded with the naked bodies of shot workers. But she had no difficulty finding the Whites' headquarters, on Gruzinskaya Street, and after the simple invention of a false identity based on mythical relatives and a missing passport, she was easily admitted.

My God! How good is the White régime on the Third Day of its Creation! How busily tap the women typists on their Remingtons, and what sweet intelligent faces they have . . .

After infiltrating the Gruzinskaya Street headquarters she hung about there for two days, before being finally admitted to the office of the notorious Ensign Ivanov, 'the Mademoiselle Fifi of White Guard Kazan, who shot soldiers and workers "for revolution" '. And from a friendly secretary there she finally discovered that Raskolnikov was alive, and Misha arrested.

But by now, life with the police chief was becoming unbearable, and he was growing increasingly suspicious. When a worker was led away from the basement to be shot, his comrades urged her to escape. Early in the morning of her third day in Kazan, she put a crust of bread in her pocket, along with a three-rouble note given to her by a worker's wife, and slipped outside, where the police chief himself gallantly escorted her off to Ivanov for questioning.

She arrived to find waiting there a group of Bolshevik sailors. After exchanging small glances with her, they were led off to be shot, after which it was her turn for the interrogation room. First she was strip-searched by a woman guard, who removed her underwear and dumped it on the dirty floor, already piled high with the possessions of previous victims. Then she was left to confront the green baize table at which sat a squirming French officer, a minute-taker and Ensign Ivanov, 'with his bald head, white as a boiled egg, his light eyes without eyebrows, his white tunic, and his clean white hands on the table'. Nudging the French officer, Ivanov winked at Reisner's underwear lying on the floor, then dismissed him and he was left alone to interrogate Larissa about Raskolnikov, her 'relatives' and her lost passport.

She was with Ivanov for several hours, while he accused, screamed and beat her with such violence that her head had to be bandaged. 'Then an extraordinary thing happened. There are moments in life of mad, divine, fairytale happiness. On that grey morning, which I glimpsed through the hopeless bars of the window, I experienced a miracle.'

Ivanov went out to the room on the right, to fetch an interrogator. At that moment, the sentry at the other door went off to light his cigarette, and she was alone. There was a third door in the middle of the room, tacked with felt. She ripped it down, nails and all, slipped out on to the staircase, tore the bandage off her head, crept past the sentry to the street, and reached the corner, where she called a cab. The driver looked at her, dazed, speechless and half-clothed, then at the Whites' headquarters, and whipping his horse he took Reisner off to his wife, Avdotya Markovna into whose motherly arms she collapsed sobbing. After feeding her and wrapping a warm shawl round her bare shoulders, Avdotya Markovna 'covered Ivanov with such curses that the cocks crowed with delight'. Two hours later, Reisner was being escorted by a peasant across the fields. After walking a mile, she met up with a Red detachment, amongst whom was one of Yudin's Cossacks, who asked her laconically whether she had 'ever found that husband of hers'.[9] Since she was still no wiser as to where he and Misha were, most of her comrades considered her entry into the Whites' headquarters at Kazan as an act of heroic but senseless self-sacrifice, and her name appeared on the enemy's counter-intelligence lists, with the words 'find and kill'.

A few days later she arrived back in Svyazhsk, to discover that Misha had been killed, but Raskolnikov, she learnt to her joy, was alive, and had left for Kronstadt. With the Soviet Republic shrunk to the size of the Grand Duchy of Moscow, Bolshevik fortunes were now at their lowest ebb. On 3 August, British troops landed in Vladivostok, as part of the grand design for a joint Allied–Czech–White Russian force; two weeks later they were joined there by the first US troop landing. By then the French fleet lay in the Black Sea, the British occupied the coast around Murmansk and had set up governments at Arkhangel and in Estonia, and British forces from Persia and Salonika were occupying the Baku–Batum railway.

At the very moment when Ludendorff was launching his last desperate offensive against Paris, the Allies had, in effect, made a coalition with Germany for the purpose of defeating Bolshevik Russia. Finnish–German troops threatened the railway to Murmansk. The Germans occupied a 350-mile line from the Gulf of Finland. General Krasnov, supported by Germany, was in the Ukraine. The German puppet, Hetman Skoropadsky, was massacring Jews and Communists in Kiev. Siberia was largely in White hands. And on the Volga, the Czechs were holding Kazan, Simbirsk and Samara, and threatening Kursk, Voronezh and Tsaritsyn.

That August, the Red Army was scourged by typhus, cholera and hunger. People existed on starvation rations, and the Revolution, strangled by intervention and blockade, was collapsing into the chaos of counter-revolution. Its fate was being decided at Svyazhsk, which barred the Czechs' access to the river-bed road from Kazan to Nizhnii Novgorod, and the rail line to Moscow.

On 8 August, two days after the fall of Kazan, and with the

Eastern Front in chaos, Trotsky had left for Kazan on his special train containing some two hundred Communists hand-picked for their determination. The French Bolshevik Victor Serge describes how the train stopped at Svyazhsk's derelict station-yard. Then the engine drove off (to emphasise that its passengers meant to stay), leaving only the carriages containing the General Staff Headquarters, the revolutionary tribunal, 'and all departments of an army that did not yet exist'. Another train followed, manned by three hundred cavalry soldiers, along with an aeroplane, a garage truck for five cars, a radio-telegraph office, a printshop and a tribunal.[10]

Shortly after Trotsky arrived at the Svyazhsk front, Raskolnikov returned from Kronstadt as Commander of the Volga Naval Flotilla, with four torpedo boats he had manoeuvred through the Mariinsky canal system. These were reinforced by several river steamers, armed with guns and machine-guns, and a tsarist yacht, the *Mezhen*, with baths, showers and clean sheets, which was to be the staff-ship. Larissa had been separated from Raskolnikov for just a week, but that week had taught her a new kind of courage and independence. Now, as she contemplated the battles ahead under Raskolnikov's command, she was impatient to put her courage to the test.

In Svyazhsk, Trotsky found units in chaos, 'sharing only a readiness to run. . . . The very soil was infected with panic'.[11] Yet it was at Svyazhsk that the advance of the Czechs and Whites was halted against a line of hastily dug trenches, 'behind which stood nothing but a will of iron'.[12] There, for a whole month, the fate of the Revolution hung in the balance. And there Larissa Reisner fought, rifle in hand, on the front line.

Svyazhsk, which later played such a great part in the recapture of Kazan, and which became the furnace in which the nucleus of the Red Army was forged, arose at the very height of retreat and panic, and was repeated and remembered as something elemental.[13]

Here was the final bastion for which Bolsheviks had to be prepared to die. Great causes raise people to this, she wrote, and make them invincible:

Those who slept on the floor, in straw strewn with broken glass, were afraid of nothing, with almost no hope of victory. Nobody wanted to know when the business would be over. . . . Each hour of life had the fullness and freshness of some miracle. A plane came to drop bombs on the station; the sickening bark of machine-guns came nearer, then receded, along with the murmur of the big guns; and the soldier in his ragged cape, with a floppy hat on his head and worn-out boots – this was the image of the defender of Svyazhsk – would consult his watch with a grin and say: 'At 0300 hours – or 0400 hours, or 0600 hours – I am still alive, Svyazhsk is still holding on, and Trotsky's train is over there, with a lamp in the window of the Political Department. Another day over.'

There were practically no medicines, and heaven knows how the doctors managed to dress wounds. The misery of our situation banished shame and fear: as the soldiers went for their soup, they passed before the dead and wounded, lying in the open on their stretchers . . .

As a Party member and commissar, Larissa Reisner had to stay with the troops, fight to the end and put backbone into the deserting masses. As a woman, she had constantly to fight the distrust of the sailors under her command, struggle for their respect, and instil dignity and discipline. This battle had to be fought over and over again, with every new group of recruits she met. One Volga Flotilla sailor who described the impact of her presence on the sailors at the Svyazhsk front was nineteen-year-old Vsevolod Vishnevsky, who later made her the heroine of his popular play 'An Optimistic Tragedy'. He recalled her, dashing and cheerful in a black jacket and fleet cap, as she visited his ship that August on a reconnaissance mission. And he described how the sailors were educated, through her own personal influence and courage, in a more enlightened view of women.

When she comes to us sailors we give her a test: we sit her down on a destroyer launch in the path of a machine-gun battery of White Czechs, and give her full speed. The destroyer leaves. We watch this female sitting there, then we order her back. 'Why?' she says. 'It's too early, we must go on!'

From that moment we were friends, and we later did much reconnaissance work with her. This person had knowledge and strength. People couldn't believe it at first. 'Look at that,' they said. 'What a woman!'[14]

The journalist and old Bolshevik Lev Sosnovsky also wrote of the 'tests' to which she was subjected:

She passed the first one. That was when, without anyone driving or sending her, she was in those places where the fate of the Revolution was decided. That was at Svyazhsk, near Kazan. That was the first test. At that time she wrote little, or else we seldom had the chance to read her . . .[15]

Later, in a letter to her family, she wrote:

Darlings, I'm writing in a great hurry, from a madhouse. Are you still alive? Tomorrow I'll send you money and flour. My dear ones, it's very hard to write.

During the day I work at the HQ, and at night Fedya and I made mad raids on the destroyers against their flotilla. We've sunk three ships and two barges under the nose of their battery. I've learnt to ride – for whole days on end. Any free time is on board the luxurious *Mezhen*, where the sound of shooting is as if in a dream. Why don't some of you come to Svyazhsk for a few days? I kiss you, my treasures. Your Lyalya.[16]

Her mother did visit her at Svyazhsk that summer, and stayed with her on board ship for a week, from where she wrote back to Moscow:

She is having a good period of *Sturm und Drang*. If she lives through it, it will do much for her soul, and her creativity might awake in writing about these extraordinary experiences. But . . . I don't think so, for she is always on the brink of destruction. . . . Our little aristocrat stands on the bridge, yielding to no one in cool courage, and the sailors silently follow her.[17]

On the night of 28 August, under cover of darkness, the Whites, led by Savinkov and Kappel (later a celebrated White general), launched a surprise cavalry attack on the Bolsheviks' rear at Tyurlyama, near Svyazhsk, killing sentries, seizing a small railway station on the line from Moscow, destroying tracks, cutting down telegraph poles, and blowing up the Red train sent to intercept them along with eighteen wagonloads of shells. With the Red sector cut in half, the regiment holding the front by the river scattered, headed by their commanders and commissars, and invaded the ships of the Volga flotilla.

With the army thrown into panic, Trotsky collected together everyone on his train – office-boys, clerks, ambulancemen, and anyone who could hold a gun – and hurled them into battle. The Bolsheviks' only hope now lay in these five hundred hastily armed recruits, against twice as many Whites, and Larissa Reisner organised a party of sailors on a reconnaissance mission to reunite the General Staff with those cut off at Tyurlyama. This dangerous operation was described by an anonymous sailor, whose words were later recorded by A. Kremlyov in an article in the Red Army paper, *Red Star*:

The enemy is moving towards the Volga, in the rear of not just our detachments but of the flotilla as well. Trotsky's train is stuck near Svyazhsk.

Order: slip through, locate and make contact with those cut off.

Larissa goes off, taking Vanyushka Rybakov, a sailor lad (just a boy!) and someone else I don't recall, and the three are off.

Night, shivering with cold, loneliness and the unknown. Yet Larissa was marching so confidently along that unfamiliar road!

At the village of Kurochkino, someone spotted them, they're fired on, they spread out, it's hard to crawl – a tight spot! And Larissa is joking, and her hidden anxiety only makes her voice more velvety.

They slipped out of the firing line, and were through!

'Are you tired, my lad . . .? Vanya, what about you?'

And in her concern, she reached an unattainable height in that moment. They wanted to kiss that marvellous woman's hands, black as they were with the grime of the road.

She walked along quickly, with long strides, and they almost had to run to keep up.

By morning they'd reached the Whites' camp. Charred ground, corpses – Tyurlyama.

From there, dropping on their feet, they made for Shikhrana, where the Red Latvian regiment was positioned, and contact could be made with Trotsky's train.

The front had been tied up. And that woman with the wan smile was the knot that tied it.

'Comrades, look after my boys. Me? No, I'm not tired!'

Then more scouting by Verkhnii Uslon, near the two Morkvashis, and as far as Pyanii Bor. Sixty miles on horseback without tiring.

Pleasures were few enough then. Yet the smile never left Larissa Mikhailovna's face in those tough campaigns.

And then Enzeli, Baku and Moscow!

And that was what a sailor from a landing-party remembered.[18]

The battle lasted several hours. The Whites, thinking they were up against a formation of crack troops unspotted by their scouts, withdrew exhausted by their forty-eight hour forced march. And the ten thousand soldiers of the newly reunited Fifth Army now gathered before Svyazhsk and the far bank of the Volga for an offensive on Kazan, whose loss would mean their destruction.

The next day, Raskolnikov and Trotsky drew up a scheme to attack and burn the enemy's fleet anchored at Kazan harbour. Larissa joined them that night aboard the torpedo boat *Durable*, which sailed with all lights out at the head of a group of ships down the Volga towards Kazan. Passing silently through the two high headlands where the Whites' batteries were mounted, they sailed on to where the river curved and broadened, and reached the harbour. On the opposite bank, Kazan lay open.

The *Durable* and its crew were the only ones to pass the narrow entrance in Kazan's harbour. Entering quickly, they aimed their artillery at a caravan of White barges, then retired without losses to watch the entire White flotilla go up in flames. The Whites fired back. The *Durable* grazed the side of an enemy ship, its rudder chain broke, and it rammed one of its own gunboats. But the Whites were so stunned by the attack that the *Durable*'s command was able to repair the damage, join up with the other ships, then pound the enemy's batteries on both shores of the Volga.

Gradually, out of the Bolsheviks' straggling horde of beaten soldiers a powerful, self-assured army emerged. This new Red Army, born of a revolutionary passion bordering on fanaticism, acted mercilessly against disorder. The day after the raid, twenty-seven Bolsheviks who had panicked and fled (including several old militants) were tried and shot. There was no alternative, wrote Reisner:

The whole army was saying that the Communists were cowards, that they were exempt from the law, that they could desert and get away with it. . . . Without the extraordinary gallantry displayed by Trotsky and the members of the Revolutionary War Council, the prestige of Communists working in the army would have been finished for ever.[19]

Gradually the situation outside Kazan improved. The Whites were beaten back again and again, fresh troops arrived from Petrograd, Moscow and elsewhere, a small airfield was laid, communications were restored, and the Reds prepared once again to enter Kazan.

Even when the rainy days of August came, our thin, badly armed lines never yielded, the bridge stayed under our control, and reinforcements began to arrive from the rear. Trotsky's organising genius now became apparent: across railways that were openly sabotaged, Trotsky got to Svyazhsk not only fresh artillery, but everything that was needed for resistance and for offensive. And this, it should be noted, was in 1918, when the sight of a squad of well-dressed soldiers walking in the streets of Moscow would cause a sensation. To do this meant to beat back the current, to fight against the weariness of four years of war, and against the stormy waters of the Revolution itself, which throughout the country was sweeping aside the old hated discipline like so much flotsam . . . And against all odds, the rations, the newspapers, the boots and the capes reached us.

From retreat and despair the new Volga flotilla was born, and the legendary Fifth Army. Reisner paid tribute to its leader, and his miracles of organisation and recruitment. But she wrote too of the calibre and nobility of its less sung heroes – of old Bolsheviks like Ivan Smirnov, 'the incarnation of the revolutionary ethic, the highest moral criterion of the Communist consciousness at Svyazhsk':

At Trotsky's side we could die in battle with the last cartridge gone, oblivious of our wounds; for Trotsky incarnated all the holy demagogy of battle, summoning up with words and gestures the most heroic pages of the French Revolution. But with Smirnov beside us we could feel calm and clear-headed when we were up against the wall, facing interrogation by the Whites in some hell hole of a prison. That is what we used to whisper to ourselves on those nights of a quick freezing autumn, lying jumbled in heaps on the floor. . . . Comrade Smirnov's exceptional purity and probity imposed themselves even on the mass of non-Party soldiers, and on Party members who'd not known him before.

Larissa herself was by this time one of the flotilla's most experienced scouts. Her work was especially valued by her old friend Nikolai Markin, and she spent much time by the mooring of the legendary battleship *Vanya the Communist*, of which he was commander. Nikolai Kartashov, one of Markin's sailors, described his first meeting with her when she arrived one evening on deck. It was at the end of the day's battle, in which his squadron had taken the village of Berezhnye Morkvashi, and the officers and men were resting on deck. Suddenly their gaze was arrested by three cavalrymen, bearing sabres and carbines, approaching the shore. One of them was invited up to the captain's bridge, and there Markin introduced the graceful young rider to his disconcerted crew as 'Larissa Mikhailovna Reisner, war correspondent and scout'.

After she had peered at the Whites' ships through her binoculars, Markin told her how the Red flotilla was disposed, and she spoke warmly of its timely arrival at Kazan and its brave attacks on the enemy's ships. But as she spoke, wrote Kartashov, the sailors below deck were discussing her with their usual noisy obscenities, and unable to contain herself any longer, she begged Markin to let them up so she could speak to them.

They crowded round her, astonished and curious, and she said: 'Comrade sailors! The pick of the bunch! I was in Kazan, and I'll never forget how the Whites dealt with our brothers . . . . But we'll have our revenge! I wish you great success, and I'll be with you at the front . . .!'[20]

This brought much applause, and she went on, smiling, to rebuke them for their language, which 'brings shame to all our heroic working women and mothers. If you need to curse, curse the White Guard filth!' And there followed a rich stream of oaths at the White Czechs. There was loud applause at this, and shouts of 'That's good! Bravo, cavalryman! Good woman!' Then she went ashore, swung on to her horse, waved and trotted off towards Berezhnye Morkvashi.

Later that evening, a destroyer launch approached the battle-ship and moored, and the sailors met her again, accompanied now by a flotilla commander, Captain Neuberg. They boarded, and Reisner requested Markin's permission to scout out the advanced White flotilla. Neuberg objected that it would be too dangerous, Reisner waved him aside, Neuberg was overruled, and the two returned to their launch. As they cut down the fairway at full speed towards the Whites' ships, Reisner stood smiling by the helm, waving her cap and shouting: 'If anything happens, open fire!' Then they disappeared from sight.

The launch soon returned, safe and unharmed. The sailors loudly applauded Reisner's courage, and she thanked them for saving them with their answering fire. 'I think we put the heat on the Whites!'

Then she turned ironically to the despondent Neuberg: 'The tragedy is that our flotilla commander is ill.' Neuberg muttered that this wasn't a woman but a sailor in a skirt, and this was the first time, devil take it, that he'd seen such an amazon.

The sailors gazed at them, relishing the situation, while Markin reassured Neuberg that it was only frightening the first time – 'look how easily Larissa Mikhailovna did it!'

Reisner's raid on the enemy zone produced unheard-of excitement and sympathy for this fearless energetic woman, who alone of all of our crew had been at Kazan. Till the day I die, I'll never forget the shining memory of Larissa Mikhailovna, the bravest of the brave, and an extraordinary Communist . . .

Neuberg was soon removed to another post.

By early September, the Volga Flotilla consisted of three des-troyers, three gunboats, eight armed steamers, several speed-boats, one floating battery and an air detachment of six planes. And as the Reds prepared for the final onslaught on Kazan, Larissa Reisner was appointed Commissar of the Reconnaissance Division of the Flotilla's General Staff.

A letter to her parents was sent from 'Political Commissar Raskol-nikova, Espionage Division, HQ of the Fifth Army, Svyazhsk':

My treasures, I've collected and armed thirty Magyars for dangerous assignments, and got them all horses and weapons, and I sometimes go out scouting with them. We talk German. We've also caught one Czech officer.

Life speeds madly. In three or four days we'll take Kazan. There are lots of soldiers, and lots of guns. We suffer terribly from dirt and insects. Eternal thanks for the scissors etc. Send my hat and my autumn coat as soon as you can – I left all my things in Kazan. I look like nothing on earth, and I'm freezing.

I kiss you all. Your wild daughter, at war with the intelligentsia, Larissa.

P.S. In Kazan I saw executions – I'll settle with them for that when we take the town.[21]

On 4 September, workers at Kazan's arsenal rose against the Whites, and were massacred. All young men were mobilised by the Constitutional Assembly Committee and were marched off by force to fight the Bolsheviks. The prison's courtyard filled with rows of fresh corpses, and the usual interminable convoys of fugitives streamed out of the town, taking with them all they had. Next day, the Reds mounted machine-guns on the hills outside the town, and went into the attack. For the next four days, bloody battles raged on either side of the river, until on 9 September Markin led a landing-party of Volga sailors into the town itself, and knocked out the Whites' battery there. They were joined next day by Azin's 28th Red Cavalry Detachment, and together they stopped the executions. The Whites, attacked on three sides, fled, and the Reds captured quantities of weapons. The Kazan victory was the Eastern Front's first successful counter-attack, and its organisers were showered with praise.

A hundred and fifty miles south of Kazan, the youthful First Army, under Mikhail Tukhachevsky, captured the town of Simbirsk. The Czech forces, exhausted and defeated, now looked desperately for help from the Japanese troops pouring into Siberia. The Whites' gold reserves moved east from Kazan to Samara, and from there ever eastward, a security without a base. By now the Whites were faced by twelve armies, stretching from the White Sea to the Black.

Chapter Four

FROM THE VOLGA TO THE CASPIAN

On 18 September 1918 the main forces of the Volga Flotilla left Kazan, under Raskolnikov's command, to pursue the Whites up the Kama, a tributary of the Volga, and for the next two months Larissa Reisner sailed up the Kama on the flotilla's warships and destroyers. Travelling mainly by night, she fought as scout, commissar and flag-secretary in fierce and daily battles for the capture of Chistopol, Elabuga and Sarapul. Every moment snatched from fighting she spent on the staff ship *Mezhen*. There she made herself at home in the imperial state-room, and seeing that the tsarina had scratched her name with a diamond on the window, she scratched it out, also with a diamond, and replaced it with her own.[1]

On the *Mezhen* she gathered, analysed and summarised the raw material of her 'Letters', worked on her correspondence, and prepared a programme of lectures on western and Russian literature for the sailors. And in the lulls between battles they would crowd on board ship to hear her talk on 'The working class in Russian literature', 'The revolutionary movement in Russian literature', 'Songs of the Revolution and their history' and 'What is literature, and why is it necessary?'[2]

It was these experiences of living under bullets with the armed masses and giving them culture that formed her as a writer. Shklovsky wrote:

Raskolnikov's torpedo boats slipped across the sandbanks and traced a red line along the Volga, and it was on these campaigns that Larissa Mikhailovna found her literary style. It wasn't a woman's style of writing. And it wasn't the journalist's habitual irony. Irony's a cheap way of being clever. Larissa Mikhailovna held dear what she saw, and took life in earnest. A little ponderously perhaps. But life itself was then as overloaded as a railway wagon.[3]

Vera Inber later described her discipline, 'her writer's cool, which she wore like a gas mask', and 'her ability, with one apt simile or metaphor, to bring distance near. . . . She wrote with a diamond-sharp pen, when others were scribbling with pencil on an envelope.'[4]

Her 'Letters from the Front' (later published as a book, *The Front*) are a series of miniatures, of fragmentary memories, fleeting characterisations and lyrical descriptions, written in haste and passion, of the battle between the Reds and the Whites. They are about the revolution for the new Russia, and against the old culture with which all Reisner's thoughts and habits were still so tied; about the struggle to be a new person, to make a new life, and a new, proletarian, literature. 'This is the violent, irreconcilable child of the materialists,' she wrote in her Preface to *The Front*:

From its life and world view, it has calmly and courageously rejected all the moderation, beauty, sweetness and consolation of bourgeois science, aesthetics, art and mysticism. . . .

Speak to the workers' faculties of 'beauty', and they'll whistle, as if you'd covered them in filth . . . . But if you want nothing to do with bourgeois individual passions and inspirations, there is the Immortality of the people who burnt themselves out in typhus, famine and fever in these delirious years.

Those *Apollo* aesthetes, those refined connoisseurs of Russian literature, frown at that magnificent naked woman Venus, and hold their nose at the Revolution. Oh, one can *say* all the crude clichés like 'heroism', 'self-sacrifice', 'the brotherhood of nations', or 'killed at his post'. But you must *do* all those rough, common, beautiful things, which so turn the stomachs of the educated![5]

Larissa Reisner *did* do those things, wrote Inber, and had 're-treated to places where there was nothing beautiful. Yet she still wanted to placate Apollo, with her "naked Venus", and "Immortality" in capitals.'[6] *The Front* is filled with the poetry, the pathos and the 'Party-spirit' of the Revolution, as well as Reisner's own revolution against her origins and the writers who had formed her. And many who met her in the summer of 1918 would never understand the experiences which had brought her from the poets of St Petersburg to the sailors of the Volga.

In the third week of September, an advanced landing-party of sailors from the warship *Kashin* stole up on the enemy's rear and seized the town of Chistopol, fifty miles south of Kazan, on the banks of the Kama. The other ships, moving more slowly, were far behind, the town was defended only by the exhausted landing-party, and the command was unable to spy out the enemy's positions. They managed to seize a stud farm of trained, saddled, cavalry horses, but none of the sailors could ride. By now Larissa Reisner rode excellently, like a man (and was often taken for one), and it was she who arrived to train a group of them as a cavalry intelligence team.

One cold, grey September dawn, recalled a sailor called Shamov, the whisper went up: 'Our Love is on board!' (This is what they called her, for Shamov had already met her at Kronstadt in 1917, and most of the others knew her from previous battles.) The sailors lined up for inspection, and she moved along the line with the commander, congratulating them on their courage and fighting spirit. Then she ordered Shamov and several others to be released from their duties, and chose horses for them. After much grumbling, the men submitted, and waited horrified for their first lesson.

She returned that evening in the pouring rain, ordered them to take their horses ashore, and there, amid much laughter from the sailors on board, she explained to them the elements of riding, grooming and feeding. When it was dark, she swung onto her prancing 'Beauty' while the men scrambled into their saddles as best they could, and after organising them into pairs, she led them into Chistopol, then ordered them to trot. Shamov and his friends bounced up and down for several miles, their rifles bumping against their backs, until they begged for a rest. Instead, she gave the order to gallop. 'What happens now is hard to describe,' wrote Shamov. 'Some of us fall off our horses into the mud, some cling to their necks, some slide onto their rumps. The reins slip from our grasp. We lose sight of one another in the dark.'

After galloping for several miles, she stopped, waited for them to catch up, then, without asking how they felt, she turned back to the town, making them first trot, then gallop. When the straggling line of riders returned despondently to their ship, Larissa Mikhailovna solemnly congratulated them on their victory. 'This did not please us,' wrote Shamov. 'We had hardly stayed in our saddles, we were beaten to a pulp, and she just pretended not to notice.' Towards dawn, after cleaning their horses, they fell into a deep sleep, from which she ordered them not to be disturbed. They awoke in agony, and the chef, feeling sorry for them, gave them two helpings of lunch.

Two days later, the exercise was repeated, not so painfully this time. And the third time, Larissa even ordered them into the attack against two enemy scouts, who took them for experienced riders and hid in a wood, and the sailors returned to their ship like heroes. She was soon able to let them go off scouting against the Whites without her, and they earned the praises even of the legendary Azin, commander of the 28th Red Cavalry Division.[7]

As the Volga Flotilla continued up the Kama, Larissa Reisner became an increasingly familiar figure, disappearing at the head of a cavalry group into a forest to reconnoitre, and talking to the sailors on board the *Kashin*, the *Lively*, the *Swift* and the *Ardent*. Many of them, like Shamov and his friends, had met her before. But new recruits were always arriving, who tended to be extremely guarded when they first met her, if not downright hostile, and she would have once again to prove herself to them in battle.

A hundred miles up the Kama from Chistopol, the flotilla came to the little town of Elabuga, where a landing-party from the *Kashin*, protected by the *Swift* and the *Ardent*, planned to infiltrate the Whites' rear, cut off their line of retreat, and destroy those trying to cross the Kama. There she met Shamov again. Scouts worked around the clock, checking their sitings of the enemy's defence-points and firing-lines, and at dawn, under the pouring rain, the landing-party disembarked. As the *Kashin* cast off, recalled Shamov, the sailors, soaked but confident, unloaded their supplies, quietly prepared for the battle ahead, and scribbled notes to their loved ones, 'promising to have their revenge on the Whites, and to return home victorious'.

Then a tug came ashore, and Larissa Reisner disembarked. Presenting herself to Gritzai, the commander, as reconnaissance commissar and representative of the Fleet's General Staff, she announced that she would be fighting under him. After that she introduced herself to the sailors, who greeted her with frank suspicion. Pretending not to notice, she joined the middle of their line, and moved off with them through the forest.

Gritzai, without any maps to guide him, led them through thick mud, and the going was unbearably hard. Shamov recalled how the sailors, exhausted, hungry and cursing, dismantled their heavy machine-guns and carried them on their shoulders, while Reisner marched on, ignoring the rising volume of oaths against the commander and his Fleet representative.

Arriving at last at a dry place, Reisner asked Gritzai if she could use the break to do some reconnaissance. ('She knew no rest, that woman!', wrote Shamov.) Borrowing a peasant shirt from one of the sailors and tying it with a belt, she threw off her boots, smeared her feet with mud and tousled her hair. Then she turned to Shamov: 'Well, my old friend, you'll make a good shepherd!' He disguised himself likewise, she approved his appearance, then told him to receive his orders from her on the way.

The two set off through the forest. 'I was enraptured by her resourcefulness and courage,' wrote Shamov. 'There was not a trace of fear on her calm face.' Thanks to their convincing disguises, they managed to get into the Whites' camp, where they found chaos and collapse, with officers being shot on the spot for the slightest disobedience, and a mass of unburied corpses, 'for the edification of others'. They returned to their detachment separately, as Reisner had given Shamov an extra assignment, and she was waiting anxiously for him to return. When he finally did so, she embraced him openly and covered him with praise.

The sailors continued on their way with a grudging new respect for the woman in their midst. Reaching the White lines earlier than expected, they started the offensive without waiting for the signal.

Larissa Mikhailovna feared neither bayonet attacks, shell bursts nor gunshots. Calm and brave in all circumstances, she was a model of revolutionary courage.

She was inseparable from us in battle . . . moving from platoon to platoon, encouraging and advising, and the sailors and commanders listened to her . . .

The Whites scattered in panic, throwing down their arms and handing themselves over as prisoners, and the sailors withdrew victorious. By now their initial contempt for her had turned into admiration, even something close to worship: 'She won their hearts, and she knew it, inspired by the knowledge that they now loved and trusted her, and that her self-sacrifice had contributed to our victory.'[8]

The flotilla left Elabuga and sailed on up the widening Kama, meandering around islands and through yellow muddy ravines, until they reached the village of Pyanii Bor ['Drunken Forest']. There they met an overwhelming concentration of Whites, and on 1 October, the battleship *Vanya the Communist* perished in unequal battle. Markin, its commander was drowned, along with half his crew. Red launches managed to get through under heavy fire and rescued fifteen sailors, who were taken to the *Mezhen*, where another fifteen survivors arrived.

Vsevolod Vishnevsky, one of those saved, was the young sailor who a month back had been setting Larissa Reisner 'tests' near Kazan. Now he met her again, on the *Mezhen*, as she bandaged their wounds, found them cabins and fed, clothed and comforted them with her 'tender maternal care'.

Our ship sinks. Thirty men survive. Larissa Mikhailovna gives us coffee and spirits, then says 'Tell me what happened.' The others push me forward. I speak. She listens, then comes up and kisses me on the forehead. The others guffaw, she looks at them and they fall silent.

It was all so simple, yet it has stayed with me all my life . . .[9]

The following year the journal *Voenmor* [Sailor] published

Larissa's poem 'Requiem', in memory of Markin and his crew, which ended:

> The destroyers have returned to the sea,
> Leaving like swans for the south,
> Sending you, fallen crusaders,
> A host of iron-winged blizzards.
>
> Upwards, upwards, frozen Markin,
> Tear the ice from your wounds,
> Whose rebellious blood in a warm slow stream
> Flows into the boundless ocean.[10]

That October, the first two of her 'Letters from the Front' were published in *Izvestiya*, daily newspaper of the Soviet, and these were followed, in June and September 1919, by three more. Larissa Reisner was one of the first writers of the Civil War, and was certainly one of the finest, and her 'Letters', with their sharp colours and frequent references to world literature, made a brilliant appearance.

Her writings were always elevated and richly adorned with bold and unusual epithets, even when describing the most tragic episodes of the war. Sailing on up the Kama, she observed its oily surface, reflecting the silver fir-trees and peasant settlements, and littered amongst them the mass graves of the White terror campaign:

Chistopol, Elabuga, Chelnya, Sarapul — all these little towns and humble villages, soaked in blood, are inscribed with burning letters into the history of the Revolution. In one town, they threw into the Kama Red Army soldiers' wives, children, even crying babes at the breast. In another, the road is still red with dried pools of blood, and traces of the massacre are reflected in the fierce flush of the nearby maples.

The wives and children of those murdered don't go running abroad to write their memoirs about the cruelty of the Cheka,* or the burning of their estates, their Rembrandts and their libraries. No one will ever trumpet to sensitive Europe about the thousands of soldiers shot on the

---

* The Extraordinary Commission for Struggle Against Sabotage and Counter-revolution

steep banks of the Kama, swept along by its current, buried under its silty shallows, and washed up on its uninhabited shores. . . . Can you recall one day when we didn't see floating past us a silent, great-coated soldier's back, his head shaven against typhus, his hand bobbing in the water?[11]

On 16 October, on a morning sharp with frost and the first hint of snow, they approached the little town of Sarapul, and learnt from the welcoming Red soldiers dotted along its shores that the Whites had just retreated. As they turned the bend into the town, crowds of people with red flags greeted them from the roads, jetties and quays, and as they moored, a rough village band struck up the 'Marseillaise'.

But the rejoicing was cut short by a young sailor's wife, who approached them sobbing with the news that the retreating enemy had loaded four hundred and thirty Soviet and Party workers on to a barge and sailed them off to be shot. The next day, Reisner, aboard the *Swift* and in her element, sailed north up the Kama with a division of torpedoes, flying white flags, to rescue the 'barge of death' from under the noses of Admiral Stark's White flotilla.

The white church of the village of Galyany came into view, with machine-guns mounted in its belfry, then they saw white tents in the bushes, and White soldiers relaxing by camp-fires. Before them the 'barge of death' lay anchored in the middle of the river, guarded by soldiers. Moving quietly forward, the commander of the *Swift* addressed the guards through the megaphone, and ordered them, in the name of Admiral Stark, to raise the barge's anchor, attach it to a tug, and follow them back down the river. The guards, trained unquestioningly to follow orders, obeyed, and the half-dead prisoners and their rescuers were welcomed at Sarapul with storms of tears and applause.

They continued up the Kama to Izhevsk and Votkinsky Zavod, where they fought alongside local factory-workers and troops of the Second Army against the officers of the Kama Constituent Assembly Committee. By early November, both towns were in Bolshevik hands.

Since ice was now forming on the Volga, the flotilla was forced to make for Nizhnii Novgorod for the winter, and the end of the summer campaign was celebrated on 7 November, the anniversary of the Bolshevik Revolution. On that day, Reisner and Raskolnikov sent the government a telegram congratulating them on the 'festival of the workers' liberation': 'The Volga Naval Flotilla is ready always to fight in the name of our great Revolution . . . until the world revolution is brought to a victorious conclusion, and the plunderers have been destroyed . . .'[12]

By then the Volga flotilla had liberated all the territory from Kazan to Izhevsk, and had driven the Whites and Czechs off the Kama and up the Belaya to Ufa, in the Urals. Leaving the main forces of the flotilla at Nizhnii Novgorod, Reisner and Raskolnikov travelled to Moscow, where Raskolnikov was awarded the order of the Red Banner and appointed to the Revolutionary War Council of the Republic.

As they arrived, thousands of women were streaming into the capital for the First All-Russian Women's Congress. The organisers, leading women Bolsheviks like Alexandra Kollontai and Inessa Armand, delivered passionate speeches on women's work and the family. Women with stern, worn faces, in bullet-riddled greatcoats, spoke of fighting at Petrograd, in Siberia and the Don. Lenin spoke at the end, to roars of applause, about the need to abolish 'domestic drudgery'. The congress ended with a resolution to set up nationwide Women's Commissions, responsible for setting up orphanages and canteens and recruiting women to the fight with the Bolsheviks. And Larissa Reisner, for her part in the Volga campaign, became the Red Army's first woman political commissar, appointed to work with Moscow's Naval General Staff.

In the winter of 1918, with daily bread rations still at only two ounces, and almost a third of the capital's inhabitants fighting at the front, Moscow was wracked by cold, toil and hunger. Counter-revolutionary plots were everywhere, and undercover British agents were reporting back daily clashes between workers and secret police, which were published in London to demonstrate the horrors of Bolshevism.

In Germany, the army had virtually collapsed under Allied

pressure; Soviets had sprung up throughout the country, taking control of several major cities, including Berlin, and the Kaiser had fled. On 11 November, a new government under Prince Max of Baden signed an armistice with the Allies, which stipulated that German troops in Russia should remain there. With the First World War over, they could now join forces in their war against the Bolsheviks, and with British backing, General Count Von der Golz, of the German High Command, set about eliminating Soviet influence in Latvia, Lithuania and Estonia.

In Moscow, Larissa moved in with her family, in their cramped freezing flat, and Raskolnikov set off for Kronstadt. He left there in late December on the destroyer *Spartak*, on a reconnaissance trip to the Estonian port of Revel (now Tallin). There he came across a British squadron of five armed cruisers, and while beating back to Kronstadt, the *Spartak* ran aground, and Raskolnikov and his crew were taken prisoner. The sailors were shipped off to a camp on the island of Norgen, where many of them died of cold and starvation, and Raskolnikov was taken to London, where he spent five uncomfortable months in Brixton jail, as hostage for British officers imprisoned by the Bolsheviks.[13] Larissa campaigned energetically for his release, and since she was working that winter with the top command of the navy, her agitation carried some weight.

Political commissars, Party members, were responsible for the well-being of their troops. They were also appointed, in a personal, supervisory capacity, to every naval and army officer of the General Staff – mainly former tsarist officers who had thrown in their lot with the Bolsheviks and needed 'a dynamic person to help them identify with the Revolution'.[14] Larissa Reisner was considered to have a special understanding of their problems in adjusting to the new régime, and in the tense political climate of 1918, she was selected for the sensitive task of discussing Bolshevik strategy with the old and aristocratic Admiral Altvater (said to be the illegitimate son of Alexander III), now Commander of the Naval Forces of the Republic. She had already earned Altvater's respect for her record on the Volga, and she soon established a good working relationship with him. Now she had to breathe the ideas of the Revolution into him, and help him to work for it.

Living again with her brother and parents must have brought a special sympathy to this 'assistance in reconstruction', as her friend Nikulin described it. Her father, although still considered an 'old liberal' by many of his Bolshevik comrades at the Commissariat of Justice, had nonetheless been chosen to draft the new Soviet Constitution, published that spring. Her brother Igor did not join the Party until the end of the Second World War, but he had an equally high-placed job at the Commissariat of Foreign Affairs, with special responsibility for Afghanistan.

It was only six months since Larissa had left her family for a new life with Raskolnikov in the Revolution. As she returned to them that winter to share their cold, hungry, hard-working life, the front seemed far away, and she was immersed in memories of her childhood and her student years. It was as she wrestled with the knots that still bound her to her past that she started writing 'Requiem', her unpublished account of her life with her parents before the Revolution.

*

In early May 1919, the British government, hearing of improvements in the conditions of British soldiers captured by the Bolsheviks, agreed to transfer Raskolnikov, under police guard, from Brixton prison to a hotel in Gower Street. There he received money from Russia via the Danish trade delegation, and he enjoyed his freedom in London, buying clothes in Oxford Street, attending meetings of the British Socialist Party, and visiting the British Museum, the Zoo and Covent Garden (to hear 'Tosca'). Two weeks later his holiday came to an end, and he left Britain by train for the Russian–Finnish border-station of Beloostrov. There, on 17 May, he was exchanged for nineteen British officers, including a Major Goldsmith of the British Military Mission in the Caucasus. A week later, Larissa was reunited with him.[15]

By then Von der Golz and his Baltic and Russian volunteers had cleared the Bolsheviks from Southern Latvia and had seized Riga. General Denikin was in supreme control of the south.

General Yudenich controlled all the territory from the Baltic Coast down to Pskov. The Germans occupied Rostov. In the south, British and Indian troops had landed at the oil-rich port of Baku, capital of Azerbaijan, and had taken over the running of the country. A major White offensive had broken through to the Don basin. And on the Volga, a British R.A.F. squadron and tank corps, joined by a number of Baron Wrangel's White troops, had captured the vital strategic steppe town of Tsaritsyn.*

As the Whites closed in on Tsaritsyn, Raskolnikov, Reisner and her new secretary, Mikhail Kirillov, left Moscow for Saratov, two hundred miles north of Tsaritsyn on the Volga. There Raskolnikov rejoined his flotilla, recently arrived from Nizhnii Novgorod, and was appointed commander of the new Astrakhan–Caspian Naval Flotilla. And there Reisner met Altvater's successor, Rear-Admiral Behrens, who had arrived to supervise the organisation of the new flotilla. She was to be his political commissar for the next nine months, during which the two developed a specially warm friendship. She was also responsible, as political commissar of the new flotilla, for organising the welfare of its greatly increased number of sailors. When the flotilla commander Andrei Babkin (a hero of *The Front*) collapsed with tuberculosis and started spitting blood, another commander, Berlin, recalled her swiftly arranging for him to be transferred to a Saratov sanatorium.[16]

By the summer of 1919, headlines in London, Paris and New York were joyfully announcing one Red defeat after another, and picturing the victory over Bolshevism as won. Soviet Russia was now being invaded by the armies of fourteen states. The French were with Pilsudski's Polish armies in the west, occupying much of the disputed territory east of the river Bug, and fighting with Denikin in the Caucasus and the Black Sea; the British were fighting with Yudenich in northern Russia and with Admiral Kolchak in the Urals; and Wrangel's troops, supported by British artillery and planes, were at Tsaritsyn.

---

* Renamed first Stalingrad, now Volgograd

But the Bolsheviks were keeping up heavy pressure on the Volga. In early June, Larissa Reisner left Saratov with Raskolnikov, Kirillov and the new Astrakhan–Caspian Flotilla, and sailed down the Volga towards Tsaritsyn. They moored some twenty miles away, and there, subjected to almost constant British air attacks, they fought in daily battles of great ferocity for the surrounding villages.

A flotilla commander called Novitsky described setting off with Reisner and some other commanders one day at the head of a squadron of torpedo boats on a deep reconnaissance exercise, to discover the extent of the threat to Tsaritsyn. She was chatting calmly on deck with her fellow-commanders, he wrote, when a few miles from the city a series of shells flew over their heads and exploded several yards from the deck. Deciding that the risk of advancing further would not be justified by the hope of getting any extra intelligence, they ordered the torpedoes back. Novitsky wrote:

It was in this tense and sensitive military episode that I observed for the first time in the Civil War a woman, and I admit I came to love and admire her. . . .

Not considering it useful in general for women to be amongst the soldiers, I must in some cases admit that the presence in the army of women like Reisner is most desirable. She didn't once lose her calm or cheerfulness under fire. Her very appearance, all in white, standing at her full height in full view of all, helped to keep order. Besides her other qualities, she was extraordinarily observant: she could quickly analyse the military situation, and more importantly, she could describe it with great skill on paper . . . [17]

The British kept up their bombardment of Tsaritsyn until 23 June when the town fell, and the flotilla sailed down the Volga to the Kazakh capital of Astrakhan, on the Caspian Sea. Astrakhan had been in Bolshevik hands since the previous January, but was now encircled by the Whites. Since the Volga route had been cut off at Tsaritsyn, they had to travel there by train, via Saratov and Pokrovsk, along a line threatened by White raids. Before leaving, Reisner had to organise train seats and a military guard for thirty-five naval commanders' wives who had been cut off from Astrakhan where their husbands were waiting for them.

In mid-July, the flotilla finally reach Astrakhan, filled with the smell of sea and wormwood and the screeching of war trains. For the next eight months Larissa Reisner lived at the flotilla's headquarters outside the town, in a dusty steppe settlement of low stone houses, inhabited by Tartars in wide hats, white stockings and silk gowns.

Raskolnikov now set about combining the river and seagoing forces of the Volga and the Astrakhan–Caspian Flotillas into one. This new combined flotilla operated over a vast area from the Volga to the Caspian, fighting a series of desperate battles under his command for the recapture of Tsaritsyn. That summer and autumn, as Reisner and Raskolnikov fought and worked together in Astrakhan, the Civil War reached its climax and their relationship seems to have achieved new passion. In a letter to her parents that summer, she described Raskolnikov's relentless courage in the battles for Tsaritsyn:

My Fedya is taking two more torpedo boats to Tsaritsyn, where he is probably now in a mess, and my heart bleeds for him, for the operations there are terribly dangerous. I had to travel there myself by train instead of him, with the head of our operational division, and the Whites have smashed everything in their path. But Tsaritsyn will be our second Kazan. . . .

I'm sending you a pile of old Chinese–Persian paintings for Behrens, and am keeping for myself a wonderful Buddha for luck, saved from a clay shrine on the blazing Kalmyk steppes. I pray to it when F.F. is in dangerous places. . . .

I miss you so much, my darlings. Has anything happened to you? Aren't you terribly cramped at home? I worry endlessly about you. Here the lull is over. If we lose Tsaritsyn, Astrakhan will be cut off. But we'll hold on to it to the end, and despite all this, and the fall of Kharkov, Fedya and I are infinitely happy. It's hard to write about. But it isn't just a sudden outburst of 'good' feelings, it's something true and straight. England has made a man of him. . . ![18]

Together with Raskolnikov, Larissa fought to drive an army of White Cossacks from the nearby village of Solodniki, and sailed two hundred miles north under his command to Guriev, on the Caspian, on a special Volga–Caspian expeditionary detachment to deliver oil from areas under White and British occupation. Her *Front* vividly evokes those months in Astrakhan. She describes seeing a ricketty Bolshevik plane sending a British bomber to its destruction, and meeting the tragic remnants of a family wiped out in another British bombing-raid. And she writes of Behrens, brooding alone in his cabin about the fall of Tsaritsyn, 'his eyes shining like those of an old man who has lost all his sons in one night'.[19]

In the autumn, the entire Ukraine was evacuated as the Whites invaded. Wrangel was in the Crimea. Petrograd was in mortal danger. Kolchak controlled Siberia. Red soldiers were starving and exhausted. But the Whites had little popular support, and gradually Bolshevik fortunes started to improve. In October, Yudenich was beaten back from Petrograd. By November, Denikin's army was in headlong retreat, and Kolchak had evacuated his Siberian capital from Omsk to Irkutsk. By the end of the month, the Red Army had recaptured Kharkov, Kiev and Rostov, and the Whites were finally beaten back from Astrakhan. As Bolshevik defeats turned into triumphs, women's part in the victory was rewarded with a new Party Women's Department, the Zhenotdel, staffed entirely by women and responsible for everything that concerned women's lives.

It was not until the following year that the Zhenotdel started working with women in the east. That autumn in Astrakhan, Larissa Reisner was involved in cultural work of a different kind, with the sailors. Pale-faced from heat and fever and exhausted by battle, they were grateful to have survived, and in the months that followed, they were finally able to relax a little. Reisner's secretary, Kirillov, staged a number of improvised plays of such talent that she urged him to go on the stage when the war was over. And Larissa herself organised poetry readings and gave lectures, and helped to set up the Astrakhan Union of Journalists. She also wrote a number of articles for the journal *Sailor*, including 'At the Front: What Tomorrow Promises Me', and a series of sketches called 'Poets of the Red Fleet', on the works of war poets like

Shmelev, Gladyshev and Plotnikov. It was then, too, that she wrote her poem 'Requiem' on the death of Markin. And on 25 October 1919, the second anniversary of the Revolution, she published another obituary, on her old student friend Semyon Roshal, who had been captured by Ukrainian officers on the Romanian front, and tortured to death.

They smashed his limbs, they broke straps over his flesh, and they imagined that the cold tormented body they threw down on the road was Roshal, and that Roshal was no more. But the murderers were wrong. Roshal cannot be killed. Let them count the wounds, the dead and the White Guard fortresses wiped off the face of the earth by red Roshal, the invincible, merciless avenger, and they'll fear our corpses: yes, the dead will rise from their graves and march, stronger than in life, at the head of the Revolution . . .[20]

By early 1920, it seemed that the war was, to all purposes, over. Kolchak was dead. Yudenich had fled to Paris, leaving the remnants of his scattered army to die of starvation and disease. The Whites and British had been driven out of Arkhangel. The Reds were in the Don and the Kuban. And the Bolsheviks had signed an armistice with Estonia. In April, the Poles launched a surprise attack on the Ukraine and captured Kiev. But, by May, they had been halted by Tukhachevsky's Fifth Army, and were being hurled back.

That spring, Reisner and her friends in Astrakhan were celebrating a series of crucial victories in the neighbouring northern Caucasus, rich in the oil needed for Russia's economic development. The previous June, the oriental princedom, or Khanate, of Khiva had been captured by Khivan Bolsheviks. In October, Askabad had gone Bolshevik. In February 1920, Bolshevik forces were in Krasnovodsk in Turkestan (now Turkmenistan). By April, the British had been expelled from Baku, and on the 25th, the Azerbaijan cabinet was overthrown by local Bolsheviks. Reisner left Astrakhan with her flotilla to celebrate Azerbaijan's new Soviet Republic, and they arrived in Baku on 1 May, to a sea of red banners and a victorious May Day parade.[21]

Just a few miles away, however, British troops were still in

Persia (now Iran) and the Caspian Sea, and ships of Denikin's White squadron, under British protection, were anchored at the port of Enzeli in Persia. Now the Bolsheviks had to consolidate their position in that area, and defend themselves against the threat from Persia, whose Shah was providing British troops with unlimited opportunities for action in the bordering strategic areas of Soviet Russia. In May 1920, therefore, the Soviet government, guided by Raskolnikov, took the big and risky decision to seize Enzeli and remove the White ships, in order, he wrote, to 'deprive Britain of its mainstay in the Caspian'.[22]

Larissa Reisner hurled herself into the Persian campaign. Leaving Baku with the main forces of the flotilla, she sailed south on the flagship-destroyer *Karl Liebknecht*. Landing on 17 May at Enzeli, she, Raskolnikov and a group of naval commanders clandestinely boarded the Whites' ships to try to persuade them to capitulate. They then went ashore to warn the Persian authorities of the attack. Finally the order was given to shell British military positions in the town and bombard Denikin's vessels. In one day, the entire White Fleet was seized with all its weapons. The British, hopelessly outnumbered, were forced to surrender and to enter into negotiations with Raskolnikov. And on 18 May, Soviet troops entered Enzeli.[23]

According to Raskolnikov, the Persian people and authorities welcomed the Soviet landing with open arms: 'All the streets and squares were packed with people,' he wrote. 'The whole city was covered in red flags.'[24] Although other accounts suggest somewhat less enthusiasm, Britain's capitulation and retreat from Enzeli did enormous damage to its anti-Bolshevik campaign and to its prestige in Persia. The Persian government resigned in confusion, in favour of one which insisted on the withdrawal of Soviet and British forces, and which made overtures to Moscow for a friendship treaty.

The flotilla stayed on in Enzeli for another few weeks, and Larissa enjoyed her freedom to wander round the town, with its narrow mud streets, camels and yellow roses, and to climb with her friends in the mountains and ravines surrounding it. For the past two years she had suffered cold, hunger and danger, not to mention the pain of her crippled foot, and now in Enzeli they at last caught up with her. And it was there that she came down with the heavy headaches and drenching sweats of her first debilitating attack of malaria.

Chapter Five

THE NEW CULTURE

In June 1920, Larissa Reisner left Persia by train for Moscow with Raskolnikov, who was warmly praised by Lenin for the brilliant success of the Enzeli campaign and awarded his second Order of the Red Banner. They stayed in Moscow for a month, in two vaulted rooms on the ground floor of Prince Dolgoruky's old mansion on Maloe Znamenskoe Street, which housed the headquarters of the grandly named ULISO, Administration of Fleet Personnel.

Their rooms, littered with guns, flags and war photographs, English cigarettes and jams, still resembled a battle headquarters, and there was always a crowd of commissars and commanders there. Larissa's secretary, Kirillov, set up his office in one corner, where he signed travel warrants and assignments, and kept contact with a troop train at the October station, on the line to Petrograd and Kronstadt. In another corner, Larissa continued her work as political commissar, and Lev Nikulin recalled her typing a letter one evening to Felix Dzherzhinsky, head of the Cheka, to intercede for the life of an arrested sailor. (The electricity went, and her friends had to light matches for her as she typed, but her intercession worked and the sailor was released.)

The past two years of war had turned her into a stern and disciplined fighter. Now she threw off her leather jacket and army cap, and started to catch up on news of her old friends from the Poetry Circle and *Rudin*. A few 'Rudinists', like Vladimir Zlobin, had emigrated, but most had joined the Red Army. Nikulin and Rozhdestvensky had fought with the Red Army in the Ukraine, Georgii Maslov and Viktor Trivus had died in battle. A few writers had managed to continue writing, doing articles for the Bolshevik press or translations for Gorky's *World Literature* series to keep alive, or lecturing at workers' classes, which earned them a small increase in their rations. But paper was scarce in those cold, hungry years: books dated 1918 or 1919 are very rare. By 1920, however, a noisy new aural literary culture was emerging from the capital's cafés, Workers' Faculties and Proletkult studios; that year saw the opening of Moscow's bold and experimental Meyerhold Theatre, of which Professor Reisner was a director. Now, with the war virtually over, people were at last beginning to think again of art and literature.

Two years before, Nikulin and Reisner had been discussing Blok at the Hermitage Park. That summer, Nikulin had returned from the Ukraine to Moscow to teach at the political department of one of its military units. And it was outside the entrance to the Hermitage Park that he again met Larissa, looking young and sunburnt in a cotton summer dress, sitting in a large open motorcar with a sailor at the wheel. Nikulin accompanied her back to Maloe Znamenskoe Street, where they slipped out of the noisy office into the shady garden, and she showered him with questions about poetry. 'We've been so cut off,' she told him.

Nikulin talked to her of the Futurists, the Imagists, the Neoclassicists, the Neoromantics and the 'Nothingists', of their old friends from the Poetry Circle, and finally of the Petrograd poets, who especially interested her, and of Blok and Anna Akhmatova (whom Reisner called Blok's 'spiritual sister'). Then Larissa talked to Nikulin of the front – of Persia, Tsaritsyn and Kazan, and of the espionage mission there which had nearly cost her life: 'I cursed you then for not getting me that cyanide,' she said. 'That *was* an emergency!' Nikulin was enchanted by her tales of the Revolution. 'Everything was charged with her romanticism,' he wrote, 'her unusual metaphors, her unexpected, eccentric word associations, and the aesthetic habits of her youth.' And he was so captivated by the atmosphere at the HQ that he resigned from his unit on the spot. Kirillov scribbled out a scrap of paper authorising him to work in the Political Department of the Baltic Fleet, and at the beginning of July, he joined

Larissa on the train to Petrograd, where Raskolnikov was appointed commander of the Baltic Fleet. He recalled their journey there, eating stale pancakes and drinking carrot tea in a carriage packed with soldiers and sailors. And when one of them,

not knowing Larissa Reisner's character, ventured to tell a rather indecent story about a young lady, the 'young lady' calmly poured a glass of rather hot tea over the joker's head, to the great satisfaction of the others, especially Gromov, a brave and gallant worker, and commissar of the Kronstadt garrison.[1]

In Petrograd, Larissa lived with Raskolnikov for the next nine months in the cold luxury of the old Admiralty Building. At the end of a long dark corridor, hung with canvases of sea battles and prim tsarist admirals, was Larissa's small room, glowing with the colours and memories of the front. A white felt Caspian nomadic tent covered the floor. The walls were hung with exotic fabrics, a ship's signal flag, a revolver and an old naval cadet's broadsword. A wide sofa was piled with English books and classical Greek dictionaries. Low oriental tables gleamed with crystal scent bottles, oriental majolica plates, and bronze jugs, boxes and Kalmyk Buddhas.

She wrote, amidst a disorder of books, rough drafts, maps and field-glasses, in another, larger room, with four windows overlooking a fine view of the river Neva and the Vasilevsky Island. It was there that the artist Chekhonin painted the uncharacteristically melancholy portrait of her which now hangs in Moscow's Tretyakov Gallery.

That summer, she plunged into the new cultural life being created in Petrograd. Hundreds of (mainly anonymous) articles and poems were appearing in local factory and Party papers, and she attended endless poetry readings, classes and meetings, at workers' and sailors' clubs, theatres and museums. She met many of her old friends again at literary gatherings in the austere white hall of the House of Art, a writers' hostel and meeting-place housed in the two top stories of the building formerly belonging to the Eliseev brothers, bakers, on the corner of the Nevsky Prospect and the Moika Canal. But she was especially involved, with Nikulin, in the Baltic Fleet's Political Department, for which she helped to organise a series of poetry classes and workshops for the sailors. She was greatly respected for her 'Letters from the Front', in which so much of the old literature survived, strangely transformed. And these writings had a great influence on the new Soviet poetry, then in its infancy and still mainly aural. Others knew her mainly for her record on the Volga, and when Nikulin was asked to do an agitational play for the Baltic Fleet, he dismayed her by writing one (published in the journal *Baltic Sailor*) called 'On the Volga', about her escape from Kazan.[2]

Many writers had fought with the Whites in the Civil War, but few had actually emigrated, and most were now trying to find some *modus vivendi* with the Bolsheviks. To promote this Larissa called St Petersburg's older poets to the Admiralty for meetings on the theme of the intelligentsia in revolution. Several poets would sit round the Admiralty's large oval conference table for this 'assistance in reconstruction'. Sergei Gorodetsky, the former Acmeist, now an ardent revolutionary, was a regular attender, as was Alexander Blok, who had followed his 'Twelve' with two anthologies of poems, about music and silence, conflagration and darkness. Blok was Reisner's most respected guest at these meetings, and she worked with especial passion to 'convert him to revolution', as his relative, M. Beketova, put it. And that summer the two would discuss poetry together on long horse rides around the islands of Petrograd, and she would challenge him to 'raise himself above his environment'.[3]

There were some who disliked the idea of the revered Blok being lectured by this young and comparatively inexperienced woman, and the image of the two on their horses, when so many in Petrograd were still hungry, sits somewhat awkwardly with the theme of revolutionary sacrifice. Her writings, too, worried many people with their bold, impressionistic, almost mystical intensity. For Lev Sosnovsky, that summer was Larissa Reisner's 'second test':

We were all workaday and prosaic. In her there was much poetry, much emotion and much of the romantic. It struck us: wasn't there just too much elegance in her writings, weren't there too many images and too much colouring? At times it would strike us, who were stumbling around in real life: was the object of her creativity just this continual juggling of colours, images, lines and juxtapositions?[4]

Others felt that she trusted people too naïvely, that she had a sometimes excessive confidence in her own judgement and often lacked vigilance. Nikulin recalls her stubbornly recommending to him and the editors of the *Red Baltic Fleet* an 'extremely experienced' journalist called L.M. Klyachko, of the pre-revolutionary school, who had 'nearly married Rasputin's daughter, so as to have first-hand information'.[5] According to Nikulin, she made a number of mistakes of this sort over the years. But in those days she was determined to turn enemies into allies; and she would work with all writers who offered their services to revolution. With those who didn't she would argue and heckle. For *Apollon* lived on in writers awaiting the restoration of the old St Petersburg, and she still remembered its language.

By mid-July 1920, Petrograd was filling with delegates from all over the world for the second congress of the Third, or Communist, International. The congress opened on 19 July at the Tauride Palace, against the background of Tukhachevsky's victorious advance into Poland, and the day was made a public holiday. On that day Nikulin drove with Larissa in her military car to the Tauride, through streets crowded with people, red banners and brass bands. On the way, she ordered the driver to stop at the House of Writers, and they entered to find Professor Karsavin lecturing a subdued audience on 'sublime, eternal, beauty'. Leading Nikulin to the front row, she listened with a sardonic smile for a while, then shouted out an exasperated riposte, and the two withdrew, amidst shouts and whistles, and drove on to the Tauride for discussions of Poland, colonialism and the European trade union movement.[6]

Two weeks later, the House of Writers moved to new premises on the Liteinii, and there, on 4 August, Reisner and Gorodetsky read their poems at the first meeting of the Petrograd Union of Poets, chaired by Blok. Blok opened the evening by talking of the

'wild, unnatural word-combination of this "Union of Poets" ',
and emphasised the difficulties of the venture. Then he concluded, more optimistically:

... it's no coincidence that at the moment when we have started to
organise our Union, two of Petersburg's most indigenous citizens, Sergei
Gorodetsky and Larissa Reisner, have returned to us . . . We haven't
heard from them for a long time, and we no longer know who they are,
but we want to believe that they will . . . listen to life's heartbeat –
difficult, but elemental, great and alive. For they are linked to life, and
contemporary Russian life is the revolutionary element.[7]

This was the stuff of Reisner's journalism then. Her experiences before the Revolution with *Rudin*, as editor, writer and
book-keeper, had given her a love of the technical side of
publishing, the rough proofs and the smell of hot metal. Now she
invariably wrote several versions of one article, and would visit
the editorial board and the printshops to make additions and
corrections. She worked at her journalism that summer with all
her usual conscientious intensity, and at a pace which brought on
a series of malaria attacks. She would often ignore the headaches
and chills which announced the onset of the fever, and it would
strike suddenly. She would then lie in bed, first shivering, sick
and blue with cold, then dizzy, half-conscious and drenched in
sweat, until the fever broke, and she would rally, much weakened, until the next attack.

Her articles always drew directly from life, and she struggled
not to betray the pains she took with them. One burning hot
Sunday in early August, Nikulin recalled visiting the Palace
Embankment, cooled by the fresh breeze from the Neva. There,
swarming around a moored barge, were hundreds of people who
had given up their free time to break it up for winter firewood for
Petrograd's children's homes. Larissa Reisner, in a worn, wet
cotton dress and a shawl thrown over her hair, came down the
granite steps laughing and wiping her wet face with her hand.
Two hours later, he wrote, she was back at her desk in the
Admiralty working on her article 'Voluntary Labour Day' for
Red Paper.[8]

She made a name for herself that summer with a number of ironic sketches based on material found on the staff-ship *Mezhen*. She was also working on a play (of unknown fate), set in a town which the Bolsheviks are forced to abandon, and involving the arguments between the heroine, a Communist's wife, who wants to follow her husband, and her relatives, who try to persuade her to await the Whites. She dictated this play to a typist, a lady of the old school, who typed obediently, 'with an expression of pained protest', wrote Nikulin, 'at the play's conclusions'.[9]

Many of Petrograd's future émigrés found shelter at the Institute of Art History, in the old palace of Count Zubov on St Isaac's Square, and she would appear at their meetings to heckle and argue with the 'masters of thought'. That autumn, Count Zubov threw a masked ball there for his friends, and hired costumes for them from the Mariinsky Theatre. Larissa Reisner managed somehow to attend this strange event, dressed in an eighteenth-century ball-dress and white periwig. She watched, amused and enraged, as Count Zubov toured the freezing ballroom, chatting condescendingly to this parade of antiquated St Petersburg snobs, and afterwards she wrote a verse about it:

> The old world gnashes its teeth
> The mother still weeps for her son
> And the much reduced gentleman of leisure
> Brings out his last dinner-jacket.[10]

By early August, the Red Army had stood at the gates of Lvov and Warsaw; but Tukhachevsky's Red troops had dangerously over-extended their lines, and they soon suffered the consequences as the Poles, helped by fresh Allied loans and supplies, drove them back along the whole front. By the end of the month the Red Army had lost the battle of Warsaw, the front had collapsed, and Tukhachevsky was hastily evacuating his troops.

The war was not over; Wrangel was still in the Crimea. Yet few in Petrograd that cold autumn could doubt that the Red Army was on the way to victory, and that spring was on the horizon. There was a round of celebrations, poetry-readings and parties, and the writers at the House of Art decided to celebrate the start of better times by offsetting Count Zubov's masked ball with one of their own. The State Theatre director, Eksuzovich, agreed that they too could borrow costumes from the Mariinsky Theatre; Petrograd's fuel and food departments were mobilised to provide heat and food, and for many weeks literary and theatrical Petrograd talked of little else. It was then that Reisner again met her old student friend Vsevolod Rozhdestvensky, now a junior commander in a Red Army division of the Petrograd garrison, and sharing a room at the House of Art with the poet Nikolai Tikhonov.

Walking to work one damp autumn twilight across the steep Dvortsovy Bridge to the Rostalny columns, he heard behind him the rustle of car tyres, and saw peering out of the car window the familiar smiling face of Larissa Reisner, 'as elegant as ever in her naval cap and greatcoat'. He got into her car, and as they drove around the Vasilevsky Island, she brushed aside his questions about her adventures on the Volga, insisting instead that they talk of the past and their old poet friends. And when she dropped him off at his garrison, she made him promise to visit her in the Admiralty with his friends to drink coffee and read poems.

Shortly afterwards, Rozhdestvensky, Osip Mandelstam and their poet friend, Mikhail Kuzmin anxiously approached the Admiralty building to take up her invitation. Once admitted, he recalled, they were so lost in admiration of its echoing splendour that they could hardly keep up with the duty-sailor who escorted them along the endless corridors to her room. Arriving at her door, they were announced so ceremoniously that shy, short-sighted Kuzmin was overcome by nerves. Then Larissa appeared, in a Cossack gown embroidered with heavy gold threads, her thick auburn hair wound around her head like a crown, and she seemed to Rozhdestvensky to resemble one of the Buddhist figures in her room.

She laughed a lot, and told them about fighting the Whites and Interventionists in Kazan, Astrakhan and Enzeli. Then the talk passed to poetry and to Petrograd's literary life, and to the forthcoming masked ball, and the important question of what to wear for it. Mandelstam made an emotional plea for her to go dressed in the costume of Artemis the hunter, while Rozhdestvensky urged her to settle for nothing less than Bakst's precious Columbine costume from the ballet 'Carnaval' – which was not, he said, for loan. This she immediately took as a challenge, as he intended her to do.

The day before the ball, recalled Rozhdestvensky, the hall was decorated with flowers raided from the Botanical Gardens and the Tauride Orangery. Artists painted a large mural depicting a crowd of European bankers baring their teeth, and World Capital, in top-hat and horn-rimmed spectacles, his huge belly pierced by a red bayonet. Then Nikifor, the Eliseevs' old servant, dragged in a sledge with a basket of theatrical costumes, the violins were tuned, and buckets of precious yellow and pink ice-cream were brought in. Rozhdestvensky, in his high officer's collar, wing-like epaulettes and white gloves, waited stiffly as the hall filled with Dniepr mermaids, Seville tobacco girls, crusaders from 'Raimonda', officers from the 'Queen of Spades' and soldiers' wives from 'Khovanshchina'. Then Larissa appeared, dressed in Bakst's Columbine costume, her hair loose and tied back with a violet ribbon. The band struck up the 'Blue Danube', and they waltzed around the hall. At that moment Eksuzovich came in, and they waltzed straight out of the door, raced downstairs, rushed by cab to the Mariinsky, and returned to the House of Art to find Eksuzovich on the telephone to its costume warehouse, unable to believe that the dress was there.[11]

For Larissa, this episode brought some badly needed light relief into the unremitting strain of her life, which was taking its toll on her health in ever fiercer and more frequent malaria attacks. Her next assignment was intended to give her the chance for a rest (though it can hardly have been anything of the sort), and to get some orthopaedic treatment for her foot.

Early in October, the Soviet government sent four delegates, headed by Adolf Ioffe, to the Latvian capital of Riga, to sign a peace treaty with representatives of the Polish government. Shortly after they left, the editors of *Izvestiya* sent Larissa Reisner to follow them, as the only Petrograd journalist covering the negotiations. The evening before her departure, Nikulin came to her room and found her lying unconscious on the divan like a wax statue, with a temperature of over 104°. 'She'd die in just over five years, but we all thought she was dying then,' he wrote. 'Next day we watched with amazement as Larissa Mikhailovna, still very pale and weak, prepared for the journey.'[12]

Riga had been occupied for the past eighteen months by a combined but bitterly divided British and German government, and was a city still at war. Approaching it by train, Larissa found it ringed by shattered factories, and ploughed by German heavy artillery into a welter of mud. Inside the town itself, she found

destroyed factories, bare of machines, and filled with starving corpses . . . the silent ruins of the workers' quarters, and the barred prison windows, through which a dim light falls on the waiting faces of the prisoners and on the hands of clocks which stopped at the only date in all time – the unshakeable 25th of October.[13]

The Bolshevik negotiators formed a tightly-knit group, in daily contact with Lenin. Reisner accompanied them to the *Schwartz-haupterhaus*, which housed the negotiations. And there, on 12 October, she witnessed the signing of the Peace of Riga (ratified the following March), in which the Bolsheviks were forced to hand Western Byelorussia and the Western Ukraine over to Poland. After the signing, she attended a round of banquets where she met Pilsudski's legionaries, still reeling from the 'miracle of the Vistula', and the French and British generals, war attachés and diplomats who had travelled to Riga from Paris and London. This was the first time in her life that she had met representatives of the capitalist states, and she stored away her impressions of them for use the following year, when she would meet their counterparts in Afghanistan. Meanwhile she enjoyed the impression she made on them, dancing a mazurka in her black evening dress with commander Egorov, a Soviet military expert, and 'driving the English women wild with envy'.

On 18 October, the war with Poland finally ended. And on 25 October, Larissa Reisner celebrated the third anniversary of the Bolshevik Revolution in an *Izvestiya* article from Riga:

Every day the Russian embassy car passes down the streets, its red flag fluttering and mocking, like a red tongue pointing at the White town . . . Today, on the third anniversary of the October Revolution, the whole town is filled with red flags, blowing brightly in the October wind . . .

She then describes her own celebration of the day, visiting a hundred ragged, starving Red Army prisoners guarded by keen-eyed foreign officers in a filthy barn outside the town; then she went on to visit an underground dungeon, where she met two hundred more prisoners lying piled half-dead on top of one another.[14]

These impressions gave a special sharpness to her next *Izvestiya* article, about her first encounter with bourgeois Riga and its Constituent Assembly, in which the Bolsheviks' enemies had placed so many hopes. She attended the large three-storey building near the station which housed this 'real, or nearly real, bourgeois parliament', and she described its deliberations in 'How the Bushy Tail Falls Off'. Here are all the traditional ingredients of Russian satire – grotesque humour, character assassination and allusion to fable. And here is Reisner's political journalism at its caustic, satirical, overblown best:

Ministers sometimes drop a few weighty words, and with the gravity of priests bearing the communion, deposit on the rostrum portfolios bulging with incredible bribes and intrigues. Mingling amongst the honoured guests is a mass of military men, in uniforms cobbled together from British, French and American aid. And amongst the spurs, the cummerbunds and daggers, are Riga ladies, sumptuous, gracious, patriotic and kind . . .

Why does this meeting of the Assembly seem so killingly funny to one who's lived through the Soviet Revolution? Because the elected take their places with all the haughty solemnity of landowners playing for the first time at government . . . This handful of financiers, rich peasants, intellectuals and speculators, with their frock-coats stretched tightly over their fat backs, their fat pink necks and ministerial bellies, are deeply and sincerely convinced that they are the power, the law and the Government. This paradise, this superabundance of power, which drips on to bald heads from the golden aristocratic ceiling of the armorial hall,

is hungrily absorbed into every fibre of this petty-bourgeois 'parliament'
. . .

I don't know the British Parliament, of which our own native consti-
tutionalists cannot speak without tears. It probably has magnificence,
tradition and a dizzying elegance.

But even here, amongst the frock-coats who have not inherited their
places, there pokes under the shadow of this exquisite political hypocrisy
the thread of historical reality, on which dangle these fetishes, phantoms,
pulcinellas and pierrots, all playing their part on history's bloody,
smoking, gilded stage.

This Constitutional Assembly, a collection of newspaper pages stuck
together with spittle, covered with a tin roof of political prejudice and the
lightning conductor of compromise, is all given over to irony, the
harbinger of tomorrow's Hurricane . . .

But these corpses have now assumed a new, unpleasant and comical
form. Under the folds of the frock-coats, humanity has suddenly
noticed, in a paroxysm of shame and laughter, that the luxuriant, bushy
parliamentary tail is falling off. In the great centres of culture they're
trying to save it. Universities, academies and laboratories argue and
create miracles. The 1914 War didn't help, nor did Versailles. Mystifiers
and charlatans have appeared. The tail is losing its flexibility. Some are
cured, others fall off. Even the bushy, fragrant tail of the brilliant Lloyd
George is rumoured to be in its last days since he read the latest Russian
communiqué and realised his tail wasn't obeying. Riga doesn't yet know.
What will happen when it does?[15]

After three weeks, Larissa returned to Petrograd, but shortly
afterwards she was sent back again to Riga to cover the negotiations following the treaty, and finally to get some treatment on
her foot.

Travelling alone in a third-class compartment of her train from
Petrograd to Riga that November was twenty-two-year-old
Andrew Rothstein, son of the Soviet diplomat Fyodor Rothstein.
Born and educated in England, he now lives in London. He had
served in the British Army during the First World War, elected in
1920 as a delegate to the founding Congress of the Communist
Party of Great Britain, and was now returning from his first visit
to his father in Moscow. As the train crawled west through the
snow-covered plains towards the Soviet–Latvian border town of

Sebezh, Skurko, the Soviet courier, announced that a woman journalist further up the train wanted to talk to him.

He went into Reisner's compartment, and was enchanted 'by her beauty, the charm of her language, and her passionate commitment to Communism'. First she questioned him about revolutionary prospects in Britain – about the mood of English workers, their 'Soviets of Action' and the prospects of a general strike, about the British Communist Party, and the students at Oxford University where Rothstein had been an undergraduate. 'It's true that everyone, from factory girls to Comintern bosses, was interested in England,' he wrote. 'But never had I been questioned by someone so refined, so cultured. She seemed to be from another world, one I'd never known before.' Rothstein then asked her about the British in Enzeli, and she spoke of the sailors and torpedoes of the Volga Flotilla, of life in Astrakhan and diplomacy at Riga.

They soon reached Sebezh, from where Ulmanis (Latvia's future fascist dictator) was to leave for Moscow as his country's first ambassador to Soviet Russia. Since Ulmanis refused to travel on the train provided for him, they had to wait several days in Sebezh, while a special diplomatic train was brought from the depths of Russia. The only food Rothstein had so far been able to buy were some green apples on Moscow's Kamenny Most, at three million roubles a pound. Now Reisner initiated him and Skurko into the secrets of Latvia's private restaurants, where they feasted on magnificent roast chicken and potatoes. She was merciless about Ulmanis and the Soviet rail authorities, recalled Rothstein, and her stories about Riga's diplomatic and political scene, and the Soviet officials there, had them in gales of laughter.

They finally arrived in Riga, where she saw an orthopaedic surgeon, and was at last able to rest. She and Rothstein visited Riga's cinemas and its National Opera, where they heard the 'Queen of Spades' in Latvian, and she took him around the town's narrow medieval streets on long shopping expeditions for hats. ('Grotesque things, in the German style,' according to Rothstein. 'Don't come to England in those,' he told her, 'You'll discredit the cause!')

They would talk after the day's work in the dining-room of the Riga hotel where the Soviet delegation was staying, and there he asked her, 'as a fraternal service', to write an article, drawn from her experiences at the front, for the new monthly *Communist Review*, of which he was editor. They spent his last evening in Riga in her room, where she talked to him of her plans for the future. And when he boarded his steamer for England the next day, she was there waving from the harbour as it cast off.

Rothstein wrote later:

Larissa Reisner was just three years older than me, but even now it's hard to realise the depths of revolutionary experience that separated her from me. Yet I always felt she was a true comrade, as enthralled by my account of the 'Hands Off Russia' campaign, or the soldiers' strikes in which I took part in January 1919, as I was by her account of her raids on White-occupied territory, or her father's work on the first Soviet Constitution.

And if I didn't fall head-over-heels in love with her, it wasn't because she didn't dazzle me with her brilliant mind and the beauty and music of her voice, but because she seemed to me, a young revolutionary, like the true ideal of an 'older sister', whose taste in hats one could criticise, with whom one could have heated arguments, and whom one could promise to send back from London her favourite scent (Houbigant's 'Rose France') – and from whom also one could learn constantly from her unswerving decisiveness, courage and conscious devotion to the business of Communism.[16]

Reisner's article 'Heroic Sailors of the Russian Revolution', translated by Rothstein, appeared in the first issue of the British *Communist Review* the following May.[17]

At the end of 1920, Larissa returned to Petrograd, rested and excited. By then the Red Army and Navy had cleared the Whites from the eastern borders and driven the British from Persia. Wrangel's forces had been hurled from the Crimea into the Black Sea, and the Allied armies were in tatters, their soldiers in no mood to fight. Japanese troops remained until the following summer in Siberia and Mongolia, but the war with the Whites and interventionists had to all intents and purposes ended. Now the Bolshevik government had to cope with the misery and chaos left by the past six years of war.

Some fourteen million people had died, and those who survived were hungry and exhausted. Railway lines were destroyed, mines were flooded, factories deserted, bridges destroyed and shops boarded up. Children were orphaned and abandoned, women were widowed, and as soldiers returned from the front, women were usually the first to lose their jobs. In the countryside, rich peasants hoarded and speculated, bandits roamed at large, Party members formed 'sowing committees' to control the sowing and harvesting on peasant holdings, and the Red Army suppressed one peasant rebellion after another. In the cities, starving workers subjected to labour conscription seethed with anger at the pre-revolutionary management techniques and privileges of the technical 'specialists' whom the Party had appointed to direct production in the factories.

In the winter of 1920–21, revolutionary hopes suppressed by war surfaced in a mass of meetings and debates. In the factories and villages, Zhenotdel workers organised political education meetings, at which women discussed their problems at work and tackled such previously unmentionable subjects as venereal disease, prostitution and abortion. And at Party and factory meetings up and down the country there were heated discussions on the relationship between the masses and their trade unions, Party leaders and 'specialists'. Various Party platforms emerged on the 'union question', with Trotsky urging the unions' integration into the state machinery; Bukharin calling for their disappearance under full Communism; Alexandra Kollontai, of the Zhenotdel and the new 'Workers' Opposition', demanding their control over all industrial production; and Lenin rounding on them all, and describing the unions' task as to 'educate their members on lines laid down by the Party'.

Raskolnikov supported Trotsky in the union debate. But by now he was ill and exhausted by the accumulated strain of six years of war, and he did so not so much from conviction, according to one western biographer, as from 'sympathy with the man he had seconded during the Civil War'. According to Nikulin, Larissa Reisner too 'attached herself to an anti-Leninist platform on the union question'. It is not known how serious this was either, or indeed which platform it was that she supported. She did visit Moscow for a large meeting held on 30 December at the Bolshoi Theatre, where union, Soviet and Party members had the chance to air their views on the question. Her secretary, Kirillov, described sitting beside her at this meeting in the orchestra pit, from which they got a close view of all the speakers, and according to him, she had no particular preference for any of them.[18]

Two months after the meeting, Raskolnikov collapsed with pneumonia. Special arrangements were made through Mikhail Kalinin, President of the Soviet Republic, for them both to take a month's holiday at the Black Sea resort of Sochi, and Kalinin travelled with them to help organise the spring sowing.

It was a long and harrowing train journey of over two thousand miles, and Raskolnikov, lying white on his berth, needed constant nursing. But as they travelled south into the sun he began to revive, and at the Black Sea port of Novorossiisk, where two years before he had scuttled the Soviet fleet, the sailors gave him a hero's welcome. From there they sailed by naval launch to Sochi, from where one of Britain's Black Sea squadrons was clearly visible, standing ready to deter the people of Georgia from rising against their Menshevik government.

Kalinin, Reisner and Raskolnikov were met by Sochi's leading Party workers and driven through the town's narrow streets, crowded with Red Army soldiers, to the district Party living quarters at the Hotel Europa. In the room next to theirs was staying the commander of the Black Sea Fleet and his wife, with whom they shared a balcony. Next door to them was the head of the local Zhenotdel, Olga Nesterovich, who had first met Reisner in December at the Moscow union meeting. ' "These people know how to live," I thought. I was astonished,' she wrote. 'I watched them, and I saw there something to learn. They lived amongst us, and it was as though they weren't there, like perfect neighbours in a communal flat.'[19]

Since Sochi was still blacked out after dark they did not socialise much in the evenings, and as Raskolnikov was still very weak they ate in their room rather than in the dining-room. But

Nesterovich often saw Reisner standing alone in the hotel meal queue, in her white blouse and blue wool skirt, and the two became friends. After two years at the front, Larissa was starved of women's company, and now she was eager to learn about what women were doing in the local party, and about the Zhenotdel conference in Tuapse, from which Nesterovich had just returned. Then they spoke about literature, and about Molière, a volume of whose works lay on her table. ('I was a heathen,' wrote Nesterovich, I'd never even heard of him.') She asked Nesterovich about local party views on the union question and gave her some printed material on the subject, 'so I wouldn't have to rely on my memory'. She also gave her the Molière, 'as my ship of happiness, she said, to help me orientate myself in the world of literature'.

23 February was Red Army Day, and a day of meetings. Since few of the local Party workers were skilled speakers, Nesterovich asked Reisner to address some meetings with her, which were held, as the day was wet, in the town's cinemas and shopping arcades. 'Some can write and can't speak,' she wrote. 'Some can speak and can't write. Larissa Mikhailovna could do both. From hearing her talk, one could learn the Russian language – strong, beautiful, rich and picturesque.'

In March, Sochi's Party workers were organised by Kalinin into 'sowing committees', to travel out to the villages and help prepare for the spring sowing. The forests seethed with White bands, who terrorised the village population and had ambushed and killed several Party members, so they walked for extra safety in groups of five. (Even then, recalled Nesterovich, the leader of the Party's local Organisation Department had taken with him his non-Party wife as a 'protective tank'.) Larissa accompanied these sowing teams several times, walking along the highway with a nonchalance that some saw as mere bravado. Nesterovich saw it differently:

I saw her immense and overflowing spiritual richness, and her lightning-fast reactions to her surroundings . . . While others were still weighing things up, she would have thought everything through, and if necessary taken charge.

Once arrived in a village, they would sit around a table with the villagers planning the sowing. In these noisy conversations, at which everyone spoke at once, Reisner encouraged the peasants to talk, one at a time, about themselves and the sowing, and she found answers to their political questions. For them, wrote Nesterovich, Reisner was like a city schoolteacher, a person from another world, seen only from afar:

But it would be wrong to think the peasants hated all intellectuals. If they saw a real person there, suffering for them, they would not only respect that person, but love them tenderly . . .

By the end of their month in Sochi, Raskolnikov had fully recovered, and in the middle of March he and Reisner returned together to Moscow.

In their absence, food shortages in the cities had become acute, with the army breaking up more and more strikes. On 24 February, a state of siege was declared in Petrograd, food supplies were rushed in and a certain amount of foraging was authorised. But the strikes continued. Four days later, these came to a head at the Kronstadt naval garrison, where sailors mutinied to demand a 'third revolution' – freedom of speech, new elections to the Soviet, political amnesty, and an end to requisitioning and official propaganda. On 8 March, as the mutiny was being crushed, the crucial Tenth Party Congress opened in Moscow's Kremlin.

With industry, the working class and its Party decimated by war, Soviet Russia faced an isolation and defeat too terrible to contemplate. Now, in four days of furious debates, the Bolsheviks struggled to hammer out an industrial strategy to restart, as quickly as possible, the country's destroyed and stagnant economy. The result was the New Economic Policy (or NEP), designed to expand large-scale industry and to 'increase at all costs the quantity of output'. This was to be done by reviving private enterprise in industry, reintroducing private trade in agriculture and considerably increasing the powers of the technical 'specialists'.

Larissa and Raskolnikov returned to Moscow after the Congress to find a staggering amount of confusion and resentment amongst their fellow Party members. Although Larissa realised that the régime of War Communism was now over, the capitalist concessions of the NEP must have seemed a cruel insult to the ideals and sacrifices of the past three years; and she may well have been drawn instinctively to the programme of the mutinous Kronstadt sailors whom she knew so well, and in whom the Revolution had such strong roots. But if she did have any doubts about the new course, she did not voice them in her writings and she remained a loyal Party member, rallying people to the Revolution and against its enemies.

In the Volga and the Caspian, she had thought sadly of Petrograd, imagining it neglected, hungry and half-destroyed. That spring, she paid a visit to the town in which she had spent her youth, and wandered for old times' sake around its islands, now overgrown like a park. And in her essay 'In Petersburg', published that summer in *Red Paper* as a postscript to her 'Letters from the Front', she celebrated 'Proletarian Petersburg, wild, deserted, but shadowed by the mark of eternity':

It was almost frightening to return here after three years of revolutionary war: what had happened to this city of Revolution and unique spiritual culture? . . . Petersburg has not died, its perspectives have gained a new severity. The luxury of its vast expanses, captured in granite, the green of its parks and the belts of its canals now wear a spartan modesty, a desertedness, a simplicity – thousands of intangible signs testifying to the town's regeneration . . .

The parks, unhindered by people, run wild, profusely making up for their past crippled springs. The Neva flows blue. The islands are a green heaven, where trees and weeds rest together, and the old wooden fences are at last thrown open to thousands of sick children and tormented slaves of toil . . .

Petersburg isn't dead, it has kept what is best and most inexpressible . . . and saved from destruction its epochs, its monuments, and its brilliant outbursts of human passion . . . [20]

Chapter Six

AFGHANISTAN

In late March 1921, Raskolnikov and Reisner were briefed by Boris Chicherin, Commissar of Foreign Affairs, for one of the first major chapters of Soviet diplomacy, in Afghanistan. It was Larissa's brother Igor, at the Commissariat of Foreign Affairs, who had helped to lay the diplomatic groundwork for their involvement there. And there they were to live for the next two years.

A small, remote land of mountains and deserts on the borders of Russia, Persia and British India (now Pakistan), Afghanistan was then inhabited mainly by semi-nomadic tribal people and ruled by a feudal Muslim Emir. As the historic invasion route to India, colonised and ruled over the centuries by a score of dynasties from Ghengis Khan to the British, it had been a key area of intrigue between Russia and Britain. It was now of enormous strategic importance to the Bolsheviks, and was at the centre of their complicated international relations with their eastern neighbours and with Britain.

After 1917, Soviet Russia had renounced all claims to the country. In February 1919, a popular new Emir, Amanullah, inspired by the growing nationalist movement in India, had declared Afghanistan independent and demanded British recognition for a radical programme of reforms. The British responded by bombing Kabul and Jalalabad. The Emir then turned to Russia, and in April 1919, Igor Reisner helped to draft the first exchange of letters between the two countries on reciprocal recognition.

In autumn 1919, Igor Reisner met an Afghan mission in

Moscow, headed by the Foreign Minister, Wali Khan, with whom he helped to negotiate the terms of a friendship treaty. The British, finally forced to recognise the country's independence, sought to recover their influence there, and in October 1920, Amanullah asked Britain's Viceroy in India to send 'trustworthy representatives' to Kabul to conclude a treaty. Then, with the mediation of the anti-British Turkish nationalist Jemal Pasha, he approached the Soviet government. That winter, Igor left for Kabul as secretary to a small Soviet mission led by Yakov Suriz, which started to lay the basis for full diplomatic relations. The presence of this mission, according to Igor Reisner's subsequent despatches, also enabled the Emir to advance his ambitions as 'Supreme Protector of all Muslims' by playing Britain and Russia off against each other.[1]

On 28 January 1921, Sir Henry Dobbs arrived in Kabul at the head of a British delegation. A month later in Moscow, an Afghan delegation finally signed its friendship treaty with Soviet Russia and agreed, in exchange for financial and technical assistance, to open Soviet consulates in Afghanistan's western districts, away from the anti-British tribal areas of the east, and to lay a telegraph-line from the Soviet border town of Kushka, through Herat, Kandahar and Kabul. This treaty, signed on 8 February 1921, was Afghanistan's first major treaty with a great power, and strengthened its hand in its dealings with Great Britain. For Soviet Russia, it meant new prestige in Central Asia, and a powerful counterweight to British interests there.

In April 1920, Raskolnikov was appointed to replace Suritz in Kabul as Soviet Russia's first full ambassador there, and Larissa Reisner, with her languages, her family connections with the country and her reputation for sensitive diplomacy, was considered the ideal person to accompany him. During their briefings in Moscow, she was instructed to make tactful diplomatic contact with the women of the Emir's harem, and convince them to accept Bolshevik promises of neutrality. Most importantly, she had to win the trust of Amanullah's mother, who was rumoured to have engineered his succession, and who dominated Afghanistan's political scene with her dreams of an Afghan-led Central

Asian Confederation. All this had to be carried out extremely discreetly and before leaving, Raskolnikov was given a letter of instruction from Chicherin, ordering him not to do anything that might annoy the British government, and to 'avoid at all costs the fatal mistake of artificially implanting Communism in that country'.[2]

The night before they set off, their family and friends threw a farewell party for them at which the poet Vladimir Mayakovsky worried that they would all be locked up on arrival. On 16 April they finally left Moscow by train at the head of a twenty-strong Soviet mission, consisting of cypher-clerks, wireless-operators, accountants, Farsi-speaking translaters, a cook and a doctor (a former Russian prisoner of war from the Austro-German army). Many old friends were there, including Larissa's secretary Kirillov, and her friend Nikulin, who was to open a consulate in Herat. Several sailors from the Volga and Baltic Fleets also went as guards, including Sergei Lepetenko, the chief commander, who kept the party in order, the gunners Astafev, Khramolov and Zentik, and Valerii Zhdanov, a broad-shouldered Ukrainian who had the reputation, according to Nikulin, of taking a wife at every stop.[3]

The journey from Moscow to the Afghan border took a month. Two hundred miles north-west of Tashkent, near Dzhuzaly, spring floods had washed away the railway line and destroyed the bridge, so that they had to spend several days at a little steppe station, and it was two weeks before they reached Tashkent. Then there was another long delay in Bukhara, the capital of Uzbekistan, on the caravan route to Persia, India and Afghanistan.

Bukhara, a former protectorate of the Russian Empire, had only the previous autumn overthrown its feudal Emir and set up the new Bukhara People's Republic. It had now become a refuge for anti-Bolshevik forces in Central Asia, and Igor Reisner's despatches from Kabul had long emphasised its economic and political importance to Afghanistan. It was to Afghanistan that Bukhara's Emir had escaped in September 1919. Amanullah, supported by the British, had then started supplying arms and troops to Bukhara's counter-revolutionary bands, or *basmachi*. By the time the Soviet mission arrived, Enver Pasha, an ex-Turkish leader sent there by the Bolsheviks to fight the *basmachi*, had gathered them into a formidable force to topple Bukhara's Soviet régime.

Larissa had developed a passionate love of the East at Enzeli. As she wandered about Bukhara's markets and mosques, and introduced herself to the women of the deposed Emir's harem, her romantic writer's eye was apparently taken more by the exoticism of the place than the plots and spies lurking beneath it. Nikulin recalled her there, in a typical excess of trust, urging the mission to take on as a cook an old woman who turned out to be an agent of Bukhara's exiled Emir.

From Bukhara, the Soviet mission travelled on to Merv, in Turkestan, and six weeks after leaving Moscow they finally reached the fortress town of Kushka, on the Afghan border, once a place of exile for erring tsarist officers. There they were welcomed into Afghanistan by a camel caravan and a pack of rough mountain ponies, which were to carry them six hundred miles, over the wild mountain paths of the Hindu Kush to Kabul. These caravan trails were the outside world's only link with Kabul, and it took two weeks for even the best riders to reach there. Since most of the Soviet mission had never been on a horse before, it took them thirty days. Larissa Reisner, who rode excellently, shone with cheerfulness and mockery at her comrades' discomfort and exhaustion, and wrote a long humorous verse about Soviet diplomacy's first lumbering steps in Central Asia, which started:

> Our troubles started at Kushka
> When a large crowd of Russians
> Without either blankets or cushions
> Climbed on a pack of wild horses . . . [4]

Lepetenko, without hat or sunglasses, rode alongside the party, recalled Nikulin, urging them on. The book-keeper had to struggle along on a prancing horse holding his precious money-box. And poor gunner Zentik, after cheerfully drinking water from a stream, was stricken with a fierce and feverish dysentery diagnosed by the mission doctor as Asiatic cholera, and could barely stay on his horse. Larissa, undaunted by the doctor's warnings and the malaria parasites in her blood, insisted on drinking from streams and swimming in the icy water of the mountain rivers. 'How many times, in the mountains and ravines, where even in hot summer the snows don't melt, you'd say to her: "Why swallow snow? Why drink from puddles?" ' wrote Nikulin. 'But she'd just shrug her shoulders and laugh.' She plunged into her new life in Afghanistan with a fierce and death-defying recklessness. Even on the journey to Kabul, wrote Nikulin, she was struck by a series of malaria attacks, and the following day she would be back in her saddle, weak but determined.[5]

On this journey to Kabul her imagination was captivated by the savage beauty of the east and its medieval Muslim customs and culture, and later, when she came to write her articles on Afghanistan, these first impressions were fixed clearly in her mind.

Here she is describing Soviet Turkestan, on the Afghan border:

Between a flat earth and flat sky smoke drifts into nothing. Pale moonlight on dead fields. Lakes and hills of melted snow. Smothered silence for hundreds of miles. Roads ravaged by the hoofs of Timur, consumed by extremes of heat and cold. Deserts which do not sleep or dream, for they do not exist. Impossible to read. Heine's scalding tears sink into the fine black earth. All fades on the steppe, where stones are made of moonlight and clouds are petrified in the emptiness.

Here there can be no history, the art of the dead. Here everything comes down to a piece of earth, a mixture of sand, salt and sunshine . . .[6]

'How far we have come,' she writes in another article, 'The Past':

Not hundreds or thousands of miles, but hundreds of years, an eternity. Here even the rocks, sands and ravines recall Tamerlane as if it was yesterday, and the squeak of his wild carts and the trudge of his cavalry lives on there, where now lies a railway.

What sun and honey the desert sheds, and what good smells. Tashkent, blazing like a dark emerald, and now at last medieval Bukhara. . . .

Covered bazaars spread over two or three miles. Inside it's cool, doves coo under the roofs, through whose chinks seeps a golden midday rain. To right and left, at the entrances to the tiny stalls, sit bright robes, turbans whiter than snow, and old men, bearded like prophets, sit with god-like ease and sniff moist roses as they tot up their profits.

Tiny donkeys run about with loads of rushes, fresh clover, veiled women and God knows what else. Sometimes one of our tall-helmeted cavalrymen passes through the crowd, and from the wall he looks like the conqueror of Jerusalem, the paladin of the Red Star . . .

And further on, in this description of a garden in Bukhara, she communicates almost physically the scents and sounds of the roses, waterfalls and palm trees:

The gardens are full of lakes, swans, tents and ancient buildings, grapevines growing close to the ground, the fragrance of roses and pomegranates, the colour of azure and the humming of bees. Then there's the smell, so strong and dense that it makes you want to shut your eyes, lie down on the blazing flagstones of the blazing courtyard, and feel yourself becoming lighter than the swallows. . . . People spread rugs under the trees and serve tea with spicy sweets. There is a silence which makes the birds dumb and the trees stop growing . . .

She continues with this description of her visit to the Bukhara Emir's harem:

A tiny courtyard with several doors leading on to it, and behind each door a white room. Its walls are decorated with peacock feathers, and contain niches in which hundreds of teapots stand in pairs, one big and one small, just like a pair of doves. And in each room lives a child-woman, thirteen to fourteen years old, and as slight as the grapevine.

They all lower their eyes, covering their smiles with their hands. Their hair is braided into hundreds of tiny plaits. They run barefoot over the carpets, and their tiny toenails are painted bright red. Sly and silent at first, these little imps in their wide pink and yellow trousers eventually settle around me and draw closer, laughing and chattering like birds, and reaching out to touch me with cool hands. I think we liked each other a lot.

Then in 'High Up', she describes the ravines and crevasses of the Hindu Kush:

Mountain cold. The road winds over summits which unite in a high plateau. From a glance, one would never guess that these gentle pyramids are the crown of a mountain range fourteen thousand feet high. Dry metallic grass rustles like wreaths at a funeral, and the mountains' rare flowers, dotted on the grey altar of this great altitude, smoulder like yellow candles with a faint, almost extinguished breath.

Beside streams like emerald velvet are the grey, clawed ruins of Macedonian fortresses, standing guard over the mountain passes and cool pastures . . .

High in the pale sky there is a snowstorm of fighting white eagles . . .

Some fifty miles from Kushka, the Soviet mission made its theatrical entry into the walled medieval Mogul town of Herat, in which the fasting month of Ramadan had just started, and life started at sunset and stopped at sunrise. From there they travelled on through the mountains to Obeh, Daulat Yar, Sar-i-Chashma. And finally, at the end of May, almost two months after leaving Moscow, they arrived in Kabul.

There they were met by Igor, with whom Larissa and Raskolnikov spent two weeks, before escorting him to the Khyber Pass on his return journey, via India, to Moscow, where he enrolled for a degree in oriental studies at the Red Army Military Academy. Perhaps Igor regretted having to leave, or felt he was being ousted, for he evidently disliked going back, and described his studies in Moscow as 'torture'. And later in letters to her parents Larissa would refer to difficulties between them in Kabul, and 'feelings of indebtedness', which she deeply repented and wept about.

By the time they arrived in Kabul, the giant Zentik had been reduced to a pile of bones. He was attended by the mission's doctor and two of his closest friends, and Larissa, defying the doctor's disapproval and the risk of infection, nursed him to the end. When, groaning in agony, he finally burned himself out, she helped to prepare the gravestone, with a hammer and sickle at the top. At his funeral, watched at a distance by a crowd of Afghans, curious to see how the Russians buried their dead, she read out the epitaph, and Nikulin received from her a postcard of his grave, on which she had written: 'This is the grave of poor Zentik, dug into stones and sand'.[7]

Soon afterwards, Raskolnikov was received by the Emir, in the presence of the British Ambassador, Sir Henry Dobbs ('hated by all Kabul', wrote Reisner to her parents):

All is settled. We were helped by the new British consul, who behaves like a boor with a whip in the colonies. All thanks to him – but how well Fedya conducted himself. Very smart! Well, that's all for now. Mother, I never stop dreaming that you'll visit. Who knows? Is it inconceivable?[8]

The Soviet mission had entered a society without radio or air communication with the outside world. Express parcels took a month to reach Moscow, Soviet newspapers were seven weeks late, and the first they heard of the famine in the Volga that year was from the Indian papers. When radio connection was finally made with Moscow, wrote Nikulin, the first message was like a message in a bottle.

In a letter to her parents that summer, Larissa described 'the "Russians in Kabul" – this psychological bluff, this Hoffman-esque mirage putting down roots under the hot Afghan sky . . .' In their diplomatic residence, at Kala i Fata, they lived on a Soviet island ('Penguin Island', she called it: Anatole France's novel was evidently being passed around).[9] Constant surveillance from the Ministries of Police and Foreign Affairs ruled out all informal social contacts, or visits to the mosque or bazaar. And despite Amanullah's strictures against the veiling of women, it is only now in the 1980s that Afghan women are throwing off their *chadris*, and Reisner was much more confined than the men. Within the mission, however, the atmosphere reminded her of nothing so much as her Petersburg *gimnazium*, and Afghan dignitaries meeting His Excellency's wife would find her singing with the sailors, or dancing the foxtrot with the mission's doctor.

Despite the difficulties of working as a journalist in these conditions, she was writing nonetheless. She returned, with a new perspective on her pre-revolutionary past, to the auto-biographical work she had started in 1919, which she now entitled *Rudin*. She also wrote voluminously to her parents, whose por-traits she hung in the Kala i Fata dining-room, and whose absence she promised to make good with letters. In these she recorded her first impressions of Afghanistan with all the lyrical intensity, and sometimes excessive lushness, of her 'Letters from the Front'. In one of her earliest letters to them, in late May, she describes her first spring there:

The first warmth floods the eternal snows with a light almost unbearable for the eyes, and fills them with sun, transparent and foaming, like unearthly wine in white crystal, while in the valleys, gardens drown in a storm of blossoms. Then the snow is shadowed by the rosy twilight of the moon, the lilacs flare up to meet it, and violet lilies soak May with a pure and intoxicating incense . . . And the clouds, racing over the sunny sky, carry caravans of shadows over the roads, sands and slopes of the dead mountains . . .

At last, in a rough heaven, hot as the desert, the cramped nomad in his tent, his *houris* reclining beside him on emerald green cushions, smokes in the heaven of Mahommet after the heat of the long, grey day . . .

But in the bazaar, in the clay streets without doors, over the cellars, where craftsmen, bent and blind from the endless darkness, embroider slippers with gold; in the long, hopeless clay wall, raised from the earth and splashed by the breath of tired laden donkeys and camels – who can deny that here, in that exhausting, pitiless wall, there is a green window, from which it may be possible to see a garden, hidden from view like a jewel inside a ring . . .[10]

Gradually she began to make friends in Kabul. She was given an Afghan stallion, whom she called Falcon, and took long rides through the town. She tended the embassy's goats. She organised diplomatic tea parties for diplomats' wives. She learned a little Farsi from the translaters. She played tennis with the Emir (with whom she spoke French). And she was at last received by his mother at the female half of the court.

In another letter to her parents, she described this first visit to the harem, cooled by the sunset and splashed by fountains. There she met the Emir's mother, in pearls and violet brocade, and his wife and mistress, curious for their first sight of a European woman. She evidently found favour with them. (They liked her, she wrote later to Alexandra Kollontai, for her 'unsoviet manners': 'So my parents' education did come in useful after all!')

Shortly after her first visit there, she was invited to a women's

banquet at which she sat next to the Emir's mother, who offered
her own plate to her as a mark of respect. After the meal some
women musicians arrived and played wild, sad music on harmon-
iums and drums. Larissa joined the women dancing, then sat on
the carpet beside the musicians, who taught her to play simple
rhythms on their drums. After the dancing, she joined the Emir's
mother on the balcony to contemplate the courtyard, with its
roses, lanterns and fountains. Summer lightning flashed in the
distant hills, Larissa cursed the British in broken Farsi, 'and the
old woman poured me a thimble-full of sweet tea, and promised
not to receive the "evil British ladies".'[11]

She became a regular guest at the banquets and festivities of the
harem, and her popularity with the women of the court soon had
the British women in Kabul interrogating her about her experiences there. But in her writings, the exotic life within its walls is
always described against the poverty, ignorance and disease
lurking outside.

Despite all the bright colours, the lustre, the superficially intoxicating
beauty of this life, I am seized with a furious hatred for the dead Orient.
Not a glimmer of innovative or creative energy. Not one book for miles
around. Decay is veiled by a splendid and monotonous flow of customs.
Nothing lives.[12]

This anger, suppressed by polite diplomacy, comes boiling out
when she describes the oppression of Afghan women's lives. In
'Science and the Harem', she describes her visit to its school,
where old courtesans taught their young charges the Koran. She
writes of these girls of the court,

taught only to love, who have created a whole science of love, a whole cult
of tender tricks: they have picked up the colours of passion, like the
bright silks on the festive carpet, and they smile like knowing priestesses,
serving the tormenting but beautiful god of desire.

And in 'The Hidden Woman and her Hidden Child', she writes of
the veiled and silent existence of the women outside:

Here, more than in any other oriental country, a woman is separated
from life by the folds of her *chadri*, gathered in thousands of folds at the

crown of the head and falling to the tips of her pointed heelless slippers, which further encumber her blind gait.

In the bright crowd following her long nomadic camel caravans on donkeys, with their bed-rolls, tents, guns and sunburnt children, the female shadow is everywhere, visibly and invisibly, present. Her face is unknown even to the infants at her breast. . . . These healthy children, with antimony on their eyes, brass rings on their fingers and toes, and hats decorated with paper flowers, are held by ghosts, immured and inaccessible, lifeless and voiceless . . .[13]

Some people later criticised her Afghanistan pieces as a mere exercise in exoticism, an attempt to conjure away the dumbness of the East. But she was writing too of the cruelty and indifference of Afghanistan's petty rulers, plump officials and smart officers, and of the British in Kabul, with their pith helmets, their disdainful free-and-easy manners, and their 'correct smiles, cutting their faces like a diametrical slash on the end of a bullet'. During her rides through the mountains outside Kabul she would stand in her stirrups, and look at the mountain range beyond which lay British India. India was at the centre of all her diplomatic encounters with the British in Kabul. 'The swinging pendulum between the Entente and Soviet Russia is evident in the way the British aristocrat, the fox, the polite murderer, masked by mean contempt for people, sweetly shakes the hand of warrant officer Fedya, and fawns to his wife,' she wrote to her parents.

A sea of blood is shed for this calculating smile, this innocent diplomatic flirtation, this semi-recognition of what might start between them and us – between the cancer eating the heart of India, and us, who will sooner or later have to tear out these bloody tentacles . . .[14]

On 25 October 1921 (the fourth anniversary of the Bolshevik Revolution), Afghanistan celebrated two years of national independence. The British and Russian missions were invited to attend the festivities, and Larissa Reisner saw the complexity of Afghanistan's relations with them acted out on the streets of Kabul. The last remaining obstacle between British bayonets and Afghan independence were the rebellious tribes of the eastern areas, in whose song, dance and music the struggle found its clearest expression. The town was filled that day with bright mountain people, and Reisner watched as the best singer, standing in the middle of a crowd of tribespeople, sang to the accompaniment of drums, while the others repeated the chorus:

'The English have stolen our land, but we'll drive them out and get back our fields and homes.'

The British ambassador, on his magnificent platform, pales and applauds ironically.

'We'll wipe you off the face of the earth like a cow licking grass – you'll never conquer us!'

A thousand eyes watch the British – and surrounding the singers a wall of silent, maliciously smiling people listen as the singer continues:

'Luckily not all Europeans are cursed *farangi** – there are the Bolsheviks who are one with the Muslims!'

And the crowd roars with laughter, and jostles towards the platform.[15]

In April 1922, she wrote to her parents of the elemental beauty of her second spring in Afghanistan, with its apples and peaches, 'masterpiece and symbol of a simple spring religion still unknown, akin to the lotus of India or the chrysanthemum of Hokkusai':

By day, spring is merciful – its blue sky is filled with flowering apple trees, old men sing at the edges of fields thick with narcissi, and women standing amongst the velvety winter crops throw back their *chadris* and smile. But the nights are terrible, powerful in their rebirth, inexorable in their love of stones, water and branches. The steady light of the moon pours in a white stream over the snow of the mountains and the flowering orchards, on the rocks and the eyelids of sleeping people, on the graveyards and the carpets of crops. All lines are sharpened, all shadows are clear in the transparent blackness. A night bird sings monotonously, sadly, shrilly . . .[16]

But her parents' letters back to her were full of sadness and even Igor's were subdued and depressed. They had little liking for NEP Russia, with its new bourgeoisie and its entrepreneurial

---

* Foreigners

vulgarity, and they had had a bad winter. Ekaterina Alexandrovna was ill, Igor hated his studies, and Professor Reisner, who was always too Marxist before the Revolution and could never be Marxist enough after it, had virtually retired from the law after being worsted in a polemic with Stuchka, Commissar of Justice, over the utility of bourgeois law. He had abandoned law for social psychology, and in his writings of those years he attempted to integrate the psychoanalytical theories of Freud with the reflexology of N. M. Bekhterev.[17] He was also closely involved in the new Soviet theatre, and had written six short satirical plays, *God and the Stock Exchange*, which entered various repertoires in Moscow and Petrograd.[18] He was particularly involved with Moscow's controversial Meyerhold Theatre, of which he was still a director. But new troubles faced him that spring at the Meyerhold too, whose repertoire had crashed after its iconoclastic production of Sukhovo-Kobylin's play *The Death of Tarelkin*.

Larissa worried about her parents in their cold, cramped, communal flat. She feared other 'psychic breaches' they were not telling her of, and felt that her absence was partly responsible for their unhappiness. And when Raskolnikov suggested, to her delight, that Igor return to Kabul as first secretary, and bring them with him, she wrote to assure them that there would be cars to take them there, not horses, and that if they came that autumn there would be no risk of malaria. But nothing came of the idea, and she wrote them almost daily letters of love, reassurance and remorse.

My father and mother, my home, my creation, if only you knew with what tender tears I think of you. . . . My only grief, you know and I needn't repeat: I miss you. You are so blessed, so disposed to eternal metamorphoses of the spirit. . . . If only I could visit you for three days, I'd tear the cobwebs from your faces, which I can't see clearly through distance, sadness and the soothing illusion of words. . . . Maybe the sun will return to you something lost in these cold terrible months . . ., the winter of papa's theatrical work and mother's utter loneliness.[19]

That winter she had finished the first draft of her autobiography and had sent it to them for their opinion. Perhaps this account of her past revealed too much and offended the family code of privacy, for their response to it was painfully cool. 'Why don't the first chapters, which seemed to me so successful, receive even justified sentence? Is it all really so loathsome?' she wrote to them. Nonetheless they were her most valued critics, and their disapproval seems to have convinced her to drop the work, the unpublished manuscript of which now lies in her archive at Moscow's Lenin Library.

Other writing seemed anyway more urgent. In the spring of 1922, more of her 'Letters from the Front' appeared in *Krasnaya Nov* [Red Virgin Soil], a new and important journal of belles lettres, criticism and theory, launched with the personal backing of Lenin and Gorky, and edited by Alexander Voronsky in an ambitious attempt to emulate the 'thick' literary political journals of the nineteenth century. Larissa was planning to turn her 'Letters' into a book, and was working that spring on its opening chapter, on the battle for Svyazhsk. In the summer she also turned her writing to the services of the Comintern, for which she became an 'Informant'. But even the Comintern could not restrain the exuberance of her prose. When she sent her first Comintern articles to her parents, asking them to publish all but those marked 'secret' in *Pravda* or *Izvestiya*, she wrote:

I can imagine with what delight they'll read my descriptions of the flowers, the clouds, the sunrises, the sunsets and all the humming-birds in the harem, without which, as you know, an old Party worker like me can describe neither revolution nor reaction.[20]

Thoughts of her family brought old contradictions to the surface. That winter she had learnt of the death seven months earlier of Alexander Blok, and in a letter of condolence to the Petrograd poet Anna Akhmatova, she described the final passing, with his death, of the old Russia.[21] With Blok gone, Akhmatova remained for her as the most moving representative of the old culture and her own past. In a letter in May thanking her parents for an issue of the Symbolists' journal *Notes of a Dreamer*, she spoke warmly of Andrei Bely's novel *The Crime of Nikolai Letaev*, and the poems of Gershenzon. Then she described the feelings evoked by the poems of Akhmatova, who 'with pain and tears has opened up old wounds, and also closed them forever':

She has poured into art all my contradictions, for which for so many years there was no escape. Now they exist outside me, like marble, and their burdens and temptations have passed into the pantheon. How grateful I am to her. . . . Her poems here both delight and disturb one – like a brief, chance return after a long absence to an abandoned house, once dear but now hateful. The floor and shelves are littered with the pages of good books, scattered sheets of old letters, comfortable, beautiful things, and the special smell of a cultured, elegant, intellectual life, now run wild. . . .

There's nothing more harmful than cemeteries, memories, and sentimental strolls around one's own ruins. They're tenacious, they smell of death, and they induce a fatal weakness. All these Petersburg writings are a sachet, with which the newly rich bourgeoisie perfumes their fine underclothes, stolen from God knows where . . .[22]

In the summer of 1922, the first of her sketches on Afghanistan were published in *Pravda*, the daily paper of the Bolshevik Party, and she wrote more in the hope of eventually turning them too into a book.[23] In June, she escaped the burning summer sun for the Emir's country residence outside Kabul, where she sat in its apricot orchards, writing up her Comintern reports. She was also 'catching up on her theoretical education', she told her parents in a letter, by reading Marx's *History of Class Struggles in France*, and the works of Bukharin, beneath whose trenchancy she found 'sociological riddles' and a 'vulgarisation of the great Marx'. 'My mental machine isn't rusting (although what comparison could there be with Goga's?)' she wrote, 'and as soon as I return home, I'll get it going!'[24] All such thoughts, however, were interrupted by a sudden crisis in Afghan–Soviet relations. In July 1922, Enver Pasha, supported by some seven thousand armed troops, finally led an uprising against the Soviet régime in Bukhara, which revived all Amanullah's dreams of a Central Asian Confederation, and Britain's demands for military intervention. Enver Pasha was killed in a skirmish with a Red Army detachment, and 'Fedya and I again felt that familiar blissful shiver up the spine, as the spiked helmets and furled flags of the

Red Army appeared over the dead quicksands'.[25] Enver Pasha's death put paid once and for all to 'the secret lusts of the Supreme Independent', and there followed days of sullen silence, in which Raskolnikov pressed for guarantees and compensations. In the middle of these negotiations, however, a sudden avalanche of British gold landed in the Emir's lap, and the Soviet mission's radio was confiscated, so that the embassy relied for its information on Afghan telegraphists returning from Russia.

In the following months of conflicts and misunderstandings, the Emir (urged on by the Italians in Kabul) was pushed into yet deeper intrigues between Britain and Russia. The Soviet mission's radio was returned, then confiscated again, British money poured in, and the Emir sent Raskolnikov a note accusing him of shooting at kittens, 'sacred animals'. Raskolnikov paid frequent visits to the Afghan Foreign Ministry, trying to restore diplomatic calm. But the Russians' main hope now lay with Turkey's new ambassador to Kabul, the old nationalist soldier Fakhri-Pasha, and Larissa was invited by him to be hostess at a banquet in his honour that July at the Turkish embassy.

By the end of the month, Soviet Russia had again replaced Britain in the Emir's affections. Larissa and Raskolnikov visited his residence in the mountains at Pagman for a festival of races, parties and parades, and when one of the parades ended in a song sung by orphans of those killed by Britain, the British contingent walked out. During another round of parties at the harem, Larissa further ingratiated the Soviet mission with the Emir by warning him of rumours of an attempt on his life by those opposed to his reforms. The next day, the distraught Emir visited her in the harem, and told her that he had heard a 'big English bird in a bush' telling people in the town that he was dead. At this, his mother 'threw herself sobbing on my neck, and I also dropped a diplomatic tear on her peach-pink shoulder'. The Emir, as a mark of his gratitude, presented her with his peaked army cap, which he ordered her to wear while riding. Larissa then took the opportunity to curse the British, 'and all in all, it was "big politics!"'[26]

But the nervous tension of this diplomatic game of chance

between Britain and Russia was taking its toll on her health in a series of malaria attacks, and when she returned to Kabul in September she collapsed exhausted and was in bed for the next two weeks. The pressure to get an agreement with the Afghans was now becoming increasingly desperate. Isolated from Moscow and from diplomatic moves at home, many in the Soviet mission were exhausted by Kabul life, and longed for home. Those returning to Russia on courier visits rarely returned now, and Reisner hated parting with them, although when her secretary, Kirillov, applied to leave for Moscow to study, she helped him to do so.

It may be that Larissa Reisner's work amongst the women of the Afghan court, and her observations of the women outside it, were not taken as seriously as they should have been by her male colleagues, and she herself tended to belittle their importance. One person, though, to whom her experiences were of immediate interest was Alexandra Kollontai, who as head of the Zhenotdel for the past two years had organised a vast educational programme amongst the women of Soviet Central Asia. In the summer of 1922, Kollontai was in Moscow awaiting her first diplomatic assignment, and when Kirillov left Kabul he took with him a letter to her from Larissa, along with her articles 'The Hidden Woman', 'Science in the Harem' and this more optimistic assessment of Afghan women's fight for liberation and their central importance in the perennial struggle to control the water supply:

Hard work and poverty long ago freed the shepherd's wife and the peasant woman from the honourable confines of her *chadri*. In the mountain passes, in secluded valleys hidden among the mountain peaks, the Afghan woman works with uncovered head, with bare arms and a neck burnt by the sun.

Her wheat field, laid out at the foot of the cliffs, is scrupulously cleared of fragments of lava, marble and granite. Silver-threaded streams, conducted there from the mountains, need constantly to be adjusted, dammed, fused with a stronger stream or divided into fine irrigation canals. In these sandy mountains in which water is life – more essential than bread or fire – men and women share equally in the hard toil of cleaning and deepening the irrigation ditches. Harmonious and dark-haired, with her Greek face, wide red linen trousers and strong golden arms, she seems fashioned out of old Tanagra clay. In the shade of the mulberry trees, languishing in the heat beside a fertilising stream covered in stones and foliage, a woman works and rests beside a man, cutting the thick acrid rushes and protecting the moisture from the intense July heat.

Every evening it is she who with a calm and open face walks around the rough walls of her home, a solitary clay fortress in the mountains, beside a road laid long ago by Timur and Alexander the Great. She turns the bundles of clover, fragrant and dried by the sun. She drives home the rams, and winds with a quick and practised movement her primeval distaff which hangs on an endless thread of camel-hair . . .[27]

After three years on the front line of the Revolution, the confinement of married life in Kabul, and her role there as the ambassador's charming wife, must have been hard for Larissa to bear. Possibly Raskolnikov enjoyed a more domestic setting for their marriage: 'I live in the love which from Fedya's side only here, under the sacred sky, has become love', she wrote to her parents. But in other letters to them that summer, there is a certain cool ambivalence, and hints at strains in their relationship.

He removes his thick dictionary from his knees, which have recently become rather plump. . . . He sits in his study conjuring with his books, and he is happy – but I don't enter into this world, for it isn't mine. Here are the roots of his Party, his law, his revolutionary shield. . . . Here is his strange holy of holies, compounded of years in prison, the titles of underground leaflets, the pseudonyms of those who have died, or become great. . . . There is no war between us, and never will be.[28]

We do not know whether Raskolnikov really was a jealous husband, as one western writer has said. He may well have resented her new friendships with women, her many deep and passionate relationships with other men, and her determination to go her own way. Perhaps she wanted children, or felt she ought to want them. Perhaps she longed again for the liberation she had known at the front. Perhaps in her first experiences as an organiser of women she was discovering a new anger on behalf of women's wasted lives. At any rate her personal life, which she keeps so hidden from us, was always, according to Nikulin, fraught with difficulties:

Maybe it was because she didn't create illusions. She told her friends to their faces exactly what she thought of them, practically from the first day of knowing them, and she would speak directly about the most precious thing she discovered in them. And some did not forgive this.[29]

There were many who quailed under her sharp tongue. Others welcomed her honest, practical criticisms, and Kirillov, who became an actor at Moscow's Meyerhold Theatre after his return there, always treasured the letter he got from her later that year, 'full of friendly concern about my path as artist':

I didn't like your first letters – don't be angry – for their disturbing complacency. . . . It's always bad when life can be made to fit through the eye of a needle. . . . If you dream one minute of the fame of Garrick, and the next of suicide, first of your power then of your worthlessness, I'll tell you that you're looking for a form, and that it's lying right in front of you, twisting, disappearing and leaving behind it a momentary gleam, a hint of how it must be 'done', according to the orders of your sacred craft. I love Meyerhold. But be careful . . . they're very oriental in their 'innovations', they trust the body (which is good), and they completely fail to understand the genius of words (which is bad).
     This is its own kind of theatrical egotism. Speech and intonation for them are the same as the soul for a good Voltairian – they don't believe in that kind of rubbish. Nor in the brain of the actor.
     But unless the brain develops a vast sensitivity and studies the complex workings of the Spirit, then I assure you, Misha, your body won't find the familiar nuances offered to the gymnastics of *ideas*, the fencing of logic, the massage of styles, which it is necessary to *know*, like a botanist knows flowers. People don't act from their heads – nor without them either. Someone who's never loved can never act love, just as someone who's never thought can't act tragedy. Keep your balance, for God's sake, don't let yourself be mutilated by the masters of formal, physical, tangible art. Spirit, spirit, spirit . . . there's nothing without it. And then the school of Komissarzhevsky will give you full, whole, human acting
. . .[30]

Larissa Reisner herself, according to Nikulin, didn't patiently endure criticism, and in Kabul the two often quarrelled. Their last argument there, 'over some trifle', said Nikulin, was shortly before he left that summer, and although they eventually made it up, they never had the chance to restore their former friendship. Nikulin finally departed for Herat, and afterwards the Russians in Kabul felt even more cut off. 'We know absolutely nothing of the Baltic,' Raskolnikov wrote to him. 'If, being nearer to Russia, you get some news before us, please let us know.'[31]

The progress of Soviet diplomacy in Afghanistan was now being rewarded by renewed British agitation for the Russians' withdrawal. In the autumn, Reisner decided to bring a little anti-British spectacle to a banquet she helped to organise at Kala i Fata in honour of Muhamed Wali Khan, the new Afghan Foreign Minister. She asked the Soviet telegraphists to construct two cardboard, battery-operated model radio stations, flying the Soviet and Afghan flags. These she had placed on the dinner-table, with leads running to her plate, to give the illusion of a working telegraph, and when she switched them on during the banquet, to communicate greetings to the Emir and curses to the British, the effect was electrifying (especially as the Soviet telegraphists had only that morning returned to their exchange). After this she organised another, women-only, banquet, for Fakhri-Pasha's wife, the Emir's mother and various other women of the Emir's court.[32]

At the end of 1922, the British, in a desperate bid to crush Afghan resistance, made use of the winter months, when the eastern tribespeople could not move, to bomb, gas and set fire to their settlements, flocks and fields. The Emir, softened by more British cash, and realising that after the tribes it would be his turn, tossed between the Russians, the British and the tribal representatives, crying for help. Raskolnikov sent increasingly urgent telegraph messages to the Soviet government for support, but he could not always be sure that his messages were being received.

Desperate neurasthenic days followed, and sleepless nights which had Reisner jumping up to chase her own shadow. Raskolnikov quarrelled with the Turkish ambassador, Fakhri-Pasha, who under the influence of 'stinking, White Guard information', demanded that Bukhara be given its independence, and the Bolsheviks 'withdraw their damned Red Army and stop oppressing good Muslims'. (Later, as a gesture of reconciliation, he sent Professor Reisner a gold embroidered cloak, 'as worn by oriental despots', wrote Larissa.)

In December, it was announced that a magnificent new motorcar would soon be arriving from Peshawar to take her home. By now she was desperate to leave. 'I've seen the East, the camels, the middle ages, the wild harem, the dances of the tribes, the eternal snows, storms of blossom and storms of snow,' she wrote to her mother:

and the reflection of these years will be with me as long as I live, and will produce many harvests. I don't regret them. What was bad was sometimes very bad: two years without you is a drought. But darling mother, I've come out of it not as a bourgeoise with the spic-and-span ethics of the Leusen-Allee, but as a mad revolutionary . . .

And our life is like our epoch, like us ourselves. From the Baltic to Novorossiisk, from the Kama to the apricot orchards of Jalalabad. We must not be judged, and there's no need for us to despair. . . . We are the great, eternal, unforgettable 1918, and the long years leading up to it, and we are happy, for we have seen it, Red, pure, naked, and rejoicing in the face of death.[33]

At the end of December 1922, Larissa and Raskolnikov left with the Emir for his winter residence at Jalalabad, fifty miles from the British-controlled Khyber Pass, on what is now the Pakistan border. The car crawled through the fierce storms of the vast mountain passes. And by the time they descended in the darkness into the valley of the Kabul river, smelling of flowers and acacias, they were exhausted and their driver's hands were stiff with cold. Finally they arrived at the Emir's palace, and late that night Larissa ran out to the garden with a candle to revive her spirits amongst the tea roses and mimosas.

Jalalabad, with its straight streets and white courtyards, its cypresses, roses and orange-trees, was the closest she would get to a real colonial town, and the impression was confirmed by the anti-British feelings amongst the people she met there. She took long walks around the town with Raskolnikov, sent her parents her piece on Svyazhsk, brooded on her recently published 'Letter' on Kazan (which she very much disliked), and started an essay on the Persian nationalist Kuchek Khan. But she couldn't write here. She had a mass of rough drafts and exotic negatives, but she needed to be at home to develop them.

From Jalalabad she wrote to Kirillov:

Here the roses flower and the air is filled with happiness, cypresses and castor-oil trees, blossoming with red torches.

This is my last month, and I'll try to live it so that I remember for the rest of my life the East, the falcons, the palm trees and those bright and carefree moments when we're happy because the fountains splash, the wind smells of stocks, and there's youth too, and beauty, and everything that's sacred, hopeful and creative. The gods lived in these gardens, and they were kind and blessed. I shall go now to pray to the flowering trees. I'll soon be home.[34]

At the end of February 1923, Larissa left Jalalabad with Raskolnikov for Kabul. More than anything else now, she longed to leave Afghanistan, with a sense of anticipated nostalgia for this episode of her life. But her departure was complicated by international developments which were to have important consequences for her life then and later.

Earlier that year, at a conference in Genoa, representatives of the western governments had announced that they would recognise the Soviet government, end hostilities against it and grant it aid only if tsarist debts were repaid and nationalised property returned to foreign investors – an estimated total of some 18.5 billion roubles, as against the 39 billion roubles of damages Russia was claiming from the western intervention in the Civil War. In addition, foreigners in Russia were to be tried in special courts, outside Russian jurisdiction, Soviet labour laws were to be abrogated, and the monopoly on foreign trade ended – a programme designed, in effect, to annul most of the Bolsheviks' socialist legislation.

In December 1922, there had been an international conference at Lausanne to work out a peace treaty with Turkey. Soviet Russia, Turkey's neighbour, was barred by the British from all but a limited section of the conference, and their proposals to close the Dardanelles to foreign warships were rejected outright.[35]

After Lausanne, the British redoubled their agitation against the Soviet presence in Kabul, which was so deeply threatening to their interests in India. In the spring of 1923, Lord Curzon, the British Foreign Minister, issued a sharply worded memorandum to the Soviet government, accusing it of committing violence against British subjects, detaining British trawlers, conducting religious persecution in the USSR and spreading anti-British propaganda in Persia, India and Afghanistan. The governments of these countries were ordered to dismiss their Soviet ambassadors within eight days, and Afghanistan's Emir was told to send Raskolnikov back to Moscow. This attempt to isolate the Bolsheviks diplomatically presaged for many a renewed military intervention against Soviet Russia, and in Britain thousands demonstrated in Trafalgar Square to demand Curzon's dismissal, while Mayakovsky declaimed his poems at huge demonstrations in Moscow.

Yet the Curzon Ultimatum, far from creating an anti-Soviet bloc in Europe and America, revealed still further conflicts between the western governments, and increased, rather than undermined, Soviet influence in Asia. The Soviet government did not respond to Curzon at once, and although Raskolnikov was instructed to tone down his anti-British statements, he was rewarded by Amanullah with the extraordinary honour of a medal for his diplomacy, and it was nine months before he finally left Kabul, when his term there was up anyway. The consequences of the Ultimatum for Larissa, however, were that when Amanullah proposed to Britain that she return via India, the British government annulled its Kabul ambassador's verbal guarantee of her safe passage. More anxious days followed, while she waited for a car, and finally, in the middle of May 1923, she said goodbye to Raskolnikov and left, via Bamian, for home.

Just before leaving, she wrote to her parents:

If now, when Afghanistan is in effect at war with Britain, when its borders are soaked in the blood of the tribes and the Emir can rely on no one but us: when all is put on the map and working Russia dares not refuse help to the tribespeople, for 100 years destroyed, for 100 years besieged – if we let this moment slip, there's nothing more for us to do here but to shut up shop. Yet now, after Lausanne, how useful it would be to remind Britain of its sore spot in the East.[36]

Chapter Seven

AFTER THE REVOLUTION – RUSSIA AND GERMANY

Within two weeks of leaving Kabul Larissa was in the Soviet border town of Kushka, where she saw barefoot Red Army soldiers peacefully washing their underwear in the river. A week later she was back in Moscow, where she was met by Party friends and taken to her new home, a small shabby room in Moscow's fifth House of Soviets. It was a grey, rainy summer, and her room was cramped and uncomfortable, but she was delighted to be back and to see her family again. Her old student friend Igor Ilinsky, whom she met on the day of her return, found her shining with happiness.[1]

Yet after two years away, there were many things she found strange about NEP Moscow, with its new neon-lit shops and factories. In those two years, the New Economic Policy had produced extraordinary results. Famine and speculation had virtually vanished; the bourgeoisie, defeated in the Civil War, were here and there resurfacing, and private businesses, restaurants and publishing houses were now doing a thriving trade. Meanwhile unemployment soared, particularly amongst women, and Larissa was shocked to see beggars sitting outside the private shops of the brightly lit Tverskoi Boulevard, down which trotted the new 'red businessmen' on their private horses. While anti-Bolshevik writers and academics hailed NEP in their new, privately funded, journals as a return to capitalism, the Party, in *Youth Pravda*, exhorted Komsomol members to donate a day's wages each month to an unemployment fund. 'NEP Russia will be Socialist Russia!' Lenin had said. But that March, Lenin had suffered his second stroke, which deprived him of the power of speech. In the Moscow of 1923, Larissa Reisner found an extra-ordinary amount of confusion amongst her old Party and writer friends about how to translate Lenin's words into reality.

The contradictions of NEP produced a mass of competing new literary currents and alignments. There was Mayakovsky and the Futurists, with their journal *Lef* [Left Front of Art], through which they aimed to make their poetry more accessible to a mass audience. There were the new Komsomol (Communist Youth League) writers and their journal *Young Guard*, which they declared to be 'inseparable from the working-peasant masses'. There were the peasant poets Esenin and Klyuev. There were the stories and novels of Boris Pilnyak, who celebrated the freshness and chaos of revolution in the provinces, and was a leading member of the Serapion Brotherhood, the 'fellow-travellers of the Revolution'. There were Shklovsky and the Formalists, Ivanov and the proletarian 'Cosmists', and a number of writers, like Khodasevich and Nabokov, who emigrated. And there was an even larger number, like Bely and Shklovsky, who practically commuted between Russia and Europe (mainly Berlin), making it hard to know if they were émigrés or not.

Larissa threw herself into a round of writers' meetings. She took a close interest in Alexander Voronsky's new journal *Red Virgin Soil*, which had published translations of the writings of Bergson, Proust and Tagore, as well as numerous original works by Soviet writers, including several pieces by Pilnyak and her own essays from Afghanistan. Three hundred pages long, it aimed to shape the Party's attitude to its fellow-travellers, and already had a large and loyal audience, mainly amongst the new Soviet intelligentsia in the workers' faculties, and the Soviet, Party and army schools. The fiercer defenders of proletarian purity denounced all such collaboration with fellow-travellers, and attacked Voronsky for opening his journal to alien, non-Communist writers. Leading the attack was the October group and their journal *On Guard*, in which poets like Alexander Bezymensky waged war on the new NEP businessmen and their supporters.

Larissa was an attentive critic of the work of Pilnyak and the

Red Virgin Soil writers. But she was especially interested in the new proletarian writers clustering around the Komsomol and *Young Guard*, and she attended many of their meetings, to praise, criticise and defend young poets from the fierce attacks of the 'On Guardists'.

With her well-cut clothes, her elegantly arranged hair and her cultured, unhurried speech, she made an incongruous appearance at these proletarian gatherings of workers, soldiers and students, most of them men, some as much as ten years younger than she. Although in discussion they found her friendly and uncondescending, many poets there preferred the more earthy roughness of speech and dress that was then in fashion, and could not at first decide whether to worship this legendary journalist and first woman commissar, or to denounce her for her bourgeois manners and for the ornamental prose of her Afghanistan articles, which many found élitist and affected. For the writer Lev Sosnovsky, these articles were the 'third test':

Wasn't this young woman being drawn towards exoticism? Wasn't she turning her face from our tedious prose and all-Russian greyness? Wasn't there here a private escape into the exoticism of bizarre lands and peoples . . . ?[2]

Red Virgin Soil had just published what was probably the first Soviet novel, Yurii Libedinsky's *A Week* and in the summer of 1923 all Moscow was arguing about his frank and controversial exploration of the dilemmas faced by a local Soviet organisation in a rural area of peasants murderously hostile to the Bolsheviks. Shortly after returning to Moscow, Larissa spent a few days with her parents at a nearby *dacha* in Kuntsevo, where Libedinsky was staying with his family. He recalled her appearing at his *dacha* one rainy afternoon, followed by her mother, who was carrying a little dog:

When she entered our wicket-gate in her simple dress and straw hat, we were struck by her beauty and delicacy – like a classical goddess or Nordic Valkyrie, and I felt that . . . to talk to her would be an extraordinary happiness.[3]

They talked for a long time that afternoon. She ardently defended Libedinsky and Voronsky against attacks from the 'On Guardists', and praised and criticised *A Week*. And when he criticised her Afghanistan pieces for their stylistic artificiality, she agreed, frowning and thumping the table: 'That's all behind me now. From now on I'm going to write differently, more simply.'

At Libedinsky's invitation, she attended several meetings of activists from Moscow's Association of Proletarian Writers (MAPP). But she was more often to be found at *Young Guard* meetings, at first in the building of the Komsomol Central Committee, where the journal was published, then in the small, dark, oak-panelled upper hall at the House of Proletarian Writers, on Vozdvizhenka, in the former residence of the industrialist Savva Morozov. She soon became a familiar figure at these gatherings in the Vozdvizhenka hall, sitting in her place by the window, a bulky briefcase on her knee, smiling, frowning and scribbling on her notepad, as Komsomol poets like Alexander Zharov and *Young Guard*'s nineteen-year-old editor, Mark Kolosov, declaimed their poems and debated with Bezymensky and the 'On Guardists'.[4]

Bezymensky recalled her attending a large literary party organised there that September by the 'Young Guardists' and 'On Guardists' for three young Ukrainian poets, Golodny, Svetlov and Yasny, who had come to Moscow to study at the capital's Workers' Art Faculty. The hall filled with workers and poetry-lovers, and Larissa made for her usual seat by the window. Then the Ukrainians arrived, and read their poems, which were enthusiastically received, especially Mikhail Golodny's conversation with his machine, which was about to be replaced:

> The machine tells me of her pain
> And of her secret grief.
> Tears don't wet the sadness
> That has gathered there since morning,
> But in my heart I understand
> My iron sister's sorrow.

After they had finished reading, Larissa approached Bezymensky, who was presiding, discreetly led him to the window, and asked him to carry out some 'battle orders' which might seem comic to him, but were in fact very serious. To her annoyance, he burst out laughing on hearing what they were.

At the next meeting for the Ukrainians the following week, Larissa arrived early, her briefcase more bulging than before, and going straight to Bezymensky, she told him to find an empty room in the building that locked from the inside, and to ask the three Ukrainians to meet her there in his presence. They arrived, and locking the door, she said, 'Comrade poets, your poems are wonderful, but your appearance isn't smart enough!' And opening her briefcase she took out three pairs of new trousers and two pairs of shoes. 'Accept this as a present. I'll be mortally offended if you refuse. I'm sure you understand what real comradeship is, in large things and small. While you make yourselves presentable, I'll busy myself here, but I won't leave. Don't worry, I won't embarrass you. I've something to discuss with comrade Sasha.'

Bezymensky concluded his story by making three observations:

1. The poets didn't reject the clothes.
2. My assignment from Larissa Mikhailovna was to find out their shoe sizes.
3. She couldn't find shoes big enough to fit Svetlov's feet.[5]

But Reisner's enthusiasm for Moscow's literary scene was shadowed by unsettled doubts about the new Russia and its disturbing affinities with the west. As Radek wrote:

Scope had to be given to the business initiative of the peasant, to obtain the raw material for industry, and if only not to die of starvation. Larissa understands this, as we all do . . . But in her heart of hearts she yearns for a heroic attempt to break through to the new social order with arms in hand. And in the summer of 1923, she is uneasy . . .[6]

Above all, she hated stagnation and calm, and that summer she longed to travel to Germany, where events were now being followed in Russia with bated breath.

Shortly after the Genoa conference the previous year, the

German government, alone of all the western powers, had concluded a treaty with Soviet Russia offering diplomatic recognition, and the reciprocal cancelling of state debts, in exchange for
vital manufactured goods. In January 1923, French occupation
forces had marched into the Ruhr to force payment of war
reparations, which Germany had been withholding from them.
The German government, supported by the Bolsheviks, had been
urging the workers there to meet the invaders with passive
resistance, and they had refused to produce goods for them. As
the government desperately issued paper money to the strikers,
inflation soared and the Deutschmark collapsed. The strikes
dragged on until September, when a new government, under
Gustav Streseman, abandoned the policy of passive resistance to
the French. That autumn, with the fate of the Weimar Republic
hanging in the balance, it seemed that if there was no revolution in
Germany now, there never would be.

At this critical moment, the Bolshevik-led Third International,
or Comintern, which had only just proclaimed a United Front
strategy to deal with the non-revolutionary climate, had to provide guidance to the precarious and divided German Communist
Party (the KPD). It was then that Karl Radek, Secretary of the
Comintern's Executive Committee, agreed, despite many mis-
givings, to support a showdown between German workers and
their government which, with the necessary determination, could
be the start of a revolution. The uprising was scheduled for early
November in Dresden, the capital of 'Red Saxony', where Communists were to infiltrate the socialist state government, as the
base from which to arm the sixty thousand or so workers pre-
sumed to be sympathetic to the uprising.

In September, Larissa Reisner visited the Comintern to ask
Radek to send her to Germany. Since she spoke the language
perfectly and could pass for a German, Radek saw her as an
obvious choice to go there. But her main asset to the Comintern,
according to him, was her pen:

Her proposal pleased me greatly. Just as the German working class
couldn't get any clear idea of what was going on in Russia, the Russian

working class thought of the German proletarian struggle in an over-simplified, schematic way. I felt convinced that Larissa, better than anyone else, could establish the link between these two proletarian armies. For she wasn't a contemplative artist, she was a fighting artist, who saw the struggle from inside and could convey its dynamics.[7]

Radek arranged for her to go to Berlin (illegally, without the necessary visitor's documents), to evoke Germany's looming civil war for her Russian readers. She was also, in the event of a power seizure in Saxony, to act as a clandestine liaison officer between local German Communists and Comintern representatives.

In early October, Radek travelled via Warsaw and Czechoslovakia to Dresden, and Reisner set off for Berlin. She arrived there on 21 October, just as General Müller was moving his troops into Dresden to depose Saxony's socialist government. Meanwhile, Communists in Hamburg had seized the town's police stations in a desperate, last-ditch show of resistance, but had been ejected by combined civil and military forces after the workers failed to support them. When Radek arrived in Berlin the day after Reisner, he had no choice but to approve the KPD's decision to retreat.

Life was very hard in Berlin after the defeats in Saxony and Hamburg, and Larissa longed to leave for Hamburg, to witness the aftermath of the revolution there. But Berlin revived all her old memories of her childhood, and she immediately felt at home. 'My darlings, of course I'm alive and well,' she wrote to her parents shortly after her arrival:

I'm eating into this new country, so familiar to me in those moments when some street reminds me of Fozanek, or when people from a different country sing the 'Internationale'. I'm not writing any more, as my boss has ordered me not to touch my pen for ten days, and to study Germany, and all that's living and dead in it. I feel splendid. Have no fears about me.[8]

She lived as an 'illegal' with a worker's family, to whom she soon grew very close, and she would take their granddaughter out to the Tiergarten, to chat with the unemployed. She also acted as a scout for the Comintern members there, who lived underground in a tight-knit group, with no chance to mix with the masses. According to Radek:

Larissa lived the life of those masses, who were as close to her as those of St Petersburg or the sailors of the Baltic fleet. . . . She whiled away many days at the dole queues and at the shops, among the crowds of unemployed and starving people trying to buy a bit of bread for millions of marks, and she sat around in hospitals packed with dead-beat working women deep in bitter thoughts and cares . . .[9]

The warmth of Radek's admiration for Larissa, unlike his frequently unflattering judgements of his comrades, is evident in everything he wrote about her.[10] And what started as a political association between them turned into a personal involvement.

Radek (born Sobelsohn) had long been known in international Marxist circles for his outrageous radicalism, his scandalous, bohemian life and his brilliant journalism for the international socialist press (which appeared under the pseudonym 'Parabellum'). For the Communist Angelica Balabanova he was 'a strange mixture of amorality and cynicism, and a spontaneous appreciation for ideas, books, music and people'. For Trotsky (of whom Radek was a fervent admirer), he was

indisputably one of the best Marxist journalists in the world. . . . But he exaggerates, and goes too far. He measures in yards where he should be looking at inches – and thus invariably finds himself either to the left or the right . . . of the correct line . . .[11]

Before Larissa Reisner met him, he had been living fairly peacefully in Moscow with his wife Rosa and their four-year-old daughter, born while he was in prison in 1919. Radek didn't believe in physical faithfulness – for men; women, particularly educated women like his wife, were expected to be monogamous, and Rosa Radek seems to have remained in the background, ignored and often discarded for other women. His affairs were numerous, indiscreet, prolonged and often very painful for her, but they never lasted. With Larissa it was different.

They made an extraordinary-looking couple – Radek with his large bespectacled head, protruding ears and thin beard, and

Reisner with her St Petersburg elegance and culture. 'Quasimodo and Esmeralda' is how Radek's biographer unkindly describes them. Rosa Levine-Meyer, Radek's friend from the German Communist Party, suggests equally unkindly that Reisner had taken Radek on the rebound from Raskolnikov – 'her real target being the inaccessible Trotsky'. Since Reisner herself tells us nothing about her personal relationship with Radek (or, for that matter, Trotsky), there is not much to be done with this piece of Comintern gossip. But Reisner was much too independent to have opted for the traditional female route to power and advancement, and had she done so she would not have chosen Radek.[12]

At the Twelfth Party Congress earlier that year, while other Bolshevik leaders had identified the Bolsheviks' successes with Lenin, Radek had paid extravagant tribute to Trotsky's military and organisational genius, raising widespread fears of his involvement in a possible Trotskyist coup. Suspicions of Bonapartism still clung to him after the doomed German revolution, based as it was on vast miscalculations of the army and working class. When Larissa Reisner met him in Berlin, his standing in the Party was not high. But he was extraordinarily clever, with a wide, practical (and frequently opportunistic) knowledge of international socialist affairs. Like her, he had a sharp, sardonic tongue and an immense, restless energy. He also encouraged (and occasionally directed) her reading, and was genuinely and generously appreciative of her writing.

The result of Larissa Reisner's experiences in Berlin was a series of articles, later published as 'Berlin in October, 1923', an appendix to her book *Hamburg at the Barricades*. Here she describes unemployed families living on 60,000 million marks a week, 'when bread cost 80,000 million the day before yesterday . . .' She describes the Reichstag, on whose red carpet 'lies scattered a multitude of assorted hands . . ., a gallery of disgraced, crumpled physiognomies, which have nonetheless managed in good time to sip from the cup of sweet power . . .' She attends the Social Democrats' 'requiem for the 1918 Revolution', which they helped to kill, and she evokes the despair and disillusion of this 'last meeting between rulers of the SPD and the masses, on which they lean for their support, and whose interests they have pledged to defend.' Finally she attends a workers' demonstration in Lustgarten, and describes how the Berlin proletariat 'proved to General Seeckt and his armoured cars the visible existence of the "banned" Communist Party'.[13]

'I'm mending my sails, whistling like an old sailor over his ancient maps,' she wrote to her parents.

I think of you: an extraordinary family, unlike any other, where a huge past – 'father, mother', those ancestral complexes usually lying like a weight on every movement, every leap forward – is inscribed into the coats of arms of the fitful, tragic, merciless muse of struggle. I love you so much . . .[14]

In November, she finally set off alone for Hamburg, 'lying on the shores of the North Sea like a big wet fish, lifted still quivering from the water'. She was enchanted by Hamburg's language, 'soaked in the sea, as salty as a cod, as slithery, rich and light as the scales of some large, rare deep-sea fish . . .'

Soon after her arrival she wrote to Radek:

After the sluggishness of Berlin you find here something solid, strong and vital. At first it was hard to fight off their distrust and prejudices. But as soon as the Hamburg workers learnt to trust me as a comrade, I could learn about every one of their great, simple, tragic experiences.[15]

In Hamburg, said Radek, 'she lived with the abandoned wives of freedom-fighters, she sought out fugitives in their hideouts, attended court hearings and Social Democratic meetings'. She went into the slums, factories and working-class districts where the uprising started – to the industrial barracks of Barmbeck, headquarters of the rising, to Schiffbeck, with its grim chemical factory and manufacturing plant, and to Hamm, where five police stations had been seized. And she wrote up the personal stories of the rising's leaders, disguising their names. People remembered her there, Radek wrote:

She disappeared into the workers' quarters, ate and slept on filthy beds, and took from there a mass of impressions and lice (poverty's the same everywhere). In the factories she visited, the engineers were mad about her. She would question them purposefully and inexhaustibly, and in a few minutes could get from any of them, man or machine, what she needed.[16]

At night she read Laufenburg, the historian of Hamburg and the Hamburg movement, and she took days off to visit the Soviet consulate, where she devoured the works of Mehring, Kautsky 'and all the best there is on Germany'.

'I'm forced to read and think,' she wrote to her parents in November.

I've never worked so hard in my life. . . . My brain creaked at first, but now it's easier. . . . I sometimes despair in the face of these skyscraper events. But if I don't enter the great revolutionary storm, I'll become completely shallow and stagnant. There's so much to learn that I'm glad of this tiny postponement which history has offered . . .[17]

Her next letter to her parents was carried back by Hans Kippenberger, head of the Communist military organisation at Barmbeck and a leader of the uprising, who was taking refuge in Moscow:

Darling mother, not since 1918 have I lived more purely, or read so much, or thought in such complete, silent solitude. The snow falls on my soul, and I stand like a tree in winter. I often pine for you and dear solitary Russia. God, what joy that Soviet Russia exists.

Worlds collapse, and classes settle their centuries-old debts. If you only knew what destruction and decomposition of a whole nation there is here. . . . In my work I start from the main thing – the stinking bourgeoisie, which smothers and leaches off the German proletariat. A genius of this hatred of the bourgeoisie is George Grosz, only his anger is almost irrational. . . . I spit on them, and try not to fill my mouth with carrion . . .[18]

In the midst of the dying revolution in Germany, she received a letter from *Izvestiya*, proposing to send her to China, where strikes, boycotts and demonstrations had brought the country to the brink of civil war. What came of this proposal is not known; perhaps she was too busy in Hamburg to consider it. By 19 November she had sent three sketches back to her parents for publication.

I fear magnificent phrases, but the stone on my heart has rolled away for ever. Do you remember, mother, that seagull in front of the destroyer just before the battle? It's always with me, flying over the abyss. Oh life, blessed and great – and roaring over my head, and over all else, the seething wave of the Revolution. I love you infinitely.[19]

At the end of 1923, Larissa Reisner left for Moscow (possibly with Radek), where she wrote up her experiences of Germany. She spent hours with Kippenberger, the exiled Hamburg Communist, going over her material with him, and corresponding with those still there when doubts arose.[20] In January 1924, the first instalment of *Hamburg at the Barricades* appeared in the journal *Zhizn* [Life], and later that year her Hamburg pieces were published together in Moscow as a book, along with 'Berlin in October', by the International Revolutionaries' Aid Organisation (MOPR). Here, accounts of the rising itself alternate with small sketches of everyday life and portraits of its leaders, to give an unforgettable picture of life in Germany just ten years before the advent of Nazism. (Shortly after the German translation appeared the following year the Reichstribunal ordered it to be burnt.)

After the publication of *Hamburg*, many writers in Russia saw Larissa Reisner with new appreciation. 'We want to live like that, or not at all!' Libedinsky said at a party at the House of the Press, where she was guest of honour. For the poet Vera Inber, *Hamburg* marked a turning-point in her work:

She wrote with incredible digestibility for those untrained in scientific truths, but without mindless popularisation either. She had the ability to bring distance near, with one apt simile or metaphor. And a whole book could be written of her comparisons.[21]

Every writer, according to Inber, has a favourite and often-repeated phrase or image, and with Reisner it is birds, mainly swans, the symbol of death. In her 'Letters from the Front', writes Inber, the 'white swans of rebirth' appear as the 'aesthetic vessels into which she tried to pour new wine'. In *Hamburg*, however, her swans no longer carry that 'aesthetic burden', since here for the first time she describes ugliness, and it no longer

frightens her. 'Here she finally abandons aestheticism and beauty
for itself, and describes the submarine depths she can no longer
deny.'

The poet Nikolai Smirnov wrote:

Like an industrious bee, she took the thick honey of her work from many
flowers, which others would avoid. But mainly, Larissa grew before our
eyes, overcoming illness, and the inevitable weaknesses of the starting
phase of our art . . .

Hamburg he described as the work not of an observer, but of a
fighter in the ranks of the world revolution.

She is always drawn to broad epic themes, and the sparkling well of her
talent has grown strong on the edge of revolution. But she is a genius too
of the miniature, and writes with a sharpened stiletto – no detail is too
small, nothing is too commonplace. She sees all the heroism, sacrifice
and pathos in the everyday details of the building of socialism.[22]

When *Young Guard*'s editor, Mark Kolosov, read her Hamburg pieces it seemed to him

as though Larissa was continuing a conversation with us, not about
poetry, but about something much bigger – the prose and poetry of
world revolution, the struggle for universal happiness, which was the
main business of her life, and the main concern of this exceptional yet
simple woman.[23]

For Lev Sosnovsky, *Hamburg* was the fourth and final 'test',
after which there could be no more doubts about her as a writer:

Now it was impossible to ignore Larissa Reisner, because there was
simply no better journalist amongst us. Had each of our Party organisa-
tions who had undergone that great revolutionary organisational and
practical Party experience possessed her pen, her sense of colour and her
sharp eye, we could have achieved ten or a hundred times more. If to this
were added her education and her European experience – which did not
pass without trace – if all that had been added to our Bolshevik temper,
we could have worked miracles . . .[24]

That winter, when Larissa Reisner's popularity as a writer was
at its height, Raskolnikov arrived back from Afghanistan and

they hastily buried their marriage. Shortly afterwards, on the morning of 21 January, Lenin suffered his last stroke. Petrograd was renamed Leningrad, and the country went into mourning. Thousands of obituary articles appeared, and Reisner poured all her grief into her article 'Tomorrow We Must Live, Today We Mourn', published six days after his death in *Izvestiya*.[25]

Larissa's break with Raskolnikov must have been a difficult one, for their paths evidently crossed frequently in literary circles. He was now working, under the pseudonym 'Petrov', as director of the Comintern's Eastern Section. Bored by his job, however, he devoted less time to politics than to his real love, literature, and he wrote several articles, stories and plays (including the play *Robespierre*, performed in 1934). He was also appointed chief editor of the *Moscow Worker* publishing house, president of Moscow's Chief Repertory Committee, and an editor of *Young Guard* and *Red Virgin Soil*.

Meanwhile Radek, blamed for his part in the German débâcle, which he had all along opposed, had returned to Moscow in disgrace. In January 1924, he was condemned by the Comintern Executive for his 'past mistakes', and four months later, at the Thirteenth Party Congress he was openly derided for his part in the failed German revolution. At the Comintern's Fifth Congress, in June 1924, he was expelled from its Executive Committee, and for the next few months he restricted his activities to journalism on non-controversial subjects.

'He was fortunate to have his trusted and beloved Larissa to support him,' wrote his biographer. 'And her love helped him face the humiliation of his fall from prominence.' According to Levine-Meyer:

Radek had vowed never to break up his marriage. But the brakes he used deliberately to put on in his relationships with other women did not work this time. Larissa Reisner proved too strong. She was young, very attractive, highly talented and ambitious. . . . Radek made one concession: he didn't 'leave' his wife, nor their common home. But it didn't help . . .[26]

Andrew Rothstein, however, who visited Radek's flat in Moscow later that year, assumes that the two were living together there, since Radek apologised to him that Larissa could not be there to pour the tea, as she was out at a meeting. At any rate, their relationship was well known, and it continued until Larissa's death.

Radek had an important influence on her work, and encouraged her to write and widen her reading with books on Russian and international economics. But she evidently continued to lead an independent life. She attended the Fifth Comintern Congress, which presided over Radek's expulsion, and wrote an article for *Pravda* about the international women's congress accompanying it.[27] She also kept in touch with her old friends, and made new ones, including the flamboyant, anarchic Boris Pilnyak and his wife, the actress Olga Sergeevna.

Her closest friend was Lydia Seifullina. Seifullina was born in 1889 into a poor family in Chelyabinsk, in the Urals, where she first earned her living as an actress and teacher. After the Revolution, she taught in a number of orphanages and delinquents' colonies in the Urals, and her first short stories were about the waifs and strays she met there, and the birth of a new children's culture. In 1923, Alexander Voronsky invited her to Moscow to join the staff of *Red Virgin Soil* and when Larissa met her, her hospitable flat on Basmannaya Street, which she shared with her husband Valerian Pravdukhin, was crowded day and night with Moscow writers. Mikhail Prishvin, in hunting boots and belted peasant shirt, would read from his latest manuscript. Victor Shklovsky, who was then writing literary criticism for Maya-kovsky's journal *Lef*, would declaim his famous aphorisms. Isaac Babel would talk of his hero Benny from Moldavanka. And Seifullina, small, bright-eyed and chain-smoking, would read from the manuscript of *Virineya*, her raw account of a woman's life in the Siberian countryside during the Revolution.

Larissa often dropped in there after Party meetings, and Seifullina, recognising her from her ring on the bell, would rush to open the door to her – 'a tall woman in a worn brown leather coat, her wonderful face slightly flushed, and her eyes shining with happiness.' Nikolai Smirnov also met her at the Basmannaya

Street flat: 'She would burst in announcing that she was tired and hungry,' he wrote, 'but she would never sit quietly or touch her food.' Instead, he recalled, she would talk ecstatically about literature, or the meeting she had just come from, leaping from the armchair to the sofa, and from the sofa to the bookshelf, throwing herself at the golden setter, Taiga, in the corner, and rushing to the writing desk to pore over Seifullina's latest story.[28]

Reisner was an ardent admirer of Seifullina's work, and the two women developed a passionate friendship which on Seifullina's side, at any rate, seems to have verged on worship. 'Sometimes the power of her literary conception glorified the significance of a picture, book or play,' wrote Seifullina. 'And at a dress rehearsal of a play that moved her, one would see this woman, so brave and so rare to cry, her face wet with tears.' Later, however, when a more dispassionate assessment of the play was needed, Larissa could be straightforward and sometimes sharp in her judgements. Many of Seifullina's friends had reservations about Larissa Reisner's writing, urging her to write more as she spoke:

Her language was often criticised for being overloaded with beautiful images, like semi-precious stones. But her style was luxurious from its huge wealth. Her insatiable literary appetite for life made her compose fuller and fuller, and describe it with more festive words. She was never afraid to search, and she would tirelessly expand her reading. And after patiently absorbing some specialist work, she would smile her astonishing smile, in which a secret light seemed to burn, and say: 'That should produce something tasty!' This meant some literary work . . . enriched with all the fullness of her emotions . . .[29]

In the summer of 1924, *Red Virgin Soil* published her 'Letters from the Front' in a separate volume, as *The Front*. Here, the bright, scattered episodes of the 'Letters' unite into a complete picture of the three-year campaign from Kazan to Enzeli, from the pools of the Volga to the Caspian Sea, from the ravines and forests of the cold Kama to the hot saltmarshes of the south.

Some of *The Front*'s heroes and heroines are mentioned by name, others are anonymous; to some she devotes several pages, to others just a few lines. But all are taken from life: Misha

Kalinin, her brave sailor friend, with his tousled hair, who died after leaving her at Kazan; the peasant Ivan Ivanovich from the village of Solodniki, near Astrakhan, with his 'diffident, magnificent smile'; the noble Markin, commander of *Vanya the Communist*; the passionate, romantic Azin, commander of the 28th Red Cavalry Regiment; young Schmidt, who found his 'mad youthful vocation' fighting for Soviet power; Kozhanov, a commander of the Volga flotilla, and of many landing-parties; and the aristocratic Admiral Behrens, who broke with his past and dedicated his life to the Revolution. She brings to life all these characters and many more, and in them she immortalises all the cruelty and magnificence of the revolutionary war.

The Front inspired many novelists of the Civil War, such as Serafimovich, Fadeev and Gladkov. Closest to it in spirit, though, and often compared to it, is *Ten Days That Shook The World*, written in the very heat of 1917 by the American Communist and journalist John Reed. Here too the Revolution is described in one breath, without any attempt at journalistic 'balance'. Like Reisner, Reed writes only what he sees, and writes himself out of the account. But where Reed is restrained and orderly, Reisner hammers out of the heat of the battle a style that is chaotic, imagistic and lush.

The Front is sometimes bombastic and often florid. Its images, piled on top of one another, are thick on the page, and sometimes squandered, 'like two riders in one saddle', wrote Inber.[30] For in this clash of styles and images she is describing her own battle with the Petersburg aesthete in her own soul. Her Introduction is partly a polemic against the *Apollon* poets, who know 'only that crude soulless beauty that the highly educated sip from a spoon'. It is partly too a manifesto for a new, more punchy, direct literary style:

To fight for three years, to march with guns for thousands of miles, to chew bread made with straw, to die, rot and shake with terror on a filthy bed in some flea-ridden hospital – and to conquer! Yes, at last to conquer the enemy who is three times stronger than we are, armed with our clapped-out rifles, our collapsing planes and our fourth-rate petrol, while all the time wretched, angry letters arrive from our loved ones at home. . . . For all this, I think we need a few verbal outbursts, don't you?[31]

The Front received enthusiastic reviews in *Pravda*, *Press and Revolution*, *The Bookseller* and other Soviet papers and journals. 'No one has described the Civil War with such inspiration, or so subtly revealed the varied essence of these years,' wrote an anonymous reviewer in the journal *Red Fleet*:

But the most important thing in this book is the psychological analysis of the ideas for which for three long years people marched through fire from the Baltic Sea to the Persian border. . . . The author has, with exceptional talent, described how people made the Revolution, and how the Revolution made them . . . Anyone who wants to know and understand this exceptional epoch must read this small but captivating book.[32]

Now Larissa was already dreaming of her next journey.

Chapter Eight

COAL, IRON AND LIVING PEOPLE

In the late summer of 1924 Larissa Reisner left Moscow as a special *Izvestiya* correspondent (or *spetskor*), and travelled a thousand miles east to the forested depths of the northern Urals. For three hundred years its rich resources of coal, iron, salt and precious stones had made this one of Russia's most industrially exploited areas, and it was there, in the 1770s, that the first serf revolt had been hatched and crushed. Under the Bolsheviks' first Five-Year Plan, from 1928 to 1932, entire cities and gigantic industrial complexes would arise there. But already new engineering, chemical and metallurgical factories were appearing, and Larissa wanted to meet the people who worked in them. According to Radek:

She had to find out what was happening in the depths of the masses, who in the final count dictate the course of history. And being a person with an immediate grasp of reality, she couldn't gain such insights by reading and debates.[1]

She stayed in the desolate coal and steelworking towns of Bilimbay, Shaitanka and Lysva, with their primitive foundries and workshops, and she went down into the mines. She visited the platinum mine at Kytlym, which means 'cauldron', and which 'resembles a huge mountain bowl, standing in the eternal snows of the mountains'. She visited Kizel, and the 'magnificent grey building' (which would soon seem so small) of the region's first electro-station.

She spends entire weeks in railway carriages, wagons and on horseback. She lives once again in workers' families, she goes down pits. She takes part in meetings of factory boards, shop committees and trade unions. And she talks – hourly, daily – with the peasants. She is feeling a way through the gloom, lending an ear close to life.[2]

Amongst the people she met and stayed with in the Urals she made a number of close friends, including Vera Inber, who was then working in the little town of Taishet as a journalist. She met families torn apart by war, women struggling on their own to support their children, and hundreds of orphaned and abandoned waifs who roamed the streets, hungry, homeless and desperate, stealing, trading and prostituting themselves for bread.

It was in Ekaterinburg (now Sverdlovsk) that she met a small, thin, twelve-year-old boy called Alyosha Makarov. Alyosha's father, a factory-worker and partisan, had been killed by the Whites, and his mother, unable to support her seven children on her own, had left him in a wretched orphanage, from which he had escaped. Stowing away with his dog on a train to Ekaterinburg, he was eventually reunited with his mother, who was working as a cleaner in the local Soviet building. But she was still unable to support him on the wages she earned. A 'comrade from Moscow' would soon be arriving, they learnt; she was their only hope. Alyosha later described to Lydia Seifullina his first meeting with Larissa, 'sunburnt and in a white dress'. 'Someone somewhere started playing the violin, she took my arm, and we stood there listening.' Then they went off to the town together, where she bought him ice-creams and took him to the cinema, to the officers of the *Peasant Paper*, and to the hippodrome, where they danced and ate. Finally, at the end of the evening, she asked him whether he would like to go back to Moscow to live with her, and he eagerly agreed.

They returned there together that winter, and Larissa re-arranged her life around Alyosha and moved an extra bed into her little room in the Fifth Soviet building. First she took him to hospital for his rickets and ringworm. Then she found a school for him, and bought him books, helped him with his work, taught him to skate and encouraged his love for music.[3]

She now had to support Alyosha too on the money she earned as a journalist, and despite her new responsibilities for him, and their cramped and uncomfortable life together, she wrote a series of articles for *Izvestiya*, *Red Virgin Soil* and *Prozhektor* [Search-light], about her experiences in the Urals. In these she describes the painful birth of industrial Soviet Russia, amidst suffering, failure and primitive machinery. She writes of the hunger, toil and superhuman sacrifices of the men and women who fought on the 'labour front'. And she conscientiously records their com-plaints – for their labours 'have earned them the right to make the widest criticisms, or rather self-criticisms. And the sharper these are, the closer they are to production and its needs, the more clearly will emerge the face of the new, post-revolutionary Russia.'[4]

Her travels in the Urals inspired Larissa with the idea of writing something bigger, and with Radek's encouragement, she embarked on a historical trilogy on the life of the workers there: on a serf factory at the time of the Pugachev serf revolt, on the exploitation of workers under tsarism, and on the building of socialism. In her visits to Moscow between trips she would devour books on the history and economy of the region. 'I won't pretend she liked figures,' Radek wrote.

When she'd worked through two or three tedious textbooks she would implore me to give her something 'tasty' about petroleum or cereal crops, and would relax over Delaisi's book on oil trusts or Norris's epic work on wheat.[5]

She sent drafts of her latest articles to the workers she had stayed with for their approval, and her archive in the Lenin Library contains a number of letters to her from them. One, from a Communist called Ivan Kochin, thanked her for helping his family, and wrote that since her visit there had been 'a swift retreat from religion'; his wife had let him throw the icons out of the house, 'and is beginning to regard faith in God as something unnecessary . . .' To another worker, Filipp Lokotsky, to whom she sent an article, she described the dry historical accounts she was reading of the Urals and its trusts and enterprises as more exciting than any novel. . . . For they are a stenographic record of their owners' desperate struggle for the peasant's purchasing power, his every working hour, his right to life, and the dizzying perspectives of his future . . .[6]

While in Moscow she visited the offices of *Izvestiya* with the manuscripts of her latest articles, and an *Izvestiya* journalist named Georgii Ryklin described how crowds would gather to meet 'our talented, beautiful Larissa Reisner, beloved by the whole staff'. Nikolai Smirnov, who was also working for *Izvestiya* then, recalled her walking in confidently, throwing off her scarf and leather coat, quickly tidying her hair, and firmly shaking hands with everyone there, including the chief editor, Stepanovich-Skvortsov, and his assistant, Boris Volin. Then she would dictate her article to the typist, changing it as she went along, and sometimes taking it away again for final revisions, for 'she was very demanding of the written word, especially her own'.[7]

Once, she told Ryklin, she had read in *Izvestiya* some friendly advice to its worker-correspondents to write 'not in pencil, but with a pen'. Her advice to him was to write 'not in pencil, not with a pen, but with the heart', and to be more bold in his criticisms of official bigotry, hypocrisy and muddle. She suggested to him any number of articles he could write on this theme, including one based on a letter she had received from a vaccination nurse she had met in Ishima, in the Urals. Each month nurse Lydia Shaburina received 26 roubles, 20 kopecks, Reisner told him, for which she was expected to:

1. Vaccinate adults and children.
2. Do night duty.
3. Politely receive visitors.
4. Not get pregnant.

Giving Ryklin the letter and some other relevant material, she sent him off to write the article, and next day he came back with a rough draft, which ended:

'You can be fruitful and multiply in education and in agriculture, but not here, for it makes people late for work. Today the nurse is pregnant, tomorrow it's the doctor, the day after it's me – and who'll work?'

But Lydia Shaburina broke the wishes of the director. She vaccinated well, she did night duty punctually, she received guests politely – but she got pregnant. So they sacked her, for giving birth against the director's wishes . . .

Larissa approved his article. 'But now you must write it with more anger,' she said, 'so it'll never happen again!'[8]

Smirnov remembered how with the first snow of winter she would walk into the office, her skates jingling, and hurry off after work to the rink. For him, Larissa's 'voice and movements suggested an irrepressible strength and liveliness'. In fact, she was slowly but surely burning herself out in a deadly cycle of recurring malaria attacks, and that winter she decided to get treatment at a special malaria clinic in Wiesbaden, near Hamburg. The evening before she left, Vera Inber, now back in Moscow, held a party for her, and she always remembered her sitting at the table with a cheerful group of friends, as she described the illness which drained her of so much strength. 'It torments not just my body,' she said. 'After an attack I'm left with a feeling of total emptiness, as though some vile animal had come and eaten all the greenery I was cultivating in my soul.'[9]

Leaving Alyosha with her parents, she set off the next day for Wiesbaden. Her fellow-patients at the clinic she later described as a crowd of 'British, French and German plunderers, adventurers and conquistadors'. She was the only woman amongst them, and the only Communist, and although they tried to be polite, they thought her very strange, and she did not enjoy her stay there (although she did enjoy outraging them by making friends with an Indian, whom they ostracised: 'You have to know your own kind!' she told Libedinsky'.[10]

She would slip away from the stuffy clinic whenever she could to visit Hamburg, where she met old friends and even took part in a Communist demonstration. And as soon as she felt well enough, she discharged herself and set off to the Ruhr, 'the arsenal of the world' and a 'concentration camp of poverty'. From these travels she produced a series of articles, published the following spring in *Izvestiya* and *Red Paper*. In these studies of workers' lives in the wake of the crushed revolution, she describes 'ragged children playing in sewage puddles around the sentry-boxes', miners toiling in derelict pits, and unemployed families surviving on 'too little to live on, too much to die on'. She records too the most intimate dilemmas of personal change and political struggle. In 'He a Communist, She a Catholic', the wife works while her unemployed husband looks after the home:

He violates her with hatred and makes her cry out loud . . . and finally sends her down for cigarettes. Never, even in the days of good money, has he loved his wife with such jealous love, or has she fancied his caresses more than now, when they have in effect to be bought.

All these miniatures of the 'army of the unemployed', however, are set within the larger framework of the giants of German industry and the industrial barons of Germany's 'national sanctuaries'. She describes her visits to the huge Ullstein newspaper plant, and to the coal mines of Westphalia; to the Junkers technical laboratories, the birthplace of Germany's aviation industry, and to the Krupp offices in Essen,

whose streets, plants and pits are all marked with the name of Krupp, just like the teaspoons and pillow-slips of some propertied family. . . .
Krupp has become a world name. Short and cast in one piece like his steel, it boomed out first in Europe and then in Asia. It was uttered wherever storm-clouds gathered. 'Krupp' meant 'war'. A new war whose horrors were still unknown to mankind, a new mode of death and a new strategy, unlike any before . . .

Caught off-balance in 1919 by the Allies' Treaty of Versailles, which had left Germany militarily crippled, Krupp was no longer making guns but false teeth and cash-registers, she wrote, and his mighty empire was toppling into poverty:

The dormitories hugging the factories hear iron crying out day and night like an infant in pain . . ., and the worker unconsciously adjusts his heart and watch . . . forward or back to be right by the works' hooter.[11]

Charged by her experiences in Germany, she returned to Moscow, where she joined Trotsky's Commission for the Improvement of Industrial Products. She also gave a series of lectures on the 1905 Revolution to the Party cell at Moscow's armoured-car school, for which she read a number of works, including the articles of Lenin, on the history of the revolutionary movement. But never one to stay put for long, she soon left Moscow again for *Izvestiya*, travelling first to the nearby textile region of Ivanovo-Voznesensk, cradle of the Revolution, then to the southern coal-mining areas of the Don basin. During this and her other trips away, Alyosha stayed with her parents.

Early in 1925, her articles on her travels around industrial Russia were published as a book, *Coal, Iron and Living People*. According to Radek,

This book marks a new artistic and ideological phase in her work. She finds her style as a writer. Her doubts disappear. She sees the working masses engaged in construction. They are building socialism, whether drenched in sweat at a blast furnace, descending half-naked down the pits or cursing their low wages, while the best of them are stoutly convinced that these torments and forced labour are all in the name of socialism . . .[12]

Vera Inber, however, thought *Coal, Iron and Living People* Larissa Reisner's least successful work. Although praising her diligence and her eye for detail and summary, it seemed to her 'as though the harsh, monotonous, sunless underground ugliness of the mines robs her of her strength, and she is weighed down by the heavy miner's cape on her shoulders'.[13]

★

At about this time, Byelorussia was shaken by a scandal in the Streshninsky district, where criminals had infiltrated official positions, carried out illegal requisitions and discredited the authority of the Party for miles around. A ragged young village correspondent called Grigorii Lapitsky, a demobilised Red Army soldier, had set out to expose them in the local newspaper, and had had his house burned down. The story reached Moscow, and in February 1925 Larissa Reisner left as *Izvestiya spetskor* for

Minsk, the Byelorussian capital, to defend Lapitsky and to cover the trial of his persecutors.

She stayed in the Europa Hotel, overlooking the former Cathedral Square and the old market, and from there she would leave early in the morning for the court. In the afternoon she would receive a stream of villagers at her hotel, listening to their complaints and encouraging them to stand as witnesses for the prosecution. And in the evening she would write up her copy for *Izvestiya* and the Minsk paper *Star*, and send it off.

A fifteen-year-old Komsomol member named Mikhail Zlatogorov, who wrote for the youth section of the local paper, described the impression these articles made on Minsk's young journalists:

We were enraptured by her sharp correspondence from the courtroom. . . . She wasn't just a journalist, she called herself the 'defender of the poor' . . ., and her writings seethed with anger – not just at the parasites in the militia, but at those idiots, many of them unfortunately carrying Party cards, whom she described as suffering from 'bureaucratic arteriosclerosis, which turns the blood of the Revolution into cheap ink . . .'[14]

She met Zlatogorov and his friends at a meeting of their Komsomol literary circle. Semyon Pilitovich, a gloomy lad from the tannery, growled out his clumsy but powerful verses, followed by a young frontier guard called Nikolai Korobkov, still wearing his soldier's shirt. Then Zlatogorov himself, the youngest, read his verses, 'mainly about my Komsomol cell and Pioneer scarf'.

Larissa listened with keen interest, and asked each of them to talk about themselves and their work. Then turning to Zlatogorov, she said: 'Well, what else do you write about? Girls? Love?' Zlatogorov was struck dumb with embarrassment: 'I did secretly write such poems, but this was my shameful secret.' Quickly changing the subject, she asked him to come to her hotel the next day and take her to Nemiga, Minsk's old ghetto, now populated by impoverished Jewish craftsmen and small traders. There a poor tailor's son called Chaim Kaplan had recently hanged himself because he had no boots to wear to school, and Larissa wanted to talk to his mother and write about it.

When Zlatogorov went to her room the next day it was so packed with villagers and local journalists that he could hardly open the door. On the table was a samovar, and sitting around it drinking tea were a crowd of shawled village women, witnesses for Lapitsky, with whom Larissa was in lively conversation. She waved to Zlatogorov to wait, and when the women finally left, he walked with her across Cathedral Square and down to the valley of the river Ptich.

As they entered the narrow streets of the Lower Market, she walked unhurriedly, he recalled, listening intently to the shouts of the women fish-traders, pausing at the doors of the synagogues to peer in, and diving into the tiny wretched shops to buy shoe laces, hairpins and cotton reels. 'Over the years I've read many books and listened to many talks about the way a writer works,' wrote Zlatogorov.

But no academic analysis could give a tiny part of the unforgettable lesson of Larissa Mikhailovna's determined, concerned investigation of living life in all its Rembrandt-like shades of light and dark.

Finally they reached the Kaplans' dark cramped room, with its long tailor's table. Larissa sat down with Chaim's mother on a decrepit sofa, and wept with her. And after a while, the woman started talking, in Yiddish and broken Russian, of Chaim's struggle to better himself, of his love of gymnastics and his school work, and of the poverty that had deprived him of textbooks and shoes. Then Larissa asked to see the boy's exercise books, and his mother brought out some scraps of newspaper, roughly sewn together and covered with columns of Russian declensions and physics diagrams.

Larissa walked back quietly, with none of her former liveliness, and Zlatogorov, in a banal effort to be positive, condemned suicide as a solution to life's tragic contradictions – 'it isn't Komsomol-like'. She reacted sharply to this ritual optimism, which denied so much complexity,

and she said one mustn't see only the bright happy things in life, and that she was ashamed that we, Chaim's comrades, had been unable to understand his spiritual crisis – that he had longed with all his heart for something new, and didn't want to grow up sick and consumptive, like generations of tailors working for the rich. He no longer believed in the Talmud, and wanted to be a sportsman and to study at a workers' high school, she said. And everything old – she swept her hand over Nemiga, now sinking into twilight – with its roots in the middle ages, was dragging him back. 'That's what drove him to the noose. How can we judge him for that?' she said.

The Lapitsky trial ended, the accused were sentenced, and just before Larissa left for Moscow, Zlatogorov went to her hotel to say goodbye. In her room, crowded as ever with Minsk Party workers, peasants and journalists, someone was telling a funny story to bursts of laughter. Thinking that she would have no time for him, he mumbled something and made to leave. But she stopped him, took a photograph out of an envelope, looked at him thoughtfully, then wrote on the back: '21.2.1925. Dear poet, comrade Mishka, Write, darling, and rejoice in life, and love the Party as you do – and listen to the old women on the streets of the ghetto. Larissa Reisner.' A month later she wrote in *Izvestiya*:

Revolution has removed from the ghetto its forbidden boundaries. But before the Jews can rise from their smouldering ruins and leave this stinking place, they suffer hunger, their necks are broken by cheap trade, and those who cannot take the gigantic step forward are mown down . . .[15]

Many people who had not read Larissa Reisner's previous works came to know her now, through her writings as an *Izvestiya spetskor*, often assuming 'Cde. Reisner' to be a man. A stream of people, mainly workers from the factories of Moscow and Ivanovo-Voznesensk, came to visit her in the paper's offices; shortly after the Minsk trial, a young man resembling a shepherd, in bast shoes, shabby coat and broad felt hat, arrived and asked to see her. It turned out to be Lapitsky himself. Her articles always provoked a lively mailbag, and her long article about the trial, 'The Forest-dweller', brought a specially large volume of critical letters, which were waved around the *Izvestiya* offices by the editor. Some complained of her description of the wheels of a car as 'the bobbin on which space is wound'. That was a matter of taste, said Skvortsov-Stepanov; more serious, he said, were the numerous complaints, including many from settled gypsies, about her description of 'the thieving gypsy eyes' of Lapitsky's chief persecutor. She was mortified at her lapse of taste and judgement.[16]

In the spring of 1925, the *Ogonyok* publishing house brought out some of her Afghanistan sketches under the title *Asiatic Stories*; later that year they were published in their entirety by the State Publishing House, in a print run of five thousand. *Afghanistan* opens with a series of short chapters, lightly sketching in the exotic images of the east, from Tashkent and Bukhara to the mountains of the Hindu Kush. From the lushness of these first mosaic-like chapters unfolds a broader panorama of the country, and a sustained and angry exposé of poverty and serfdom, slave labour and veiled women. Larissa Reisner was one of the first Soviet writers to apply to the East the measure of the Russian Revolution, and all her observations of Afghanistan are set against this new, more hopeful, period of history. She describes the century-long independence struggle of the wandering mountain tribes, and the comparative independence of their women. She writes of the workers in Kabul's new factories, and of the birth of a new critical literature. And she writes of the British in Afghanistan. The gangster politics of colonialism are described with grotesque satire in a brilliant concluding essay, 'Fascists in Asia':

The body of India is thickly planted with white leeches. With a desperate heave she manages from time to time to tear from her bloody sides a heavy, bloated cluster of suckers. . . . But along come punishing detachments, armoured cars and artillery. . . .

These grabbers and speculators, with heavy faces like flat-irons, on which mouths and eyes lie like traces of something squashed . . ., these strapping, morning-suited thugs, casting their contemptuous monocles at this stern country so unripe for speculation, seem no different from a million others like them. But in fact their adventurism is marked by a convinced and aggressive fascism. . . . For their brazen motto isn't simply 'your money will be ours', but 'we'll tear the coats off your backs in broad daylight, we'll thrash you with our white, well-groomed hands, which contain the strength and agility of two well-fed beasts – and no legal, parliamentary or religious rubbish will stop us'.[17]

Afghanistan had a mixed reception. Many felt the book's exotic style to be incompatible with a Bolshevik world view and inaccessible to a mass readership. 'Like an ageing woman looking in the glass and seeing more wrinkles on her face, Larissa looks into her soul and sees new cavities,' wrote one malicious critic. Others defended the book. Alexander Voronsky, who had first published the pieces in *Red Virgin Soil*, wrote:

Each sketch resembles a tree, loaded with an abundance of fruits, and as in a vast and varied flower garden, the eye is sometimes dazzled by its wealth of similes and images, its sharp and unexpected descriptions, its oriental brightness, colour and saturation. Sometimes it seems like mere preciosity, for she has mastered the culture of the literary word, and knows all its secrets. But it isn't preciosity, it's the generosity of one who lightly scatters handfuls of what she possesses in such abundance . . .[18]

Her friend Nikolai Smirnov, who had warmly praised *The Front*, also defended *Afghanistan*'s style, as 'fully and naturally determined by the brilliance of the life reflected in it. . . . It belongs amongst those literary works smelling more of gunpowder than of the roses of the orient.' And her old university friend Igor Ilinsky, now a literary critic, praised the work for revealing, 'the tireless, ineradicable hatred between the two worlds that lies beneath diplomatic politeness, etiquette and ceremony . . .'[19]

In the summer of 1925, she was involved in diplomacy of rather a different kind, with China. As the revolution there spread, the Comintern had finally thrown its support behind Sun Yat Sen and the Kuomintang. The Chinese Communist Party agreed to join them, on condition that a school was set up in Moscow to train Chinese students as future Kuomintang cadres, and 1924 saw the opening of Moscow's Sun Yat Sen University, run in consultation with Sun Yat Sen's successor, Chiang Kai-Chek. Radek, finally forgiven his mistakes in Germany, was appointed provost, and in the summer of 1925, he appointed Larissa Reisner to lecture there in Russian Literature. Together they were involved in the training of some six hundred Chinese students, including many future leaders of the Chinese Communist Party, and the job carried great prestige. Teaching there entitled Larissa to accommodation in a large room in a communal house on the Volkhonka, but it is not known whether she took this up.

Despite their new work together, Larissa's roving life as a journalist and her responsibilities for Alyosha, not to mention Radek's wavering commitment to his wife and daughter, evidently brought new strains and complications to their relationship. According to Rosa Levine-Meyer, Karl and Rosa Radek were still living together. When she visited them in their flat, she found him

the same matey informal man I knew before, and one of the few on whom power left no trace. But all was not right in his household. I found him very subdued and lacking his former brilliance. And the proud, beautiful woman I'd known only three years before now seemed, with her tight-pressed, unsmiling lips and empty eyes, to be drained of life.[20]

Whatever the state of Larissa's relationship with Radek, it does not seem to have interfered with old friendships. Lydia Seifullina had recently left Moscow for Leningrad with Pravdukhin to supervise the dramatised version of her *Virineya*, and Larissa missed her deeply. But she again met Olga Nesterovich, her friend from the Sochi Women's Department. Shortly after her first meeting with Reisner, Nesterovich had left Sochi for Leningrad University where she had done a history degree. Now she was an editor at Leningrad's Obllit publishing house. 'Now the "ship of happiness" Larissa had given me was filled not just with political and scientific works, but with literature, too.'[21]

One evening after work, Nesterovich set off with Reisner and her friends in an open car for Zagorsk, to visit Voronsky at the *dacha* he had rented there with Isaak Babel. They sat around the samovar with their hospitable hosts until late into the night, discussing Babel's *First Cavalry* and 'Salt', which Reisner praised for their heroic form, and described as new classics in Russian literature. Then the discussion turned to Proust, whom Nesterovich had bravely disinterred for publication. But Reisner's imagination was particularly caught by a small book Nesterovich had recently published called *The Tales of Pushkin, From the Mouth of his Friend P.I Bartyonev*. They read some of these stories aloud, including one about Pushkin's last visit to Moscow, in which he foresaw his death. Larissa was deeply moved by this, according to Nesterovich. ' "What phenomenal premonition," she said. "It has nothing to do with superstition. It has to do with the form of experience that moulded people then." And she shuddered with sadness, and with premonitions of the inevitable.'[22]

They returned to Moscow early the next morning to start the day's work, and as they drove along the quiet, forested, country roads, bathed in sun and dew, the men started humming popular songs, 'Overgrown Paths' and 'Along the Don walks a Young Cossack'. Larissa sat quiet and thoughtful, not joining in the singing. Then someone put music to Esenin's poem 'Song':

> The best song the nightingale has
> Is a funeral song over my head . . .

'And Larissa said that they had found the right music for it, from the melody of the verse itself.'[23]

Inspired perhaps by the Pushkin stories, she started reading about Russia's first revolutionaries, the Decembrists, with whom Pushkin had been associated. And that autumn she started work on a jubilee monograph to mark the centenary of the 1825 Decembrist uprising. She accumulated a mass of material, buried herself in archives, and travelled to Leningrad to see a well-known historian, who was said to have volumes of material on the uprising.

This visit to Leningrad may have been partly an excuse to see Lydia Seifullina. Moscow was not the same for Larissa without her and her hospitable flat. Seifullina, too, felt lost in Leningrad, and wrote to her:

Where are you, you extraordinary, magnificent woman? I long to see you. From a Marxist viewpoint, you're a great pig, but as I'm a fellow-traveller with a complex ideology, you're on the whole an angel, and I love you as ever . . . Please write to me about yourself. . . . Yours in spirit only, for my body is here . . .[24]

Late one evening, Seifullina recalled, the bell rang, and there at the door stood Larissa. She told them about her Leningrad professor, who had refused to lend her any material, and would apparently need three dinners to change his mind. They talked about the work of Leonid Andreev, and Larissa suggested that they co-edit an almanac of memoirs on him, entitled 'My First Love'. Then she spoke of her recent visit to Germany, 'and in just two or three words she would describe a German working woman – and one would see her with her eyes.'[25]

When Seifullina reminded her that people in Moscow had always urged her to write as she spoke, she said, 'That's how I write now.' And her next articles, on the Decembrists, were written much more sparingly than usual. In January 1926, *Izvestiya* published '14 December 1925' and 'Prince Sergei Petrovich Trubetskoi', literary portraits of people 'whose blood flashed on the icy immensity of tsarist despotism'.[26] According to Igor Ilinsky:

She tirelessly perfected her style, discarding, adding and improving. And in these, her last writings, there is a new severity and straightness of line, promising drawings wonderful in their clarity and simplicity . . .

Born eighty years earlier, Ilinsky wrote, she would have been caught up in the fanatical idealism of the revolutionary terrorists of the People's Will. Had she been of Pushkin's generation, she would have been a Decembrist:

For this is more than just the restoration of an epoch by the skilful hand of a brilliant artist. She has a special spiritual affinity for the period. . . . But although entranced by the past, she lives in the present, in an epoch beside which the plot of 14 December, and the iron passion of the People's Will, pale into insignificance.[27]

Early in 1926, her *Izvestiya* sketches on the Ruhr were published separately as a book, entitled *In Hindenberg's Country*.[28] Many, including Vera Inber, considered these essays her best writing:

People, things and ideas are described by a pen which has now achieved brilliance and maturity. Her last essays on Essen are extraordinary –

here the characteristic beauty and refinement of her language are turned into the wealth of a mature pen, unafraid to write well today, knowing that it will be better tomorrow.

Inber especially singles out Reisner's essay on Junkers, the architects of German aviation:

She describes 'the enrapturing moment of single combat at a height of 5,200 metres, where air lies dissolved in space like a diamond in water.' It doesn't matter whether or not a diamond really does dissolve in water: it's usually a pearl in vinegar. But she takes it thus – transparency and hardness. And this is what characterises her – a stone dissolved in the fire of the Revolution for which she writes.[29]

In the summer of 1925, *Pravda* had issued a statement of the Party's policy on literature, which criticised some proletarian writers for their arrogance and urged them to be more discreet in their treatment of 'fellow-travellers'. A few months later, the journal *Novy Mir* published an article harshly attacking the writings of Seifullina, Babel, Pilnyak and others as excessively negative. And in January 1926, Larissa Reisner entered the battle against philistinism with her article 'Against Literary Banditry'. Here she defends the duty of all writers to describe the contradictions of the life around them 'without adornment and varnish', and she praises Seifullina's truthful and naturalistic portraits of Siberian life:

We understand what value these books, born of the Revolution, have for the future, for they are incorruptible eye-witnesses of its sufferings, heroism and dirt, its poverty and magnificence. . . .

And now the daubers are creeping up on them, dipping their critical broom into the bucket of cheap idealism, and trying to colour, shade and sweeten . . .

And she defends those writers, like Seifullina, who learnt to see the Revolution as it really was:

The intelligent eyes of the romantics and idealists often find it painful to look at the blazing furnace in whose flames . . . whole strata of the old familiar culture have turned to dust. Yet they have looked without flinching, and have drawn with great honesty the shocking, formless and incomparably beautiful face of the Revolution . . .[30]

That winter of 1925–26, Larissa was full of plans. She wanted to visit Paris, and then to fly to Teheran on a special flying expedition. She was still working on her Urals trilogy, and was also planning a portrait gallery of the precursors of socialism – Thomas More, Munzer, Babeuf, Blanqui and the unsung heroes – starting with the first steps of the handicrafts workers, and finishing with the revolutionary struggles of her own lifetime. 'At times she took fright at the tasks she had set herself,' wrote Radek. 'She was very modest and doubted the power of her talents. . . . Yet that power was growing within her every day.'[31] To many of her friends then, she seemed charged with new energy. Nikolai Smirnov met her one frosty afternoon in December, striding down Tverskoi Boulevard, wrapped in a coat of soft Siberian silver fur, her 'Snow-maiden' skates jingling in her hands.

Seeing me, she smiled, looked around and said: 'What a wonderful day!' Everything seemed magical to her: the silver hoarfrost on Moscow's old lime-trees, the screech of sledges on the sugary snow, the mirror-like surface of the skating rink at Patriarch ponds, and the low, mother-of-pearl sun, which gilded the statue of the thinking Pushkin. When we parted, she shook my hand as firmly as ever, and hurried on. Then she turned back, and said: 'How extraordinary to be alive in this world . . .!'[32]

Yet with each new malaria attack, the power was draining from her, and with it her enthusiasm for life, travel and experience. This she had sought with Radek, but now their relationship was evidently collapsing. 'Thirty years after her death,' wrote Nikulin later, 'one can say that Larissa, so beautiful, talented and intelligent, was not happy in her personal life.'

He recalled walking down Nikitin Boulevard with her one day that winter, and she talked of her forthcoming trip to Paris.

Then, she began with her old simple candour to talk about herself, and about the man she was close to: 'Ah that *burger Gemütlichkeit*!* Isn't it strange that a revolutionary and fighting journalist can suddenly be such a narrow, petty-bourgeois philistine in his private life. . . . But that's all over now.'[33]

Others also found her strangely quiet and reserved. Her old friend Rozhdestvensky met her that winter at the opening of Herzen House on Tverskoi Boulevard. All Moscow's literary world was there, as well as a large delegation from Leningrad, and the evening ended with a noisy banquet which continued until late into the night. When Larissa Reisner appeared, she was greeted by happy exclamations and oustretched hands.

She was friendly and unaffected as ever. But she seemed distant from this noisy and rather drunk literary gathering. Even her glass was held unwillingly, and rarely touched her lips . . .

Leaving her place, she moved quietly from group to group. When she reached Rozhdestvensky, she asked him to recite his latest poems to her.

And I looked at her, and thought: what beautiful intelligent eyes she has, and how much youth, as though the stormy experiences of her life haven't touched the pure lines of her brow, the fine, slightly ironic curve of her mouth, and her bright chestnut hair. . . . But then sometimes her attentive gaze would be clouded by a shadow of anxiety, or simply tiredness . . .

Later, as the guests were leaving, she stretched out her hand to him, 'and it's as though I can still feel in my hand the warmth of her strong, thin fingers . . .'[34]

*

This was Rozhdestvensky's last meeting with her. Shortly afterwards, she was assailed by headaches and heaviness. Then suddenly the headaches became intense, and she became drowsy and delirious. Her family rushed her to the Kremlin Hospital, where doctors diagnosed typhus, caught probably from drinking a cup

---

* Bourgeois cosiness

of unpasteurised milk. Her eyes became heavy, and she sank
further into feverish delirium, broken at first by bouts of restless
energy in which she grabbed her pen and started on a story:

She was dying slowly, long after the illness had lost its danger and
acuteness, dying simply from a weak heart. Sometimes she was too weak
even to lift her arm. She felt flies crawling on her eyelids. She was
tormented by thirst, heat and an inexplicable sadness for a life she had
suddenly forgotten . . .[35]

The story was never finished. Robbed of her last strength, wrote
Inber, 'she slowly drifted from life, like on an ice block which
cannot detach itself from the beloved mainland.'

She spent her last days, barely conscious, amongst her family
and friends at the Kremlin Hospital. 'Shortly before her death,'
wrote Inber, 'as the dark waves of fever carried her away forever
from the fragile island of life, she dropped her pen. Then she
regained consciousness, and said: "Now I understand what
danger I am in."'[36] Radek wrote:

Amidst her last flickerings of consciousness, she exulted in the sun whose
rays were sending her a last farewell. She spoke of how good it would be
for her in the Crimea where she was going to convalesce, and how lovely
it would be when her weary head filled up again with new ideas. She
vowed that she would fight for life to the end, and she only abandoned
that fight when she finally lost consciousness.[37]

She died three months before her thirty-first birthday, on 9
February 1926, and for two days her body lay in state at the House
of the Press, guarded by soldiers and wept over by her family and
friends. Lydia Seifullina rushed back from Leningrad, and saw
her 'dead and unrecognisable in her red coffin'. Vera Inber,
seeing her 'severe wax face, under its white bonnet, like Dante's
headgear', remembered her 'dimpled cheeks and braided hair,
whose gold defied photographs'.[38]

On 11 February, her coffin was carried through the streets of
Moscow by Radek, Volin, Pilnyak, Lashevich, Commissar for
War, Enukidze, of the Party Central Committee, and Ivan
Smirnov, with whom she had fought at Svyazhsk. She was buried

in state on the Square of the Communards at the Vaganka Cemetery, and her death was mourned in more than fifty obituary articles.

According to one, 'she should have died on the steppe, the sea, the mountains, with a pistol clenched in her hands'. But according to Inber,

We cannot choose our death, as we can choose where to live or whom to love. Neither a Volga bullet, nor a flea-ridden greatcoat at Svyazhsk, nor Ensign Ivanov at Kazan could harm her, and instead she died on a hospital bed of typhus.[39]

Eight days after her death, her family and friends organised a memorial evening at the House of the Press. Lydia Seifullina wept inconsolably: 'Beauty is dead!' Others talked seriously and at length of how wrong it had been ever to doubt her. Her path had not been an easy one, said Inber:

Her extraordinary beauty and joy, on the gloomy background of every-day work, often aroused censure and doubt, and many who had passed through the hard school of prison and the underground doubted if it was right for so many rare qualities to be combined in one person. But with every year that passed, and each new book, these people diminished. 'She always seemed slightly strange to us,' they said, 'But we under-valued her. And now we know we were wrong . . .'

I remembered that phrase about the 'greenery in her soul' word for word and forever, but I never thought I'd have to repeat it at such a bitter time. . . . It makes me think of fresh, strong leaves, washed by the rain, shining from the sun's energy . . .[40]

'She did all for the proletarian revolution that a person from another class could,' wrote Rozhdestvensky.

Remembering everything about her, I am filled with sadness that we did not meet more. . . . For I saw her only in the lulls in her life, never at its most important periods, which she wrote about in her books. So my memories of her are rather one-sided, and touch only that part of her rich and generous soul which found a place for memories of our university years. . . .

She had a bright, complex nature, enriched by the culture of the past and by the experience of revolutionary struggle. When I think of Larissa Reisner as a person, a fighter and a literary artist, I see harmoniously fused in her image all the features of that active, heroic, inspired epoch which she herself would have called 'The Youth of the Revolution'.[41]

'I still feel the icy grip on my heart that I felt when I heard she had died,' wrote Andrew Rothstein. 'And to the end of my days I shall consider myself lucky to have met her.'[42]

'Don't grieve for us,' her mother wrote to Lydia Seifullina in November, '9 February is over, and now we must endure the consequences. Each of these I meet calmly. And if you hear that I have given up the ghost, be a good friend and rejoice for me.'

Ekaterina Alexandrovna Reisner died early one morning the following January, and two years later, Professor Reisner died of heart disease. Igor Reisner moved into their flat with his wife, Violet Lansbury (daughter of the British socialist George Lansbury), and Alyosha passed into their care. But Seifullina could not rejoice. On the anniversary of Larissa's death, she wrote:

I can overcome the horror of knowing that the words 'Larissa Reisner' are just an idea, not a living person. I can overcome this only by remembering the way she valued every moment of life, and treasured all its gifts and possibilities.[43]

Five years after her funeral, Nikulin returned to her grave at the Vaganka Cemetery,

and I saw a girl with plaits wound like a ring around her high clear forehead, and I heard her laugh, ringing like steel. . . . She will enter the history of the new world as a beautiful model of a new human type, a person standing on the edge of the old and the new worlds. All her weaknesses and mistakes were from that old world. But they are reduced to ashes by her courage and loyalty to the struggle for the new.[44]

*

Aristocratic and urbane, Larissa Reisner rejected the privileges of her class and her past, and lived until her death on the front line of the Revolution. Shutting the door on the powerlessness and containment of family life, and all the female compromises and adjustments which had crippled women of her mother's generation, she demanded a new partnership, sexual frankness and dynamic simplicity from the men she loved and worked with. Patriarchy was dead and buried. Now it was up to her and a new generation of women to put something better in its place.

The supreme sacrifices demanded of the revolutionary movement – and the special urge to self-sacrifice instilled in the women who had joined it since its birth in the 1860s – make her reticent about the more intimate experiences of the 'new women' of the Revolution. She struggled throughout her life as a revolutionary against the traditional patriarchal values that underpinned the old order and lingered on into the new. Yet for feminists now, her self-determination as a woman may often seem in conflict with her own personal needs, her sense of identity and her sexuality. She was never primarily an organiser of women, although she was an inspiration to women then and later who were. Because she always operated mainly in the world of men, she isolated herself from the strong constituency of women making their own demands of the Revolution. And her frequent travels meant that she never stayed put for long enough in one place to get immersed in any one struggle. On her return from the front, she was deeply involved in journalistic and writers' circles, amongst which she had many friends, yet she rejected marriage and lived most of the time alone, in a series of small and shabby rooms. And in the last six years of her life, she gradually lost her power and control over life in a relentless struggle with illness.

It was through writing that she cut through the tensions of her condition and transformed them, for it was writing that tied her to life, and she dropped her pen only in dying. Her writings are so tied to her times that much of their original polemical sharpness is now lost, but there remains the unusual tone of her fine phrases – romantic, haughty, satirical, often florid. In her first literary attempts before the Revolution she began to find her way into the world of work and economic independence, and it was writing that later gave her the right to travel freely, assert herself and intervene in politics. During her lifetime, she was respected, celebrated, even revered, as a writer, and shortly after her death,

Hamburg at the Barricades was turned into a film,[45] and the Historical Department of the Red Fleet organised an exhibition in honour of her memory at Leningrad's Naval Military Museum.

Many of Larissa's writer friends, like Nikulin, Rozhdestvensky, Inber and Seifullina, went on to become some of the Soviet Union's most popular writers; Igor Reisner established himself as a distinguished orientalist, whose work is quoted and respected in the Soviet Union to this day. Others of her friends, however, fell victim to the Stalinist excesses of the 1930s. Ivan Smirnov, her pall-bearer, was sentenced to death in the first Moscow Trial of 1936. Radek was sentenced the following year to ten years' imprisonment, and died in prison. Raskolnikov died in Nice in 1939 in suspicious circumstances. And as Soviet Russia geared itself up for its immense industrialisation programme, women's autonomy was repressed, the Zhenotdel was closed and Larissa's writings fell into disfavour.

But the optimistic reconstruction of Soviet life now under way has started to discover fresh sources of strength from its revolutionary origins. New insights are being brought to bear on the history of the Revolution, its heroes and heroines are being resurrected and rehabilitated, and history-books are being re-written. Raskolnikov's memory has now been properly honoured, and his rehabilitation has been followed by a renewed interest in Larissa Reisner.

For socialist feminists now, Larissa Reisner is a pioneer and a model of female strength. Her writings evoke an entire epoch, the 'spirit of October'. Her headlong life and early death is the story of the 'new woman' born of October: 'a completely new kind of woman,' wrote Alexandra Kollontai, 'proud and conscious of her rights – a citizen of Soviet Russia.'[46]

NOTES

Three books are cited frequently, and are therefore referred to here in abbreviated form:

Larissa Reisner, *Sobranie sochinenii* [Collected Works], Moscow/Leningrad, 1928: *Sob. soch.*

Larissa Reisner, *Izbrannoe* [Selected Works], ed. A. Naumova, Moscow, 1965: *Izb.*

Larisa Reisner v vospominaniyakh sovremennikov [Larissa Reisner Remembered by Her Contemporaries], ed. Yu. Tomashevsky, Moscow, 1969: *Vosp.*

Introduction

1 L. Nikulin, *Gody nashei zhizni* [Years of Our Life], Moscow, 1966, p. 190.
2 *Hamburg at the Barricades, and Other Writings on Weimar Germany*, trans. and ed. R. Chappell, Pluto, London, 1977; *Russkie sovetskie pisateli prozaiki* [Russian Soviet Prose-writers], ed. O.D. Golubeva et al., Vol. 7, Leningrad, 1972.
3 K. Radek's short biography of Larissa Reisner, in 'Deyateli SSSR i Oktyabrskoi Revolyutsii' [Activists of the USSR and the October Revolution], in *Entsiklopedicheskii slovar Russkogo Bibliograpfiches-kogo Instituta Granat* [Encyclopaedia of the Granat Russian Bibliographical Institute], 7th edn., Moscow, 1927–9.
4 Boris Pasternak, 'V pamyati Reisner' [In Memory of Reisner], in *Stikhotvoreniya i poemy* [Verses and Poems], Moscow, 1965; trans. R. Chappell, in *Hamburg*.
5 *Sob. soch.*; Larissa Reisner, *Izbrannoe*, Moscow, 1958; *Izb.*; *Vosp.*
6 L. Sosnovskii, 'V pamyati Larisy Reisner' [In Memory of Larissa

Reisner], in *Lyudi nashego vremeni* [People of Our Time], Moscow, 1927; trans. R. Chappell in *Hamburg*.

7   K. Radek, Introduction, *Sob. soch.*, p. 4.

Chapter One: Childhood

1   A short biography of M.A. Reisner is contained in *Vestnik kommun-isticheskoi akademii* [Herald of the Communist Academy], Moscow, 1928.

2   V. Andreev, 'V seme Reisnerov' [With the Reisners], in *Vosp.*, p. 44.

3   Ibid., p. 46.

4   M. Reisner's account of the trial is in *Sudebnyi protses Karla Libknekhta protiv russkogo tsarya* [Karl Liebknecht's Trial Against the Russian Tsar], Ryazan, 1925.

5   A letter from Lenin to Mikhail Reisner, dated 4 October 1905, is in V.I. Lenin, *Complete Works*, 4th edn., Vol. 36, Moscow, 1957, p. 121; M. Reisner, *Russkii absolyutism i evropeiskaya reaktsiya* [Russian Absolutism and European Reaction], St Petersburg, 1906.

6   Reisner popularised the ideas of Petrazhitsky in his book *Teoriya L.N. Petrazhistkogo marksisma i sotsialnoi ideologii*, [L.N. Petra-zhitsky's Theories on Marxism and Social Ideology], Moscow, 1908.

7   K. Radek, Introduction, *Sob. soch.*, p. 6.

8   Ibid.

9   'Requiem' (later titled 'Rudin'), quoted by S. Zhitomirskaya, in 'Muzyka revolyutsii: po stranitsam rukopisei Larisy Reisner' [The Music of the Revolution: from the Pages of Larissa Reisner's Manuscripts], *Literaturnaya gazeta* [Literary Gazette], 21 May 1975.

10   Reisner made a critical appraisal of the work of Andreev in his book *L. Andreev i ego sotsialnaya ideologiya* [L. Andreev and his Social Ideology], Moscow, 1909.

11   M. Reisner, *Gosudarstvo. Posobie k lektsiyam po obshchemu ucheniyu o zakone* [The State. A Textbook of Lectures on General Law Studies], St Petersburg, 1912.

12   V. Andreev, 'With the Reisners', *Vosp.*, pp. 47–8.

Chapter Two: Poetry and Revolution

1   Letter dated 1913, *Izb.*, p. 511.

2   V. Rozhdestvenskii, '*Yunost nashikh dnei*, [The Youth of Our Days], *Vosp.*, pp. 15–17.

3   I. Ilinskii, 'Granyonyi talant' [A Cut-glass Talent'], *Vosp.*, pp. 119–20 (first published in *Pechat i revolyutsiya* [Press and Revolution], 1926, no. 3).

4   V. Inber, 'Evolyutsiya lebedya' [The Evolution of a Swan], Vol. 4, *Complete Works*, Moscow, 1966, pp. 274–5 (article first published as 'Larisa Reisner', *Krasnaya Nov.*, 1927, no. 2).

5   V. Andreev, 'With the Reisners', *Vosp.*, p. 50.

6   V. Rozhdestvenskii, 'The Youth . . .' *Vosp.*, p. 19.

7   I. Vasileva, *V. Rozhdestvenskii, ocherk zhizni i tvorchestva* [V. Rozhdestvenskii, a Brief Account of his Life and Work], Leningrad, 1983.

8   Poems quoted in V. Rozhdestvenskii, 'The Youth . . .', *Vosp.*, pp. 22–4.

9   L. Nikulin, *Years of Our Life*, p. 168.

10   This and the following quotations: V. Andreev, 'With the Reisners', *Vosp.*, pp. 44–5.

11   'Zhenskie tipy Shekspira: Ofelia i Kleopatra' [Shakespeare's Female Characters Ophelia and Cleopatra], *Nauka i zhizn* [Science and Life], nos. 25 and 34, Riga, 1913.

12   V. Rozhdestvenskii, 'The Youth . . .', *Vosp.*, pp. 24–5.

13   V. Inber, 'Evolution . . .', pp. 269, 272.

14   E. Solovei, 'Rudin', *Neva*, 1957, No. 3.

15   Ibid.

16   Quoted in I. Vasileva, *V. Rozhdestvenskii . . .*, p. 190.

17   'Pesnya krasnykh krovavykh sharikov' [Song of the Red Blood Corpuscles], *Rudin*, No. 5, 1916; quoted by Rozhdestvensky, *Vosp.*, p. 23.

18   *Rudin*, 1915, no. 2; no. 3; no. 1; quoted in I. Vasileva, *V. Rozhdestvenskii . . .*, p. 192.

19   'Cherez Al. Blok k Severyaninu i Mayakovskomu' [From Blok to Severyanin and Mayakovsky], *Rudin*, 1916, no. 7; quoted *Izb.*, pp. 495–9.

20   L. Nikulin, *Years . . .*, pp. 165–9.

21   *Izb.*, p. 512.

22   V. Shklovsky, 'Bessmyslneishaya smert' [A senseless death], in

Gamburgskie schety [The Debts of Hamburg], Leningrad, 1928, pp. 60–1. Gumilyov's letter, of June 1917, is quoted in L. Nikulin, *Years . . .*, p. 191.

23 Reisner's bibliography contains over a dozen articles on popular culture for *New Life*, including this one, 'Narodnyi dom i ego preobrazhenie' [The People's House and its Transformation], *New Life*, 19 September 1917.

24 N. Sukhanov, *The Russian Revolution, 1917*, trans. J. Carmichael, Oxford University Press, London, 1955, p. 275; Asian Communist quoted in *Makers of the Russian Revolution*, ed. G. Haupt and J.J. Marie, George Allen & Unwin, London, 1974, pp. 206–7.

25 V. Inber, 'Evolution . . .', p. 280.

26 'V. Zimnem dvortse' [In the Winter Palace], *New Life*, 11 November 1917; *Izb.*, pp. 425–8.

27 'From the Editor', *New Life*, 16 November 1917; incident described by A. Naumova, *Izb.*, p. 567.

28 V. Inber, 'Evolution . . .', p. 273.

29 'Requiem' (later 'Rudin'), quoted by S. Zhitomirskaya, 'Music of the Revolution . . .'

Chapter Three: Civil War

1 Robert Rhodes James, *Churchill, A Study in Failure, 1900–39*, p. 105; *Dokumenty vneshnei politiki SSSR* [Documents of USSR Foreign Policy], Vol. 1, Moscow, 1959, pp. 546–8.

2 All three women quoted in *Pravda stavshaya legendoi* [Truth Become Legend], ed. M.D. Konyushenko, Moscow, 1969, pp. 90, 116.

3 *Makers of the Russian Revolution*, p. 408.

4 L. Nikulin, *Years . . .*, p. 171.

5 V. Shklovskii, 'A Most Absurd Death', p. 61.

6 L. Nikulin, *Years . . .*, pp. 169–70.

7 V. Shklovskii, 'A Most Absurd Death', p. 61.

8 These and the following quotations (up to p. 64) from 'Kazan', in *Front* [The Front], *Sob. soch.*

9 Reisner gives a completely different account of her escape in a letter to her parents (in *Izb.*, p. 513).

10 Victor Serge, *Year One of the Revolution*, trans. and ed. Peter Sedgwick, Allen Lane/Penguin, London, 1972, p. 292.

11 L. Trotsky, *My Life*, p. 412.

12 Victor Serge, *Year One . . .*, p. 492.

13 This and the following quotations from 'Svyazhsk', in *The Front*, *Sob. soch.*, p. 32.

14 'An Optimistic Tragedy' was broadcast on BBC Radio Three on 18 November 1986 (translated by Faynia Williams and Richard Crane, and produced by Ned Chaillet). Its heroine's experiences are closely based on Reisner's experiences on the Volga, but unfortunately she was not acknowledged as the play's inspiration. Vishnevsky's recollections are from a recorded speech he gave to actors rehearsing the play at Moscow's Kamerny Theatre. This was printed as an Introduction, published that year; it is contained in *Vosp.*, pp. 103–4; 'Ostalalas v pamyati na vsyu zhizn' [Remembered All My Life].

15 L. Sosnovskii, 'In Memory of Reisner'.

16 Undated letter, *Izb.*, p. 514.

17 Quoted by S. Zhitomirskaya, 'Music of the Revolution . . .'.

18 'Pod Tyurlyama' [Outside Tyurlyama], *Krasnaya Zvezda* [Red Star], 14 February 1926.

19 This and the following two quotations from 'Svyazhsk', in *The Front*, *Sob. soch.*, pp. 34–5, 39.

20 This and the following quotations from N. Kartashov, 'Bravo kavaleristu!' [Bravo Cavalryman!], *Vosp.*, pp. 83–7.

21 Undated letter, *Izb.*, pp. 512–3.

Chapter Four: From the Volga to the Caspian

1 Recalled by the naval commander I. Berlin, 'Delo sluzheniya narodu' [The Business of Serving the People], *Vosp.*, p. 80.

2 Ibid., p. 78.

3 V. Shklovskii, 'A Most Absurd Death', pp. 61–2.

4 V. Inber, 'Evolution . . .', p. 276.

5 Introduction to *The Front*, *Sob. soch.*, p. 20.

6 V. Inber, 'Evolution . . .', p. 276.

7 V. Shamov, 'Nasha Lyubov' [Our Love], *Vosp.*, pp. 88–93.

8 Ibid., pp. 93–8.

9 V. Vishnevskii, 'Remembered . . .', *Vosp.*, p. 104.

10 'Na gibel voennogo korablya *Vanya-kommunist*' [On The Sinking of the Warship *Vanya the Communist*], *Voenmor* [Sailor], 19 November 1919.

11   *The Front, Sob. soch.*, pp. 55–6.
12   The telegram is contained in the Archives of the October Revolution; see notes to *The Front*, in *Izb.*, p. 560.
13   A.P. Konstantinov, *F.F. Ilin-Raskolnikov*, Leningrad, 1964, pp. 76–7.
14   K. Radek, *Granat*.
15   See B. Pearce's Introduction to his English translation of Raskolnikov's book, *Kronstad i Petrograd v godu 1917* [Kronstadt and Petrograd in 1917], New Park, London, 1982, for details of Raskolnikov's time in London.
16   Recalled by L. Berlin, 'The Business of Serving the People', *Vosp.*, p. 82.
17   F. Novitskii, 'Na minonostse' [On The Torpedo Boat], *Vosp.*, pp. 101–2; article first appeared in *Izvestiya*, 11 February 1926.
18   Undated letter of 1919, *Izb.*, pp. 514–5.
19   'Astrakhan', *The Front, Sob. soch.*, pp. 73–92.
20   'Doroga iz Oranienbauma v Kronstad' [The Road From Oranienbaum to Kronstadt], *Krasnyi Baltiiskii Flot D* [Red Baltic Fleet], 1919, no. 5, *Izb.*, pp. 428–30.
21   'Astrakhan–Baku', *The Front, Izb.*, pp. 112–17.
22   Raskolnikov, interview in *Petrograd Pravda*, 15 July 1920; quoted in Harish Kapur, *Soviet Russia and Asia, 1917–27*, Michael Joseph, London, 1966, p. 167.
23   'Baku–Enzeli', *The Front, Sob. soch.*, pp. 118–28.
24   Kapur, *Soviet Russia and Asia*, p. 167.

Chapter Five: The New Culture

1   L. Nikulin, *Years . . .*, pp. 172–3.
2   Ibid., p. 178.
3   Ibid., p. 176.
4   L. Sosnovskii, 'Memories of Reisner'.
5   L. Nikulin, *Years . . .*, p. 181.
6   Ibid., pp. 176–7; she may also have attended the First International Conference of Communist Women, held in conjunction with the Second Congress, which set up a secretariat for work amongst women.
7   Blok's speech is reprinted in his *Collected Works*, Vol. 6, Moscow, 1962, p. 437.

8   L. Nikulin, *Years* . . ., p. 174; Reisner's article, 'Subbotnik' [Voluntary Labour Day], appeared in *Krasnaya gazeta* [Red Paper], 5 August 1920.

9   L. Nikulin, *Years* . . ., p. 179.

10 Ibid., p. 181.

11 V. Rozhdestvenskii, 'The Youth . . .', *Vosp.*, pp. 29–36.

12 L. Nikulin, *Years* . . ., p. 179.

13 'Putevye zametki' [Traveller's Notes], *Izvestiya*, 12 November 1920.

14 '25 oktyabrya v Rige' [25 October in Riga], *Izvestiya*, 14 November 1920.

15 'Kak otvalivaetsya pushistyi khvost' [How the Bushy Tail Falls Off], *Izvestiya*, 14 November 1920; manuscript from Andrew Rothstein.

16 A. Rothstein, 'Schastliv, chto znal ee . . .' [Happy to Have Known Her . . .], *Vosp.*, pp. 145–52, and private conversation with the author.

17 'Heroic Sailors of the Russian Revolution', trans. A. Rothstein, *Communist Review*, no. 1, May 1920.

18 M. Kirillov, 'Shchedroe serdse' [A Generous Heart], *Vosp.*, p. 133.

19 This and the following quotations from O. Nesterovich, 'Korablik schastya' [The Ship of Happiness], *Vosp.*, pp. 152–62.

20 'V Peterburge' [In Petersburg], *The Front*, *Sob. soch.*, pp. 129–31.

Chapter Six: Afghanistan

1   Igor Reisner's book *Afghanistan*, published in Moscow in 1929, was one of the first scholarly accounts of the country's economy, culture and historic importance to Russia.

2   Quoted by Harish Kapur, *Soviet Russia and Asia*, p. 233.

3   L. Nikulin, *Years* . . ., pp. 183–4; Nikulin's account of the Soviet mission's experiences in Afghanistan, *14 mesyatsev v Afganistane* [14 Months in Afghanistan], Moscow, 1923.

4   L. Nikulin, *Years* . . ., p. 184.

5   Ibid., pp. 179, 188.

6   This and the following quotations from *Afghanistan* (the book version of her articles), State Publishing House, Moscow–Leningrad, 1925, pp. 4–5.

7   L. Nikulin, footnote to an excerpt from *Years* . . ., in *Vosp.*, p. 70.

8   Letter of 5 April 1921, in 'Pisma Larisy Reisner' [Larissa Reisner's Letters], *Novy Mir* [New World], no. 10, 1963, p. 205. (The dates on these first letters from Kabul do not tally with the dates of the Soviet mission's arrival there as given by Nikulin and others.)

9   Letter of 28 May 1921, *Izb.*, p. 517.

10 Ibid.

11 Letter of 7 May 1922, *Izb.*, pp. 522–3.

12 'The Past', *Afghanistan*, pp. 5–6.

13 *Afghanistan*, pp. 50–54, 60–68.

14 Letter of 1 May 1922, *Izb.*, pp. 521–2.

15 *Afghanistan*, pp. 25–8.

16 Letter of 10 April 1922, *Izb.*, p. 525.

17 This was the subject of his book *The Bourgeois State and the RSFSR*, Moscow, 1923; Reisner's writings on social psychology had a great influence on the Soviet psychologist A. R. Luria.

18 *Bog i birzha. 6 revolyutsionnykh pes* [God and the Stock Exchange. Six Revolutionary Plays], Moscow, 1921.

19 Letter of 10 April 1922, *Izb.*, pp. 524–5.

20 Undated letter, *Izb.*, pp. 519–20.

21 Letter of 24 November 1921, *Izb.*, pp. 518–9.

22 Letter of 7 May 1922, *Izb.*, pp. 522–3.

23 She originally thought of calling it 'In the East'.

24 Letter of 1–2 July 1922, *Izb.*, pp. 528–9.

25 Letter of 12 July 1922, *Izb.*, p. 535.

26 Letter from Pagman dated middle of August 1922, *Izb.*, pp. 539–61.

27 Undated letter to Alexandra Kollontai, *Izb.*, pp. 533–4; 'On the Afghani Woman, the Grape Harvest and the Dance of the Tribes', *Afghanistan*, pp. 22–9.

28 Letter of 6 June 1922, *Izb.*, p. 527.

29 L. Nikulin, *Years . . .*, p. 189.

30 M. Kirillov, 'A Generous Heart', *Vosp.*, pp. 134–6.

31 L. Nikulin, *Years . . .*, p. 186.

32 Letters of 23 August and 19 September 1922, *Izb.*, pp. 538–9, 543–4. Wali Khan had headed the first friendship mission to Moscow in October 1919.

33 Letter dated end of 1922, *Izb.*, pp. 545–6.

34 M. Kirillov, 'A Generous Heart', *Vosp.*, p. 136.

35 *Dokumenty vneshnei politiki SSSR* [Documents of USSR Foreign Policy], Vol. V, pp. 110–11.

36 Letter of 29 January 1923, *Izb.*, p. 551.

Chapter Seven: After the Revolution – Russia and Germany

1 I. Ilinskii, 'A Cut-glass Talent, *Vosp.*, p. 119.
2 L. Sosnovskii, 'In Memory of Larissa Reisner'.
3 Yu. Libedinskii, *Sovremenniki* [Contemporaries], Moscow, 1958, pp. 42–4.
4 M. Kolosov, 'Larisa Reisner i *Molodaya Gvardiya*' [Larissa Reisner and *Young Guard*], *Vosp.*, pp. 169–75.
5 A. Bezymensky, 'Vot chto okazalos v portfele' [Look what turned up in the Briefcase'], *Vosp.*, pp. 176–9.
6 K. Radek, Introduction, *Sob. soch.*, pp. 11–12.
7 Ibid., p. 12.
8 Undated letter from Berlin, 1923, *Izb.*, p. 551.
9 K. Radek, Introduction, *Sob. soch.*, p. 14.
10 See, for example, Radek's political sketches, *Portrety i pamflety* [Portraits and Pamphlets], Moscow, 1934.
11 A. Balabanova, *My Life*, London, 1938, p. 246; L. Trotsky, *Contre le Courant* [Against the Current], 10 June 1929.
12 Warren Lerner, *Karl Radek. The Last Internationalist*, Stanford University Press, California, 1970, p. 124; Rosa Levine-Meyer, *Inside German Communism*, ed. D. Zane Mairowitz, Pluto Press, London, 1977, p. 104.
13 'Berlin in October, 1923', *Izb.*, pp. 235–48.
14 Letter of 20 October 1923, *Izb.*, pp. 551–2.
15 K. Radek, Introduction, *Sob. soch.*, p. 14.
16 Ibid.
17 Undated letter to her parents of November 1923, *Izb.*, p. 553.
18 Another undated letter, *Izb.*, p. 553.
19 Letter of 19 November 1923, *Izb.*, p. 552.
20 In *Hamburg at the Barricades*, Kippenberger's identity is disguised as 'Kb'. That May, he wrote his own account of the rising, contained in A. Neuberg, *Der bewaffnete Austand*, 1928; trans. as *Armed Insurrection* by Quintin Hoare, New Left Books, London, 1977. 'A. Neuberg' was the pseudonym for Kippenberger and three other Comintern officers: Mikhail Tukhachevsky, O. Pyanitsky and Ho Chi Minh.
21 V. Inber, 'Evolution . . .', pp. 276–88.
22 N. Smirnov, 'Neotrazimyi obraz' [An Irresistible Image], *Vosp.*, pp. 141–2; first published as 'Pamyati Larisy Reisner' [Memories of Larissa Reisner], in *Novy Mir* [New World], 1926, no. 23.

23   M. Kolosov, 'Larissa Reisner and *Young Guard*', *Vosp.*, p. 175.

24   L. Sosnovskii, 'In Memory of Larissa Reisner'.

25   'Zavtra nado zhit – segodnya gore' [Tomorrow We Must Live, Today We Mourn], *Izvestiya*, 27 January 1924.

26   R. Levine-Meyer, *Inside German Communism*, p. 104.

27   'Na mezhdunarodnoi konferentsii kommunistok' [At the International Conference of Communist Women], *Pravda*, 15 July 1924.

28   L. Seifullina, 'Larissa Reisner', *Collected Works*, Vol. 4, Moscow, 1969, p. 159; first published in *Leningrad Pravda* on 9 February 1927. Also N. Smirnov, *Lidia Seifullina v vospominaniyakh sovremennikov* [Lydia Seifullina Remembered by her Contemporaries], Moscow, 1961, p. 158.

29   L. Seifullina, 'Larisa Reisner', p. 159.

30   V. Inber, 'Evolution . . .', p. 289.

31   Introduction to *The Front*, *Sob. soch.*, p. 21.

32   'N', *Krasny Flot* [Red Fleet], 1924, no. 7, p. 95.

Chapter Eight: Coal, Iron and Living People

1   K. Radek, Introduction, *Sob. soch.*, p. 15.

2   Ibid.

3   L. Seifullina, 'Alyosha', in *Prostye rasskazy* [Simple Stories], Moscow, 1928.

4   *Ugol, zhelezo i zhivye lyudi* [Coal, Iron and Living People], Moscow/ Leningrad, 1925.

5   K. Radek, Introduction, *Sob. soch.*, pp. 16–17.

6   In Naumova's notes to *Coal, Iron . . .*, *Izb.*, p. 563.

7   N. Smirnov, 'An Irresistible Image', *Vosp.*, pp. 139–40.

8   G. Ryklin, 'Ne karandashom i ne perom . . .' [Not in Pencil, and Not With a Pen . . .], *Vosp.*, pp. 165–7; first published in Ryklin's book *Esli pamyat ne izmenyaet* [If My Memory Doesn't Deceive Me], Moscow, 1968.

9   V. Inber, 'Discipline . . .', *Vosp.*, p. 196.

10   Yu. Libedinsky, 'A Firm Passion', *Vosp.*, p. 118.

11   'On Kommunist, ona Katolik' [He a Communist, She a Catholic]; and 'Krupp i Essen' [Krupp and Essen], *Izb.*, pp. 260, 257; the translations of Reisner's German pieces are mostly those of R. Chappell in *Hamburg at the Barricades*.

12   K. Radek, Introduction, *Sob. soch.*, p. 15.

13 V. Inber, 'Discipline . . .', *Vosp.*, p. 190.

14 This and the following quotations from Mikhail Zlatogorov, 'Pamyatnaya vstrecha' [A Memorable Meeting], *Vosp.*, pp. 124–32.

15 'Nasledie getto' [The Heritage of the Ghetto], *Izvestiya*, 24 March 1925.

16 'Lesnoi chelovek' [The Forest-dweller], *Izvestiya*, 15 February 1925; G. Ryklin, 'Not in Pencil . . .' *Vosp.*, p. 166.

17 'Fashisty v Azii' [Fascists in Asia], *Afghanistan*, pp. 98–102.

18 A. Voronskii, *Literaturnye Zapisi* [Literary Record], Moscow, 1926, pp. 159–60.

19 N. Smirnov, 'Pamyati Larisy Reisner' [Memories of Larissa Reisner], *Novy Mir*, 1926, no. 3; I. Ilinsky, article in *Pechat i revolyutsiya* [Press and Revolution], 1926, no. 3, p. 70.

20 R. Levine-Meyer, *Inside German Communism*, p. 104.

21 O. Nesterovich, 'The Ship of Happiness', p. 159.

22 Ibid., p. 160.

23 Ibid., p. 161.

24 F. Levin's notes to L. Seifullina, 'Larissa Reisner' *Collected Works*, Vol. 4, p. 396.

25 L. Seifullina, 'Larissa Reisner', p. 161.

26 From 'Dekabristy' [The Decembrists]: 'Den 14 dekabrya, 1825 goda' 14 December 1825 and 'Knyaz Sergei Petrovich Trubetskoi' [Prince Sergei Petrovich Trubetskoi], *Izvestiya*, 1 and 5 January 1925; 'Baron Shteingel' and 'O Kakhovskoi' [About Kakhovskoi], *Red Virgin Soil*, 1926, no. 11.

27 I. Ilinskii, 'A Cut-glass Talent', *Vosp.*, pp. 121–2.

28 *V strane Gindenburga* [In Hindenburg's Country], *Izvestiya*, 1925, nos. 185, 187, 201.

29 V. Inber, 'Evolution . . .', p. 280.

30 G. Yakubovskii, 'Sochineniya L. Seifullinoi i ee kritiki' [The Works of L. Seifullina and her Critics], *Novy Mir*, 1925, no. 10; L. Reisner, 'Protiv literaturnogo banditizma' [Against Literary Banditry], *Zhurnalist* [Journalist], 1926, no. 1.

31 K. Radek, Introduction, *Sob. soch.*, p. 18.

32 N. Smirnov, 'An Irresistible Image', *Vosp.*, p. 144.

33 L. Nikulin, *Years . . .*, p. 189.

34 V. Rozhdestvensky, 'The Youth . . .', *Vosp.*, pp. 40–1.

35 Story quoted in L. Seifullina, 'Larissa Reisner', p. 158.

36 V. Inber, 'Discipline . . .', *Vosp.*, pp. 196–7.

37   K. Radek, Introduction, *Sob. soch.*, p. 18.
38   V. Inber, 'Evolution . . .', p. 271.
39   Ibid., p. 282.
40   Ibid., p. 280.
41   V. Rozhdestvensky, 'The Youth . . .', *Vosp.*, p. 42.
42   A. Rothstein, 'Happy to Have Known Her . . .', *Vosp.*, p. 151.
43   L. Seifullina, 'Larissa Reisner', pp. 158–9, 162.
44   L. Nikulin, *Years . . .*, p. 189.
45   *Hamburg*, VUFKU film studios, 1926, directed by Ballyuzek, script by S. Schreiber and Y. Yanovsky.
46   A. Kollontai, 'Gorod pervykh "buntarei" ' [The Town of the First 'Rebels'], *Pravda*, 3 October 1918.

SELECT
BIBLIOGRAPHY

(including a representative, but limited, number
of Larissa Reisner's works)

G. Alakhverdov et al. (eds), *Kratkaya istoriya grazhdanskoi voiny v SSSR*
[A short history of the Civil War in the USSR], Moscow, 1960.

G. Ambernadi et al. (eds), *Oktyabrskie stranitsy* [Pages of October],
Moscow, 1970.

A. Balabanova, *My Life*, Hamish Hamilton, London, 1938.

A. Blok, *Complete Collected Works*, Vol 6, Moscow, 1962.

J. Bradley, *Allied Intervention in Russia*.

Dokumenty vneshnei politiki SSSR [Documents of USSR Foreign Policy],
Vols i and v, Moscow, 1959.

I. Ehrenburg, *First Years of the Revolution, 1918–21* (trans. A. Bostock
and Y. Kapp), Macgibbon Kee, London, 1962.

Yu. Gerasimov et al. (eds), *Zapiski otdela rukopisei* [Notes of the
Manuscript Department of the Lenin Library], Vols 27 and 29,
Moscow, 1965 and 1967.

O.D. Golubeva et al. (ed), *Russkie sovetskie pisateli prozaiki* [Russian
Soviet Prose-writers], Vol 7, Leningrad, 1972.

G. Haupt and J.J. Marie (eds), *Makers of the Russian Revolution*, Allen
& Unwin, London, 1974, pp. 206–7.

I. Ilinskii, 'Granyonyi talant' [A Cut-glass Talent'], *Pechat i revolyutsiya*
[Press and Revolution], 1926, no 3.

Vera Inber, *Complete Works*, Vol IV, Moscow 1966.

———— , 'Larisa Reisner', *Krasnaya Nov*, 1927, no. 2.

H. Kapur, *Soviet Russia and Asia 1917–27*, Michael Joseph, London,
1966.

A. Kollontai, *Iz moei zhizni i raboty* [From My Life and Work], Moscow,
1974.

A.P. Konstantinov, *F.F Ilin-Raskolnikov*, Leningrad, 1964.

M.D. Konyushenko (ed), *Pravda stavshaya legendoi* [Truth Become
Legend], Moscow, 1969.

V.I. Lenin, *Complete Collected Works*, 4th edn, Vol 36, Moscow, 1957.

W. Lerner, *Karl Radek: The Last Internationalist*, Stanford University Press, California, 1970.

R. Levine-Meyer, *Inside German Communism* (ed. D. Zane Mairowitz), Pluto, London, 1977.

Yu. Libedinskii, *Sovremenniki* [Contemporaries], Moscow, 1958.

A. Neuberg, *Armed Insurrection* (trans. Quintin Hoare), New Left Books, London, 1977.

L. Nikulin, *Gody nashei zhizni* [Years of Our Life], Moscow, 1966.

———, *14 mesyatsev v Afganistane* [14 Months in Afghanistan], Moscow, 1923.

B. Pasternak, *Stikhotvoreniya i poemy* [Verses and Poems], Moscow, 1965.

'Pisma Larisy Reisner' [Larissa Reisner's Letters], *Novy Mir* [New World], No. 10, 1963, p. 205.

K. Radek, *Portrety i pamflety* [Portraits and Pamphlets], Moscow, 1934.

———, 'Larisa Reisner', in 'Deyateli SSSR i Oktyabrskoi Revolyutsii' [Activists of the USSR and the October Revolution], in *Entsiklopedicheskii slovar Russkogo Bibliograpficheskogo Instituta Granat* [Encyclopaedia of the Granat Russian Bibliographical Institute], 7th edn, Moscow, 1927–9.

F. Raskolnikov, *Kronstad i Petrograd v godu 1917* [Kronstadt and Petrograd in 1917], Moscow, 1923.

I. Reisner, *Afghanistan*, Moscow, 1929.

L. Reisner, *Sobranie sochinenii* [Collected Works], Moscow/Leningrad, 1928.

———, *Izbrannoe* [Selected Works], (ed. A. Naumova), Moscow, 1965.

———, 'Zhenskie tipy Shekspira: Ofelia i Kleopatra' [Shakespeare's Female Characters: Ophelia and Cleopatra], *Nauka i zhizn* [Science and Life], nos. 25 and 34, Riga, 1913.

———, 'Putevye zametki' [Traveller's Notes], *Izvestiya*, 12 November 1920.

———, '25 oktyabrya v Rige' [October 25 in Riga], *Izvestiya*, 14 November 1920.

———, 'Kak otvalivaetsya pushistyi khvost' [How the Bushy Tail Falls Off], *Izvestiya*, 14 November 1920. (Manuscript from Andrew Rothstein.)

———, 'Heroic Sailors of the Russian Revolution' (trans. A. Rothstein),

Communist Review, no. 1, May 1920.

———, *Afghanistan*, State Publishing House, Moscow/Leningrad, 1925.

———, *Hamburg At the Barricades, and Other Writings on Weimar Germany* (trans. and ed. R. Chappell), Pluto, London, 1977.

———, *Ugol, zhelezo i zhivye lyudi* [Coal, Iron and Living People], Moscow/Leningrad, 1925.

———, 'Protiv literaturnogo banditizma' [Against Literary Banditry], *Zhurnalist* [Journalist], 1926, no. 1.

M. Reisner, *Sudebnyi protses Karla Libknekhta protiv russkogo tsarya* [Karl Liebknecht's Trial Against the Russian Tsar], Ryazan, 1925.

———, *Russkii absolyutism i evropeiskaya reaktsiya* [Russian Absolutism and European Reaction], St Petersburg, 1906.

———, *Teoriya L.N. Petrazhistkogo marksisma i sotsialnoi ideologii*, [L.N. Petrazhitsky's Theories on Marxism and Social Ideology], Moscow, 1908.

———, *L. Andreev i ego sotsialnaya ideologiya* [L. Andreev and His Social Ideology], Moscow, 1909.

———, *Gosudarstvo. Posobie k lektsiyam po obshchemu ucheniyu o zakone* [The State. A Textbook of Lectures on General Law Studies], St Petersburg, 1912.

———, *Bog i birzha. 6 revolyutsionnykh pes* [God and the Stock Exchange, 6 Revolutionary Plays], Moscow, 1921.

R. Rhodes James, *Churchill. A Study in Failure, 1900–39*, Weidenfeld & Nicolson, London, 1970.

A. Rothstein, *When Britain Invaded Russia*, Journeyman Press, London, 1979.

G. Ryklin, *Esli pamyat ne izmenyaet* [If My Memory Doesn't Deceive Me], Moscow, 1968.

L. Seifullina, *Complete Collected Works*, Vol. 4, Moscow, 1969.

———, 'Alyosha', in *Prostye rasskazy* [Simple Stories], Moscow, 1928.

Lidia Seifullina v vospominaniyakh sovremennikov [Lydia Seifullina Remembered by Her Contemporaries], Moscow, 1961.

V. Serge, *Year One of the Revolution* (trans. and ed. Peter Sedgwick), Allen Lane/Penguin, London, 1972.

V. Shklovskii, 'Bessmyslneishaya smert' [A Senseless Death], in *Gamburgskie schety* [The debts of Hamburg], Leningrad, 1928, pp. 60–1.

N. Smirnov, 'Pamyati Larisy Reisner' [Memories of Larissa Reisner], *Novy Mir* [New World], 1926, no. 23.

E. Solovei, 'Rudin', *Neva*, 1957, no. 3.

L. Sosnovskii, 'V pamyati Larisa Reisner' [In Memory of Larissa Reisner], in *Lyudi Nashego Vremeni* [People of Our Time], Moscow, 1927.

R. Stites, *The Women's Liberation Movement in Russia*, Princeton University Press, Princeton, 1978.

N. Sukhanov, *The Russian Revolution, 1917* (trans. J. Carmichael), Oxford University Press, London, 1955.

Yu. Tomashevskii (ed), *Larisa Reisner v vospominaniyakh sovremennikov* [Larissa Reisner Remembered by Her Contemporaries], Moscow, 1969.

R. Ullman, *Intervention and the War*, Princeton University Press, Princeton, 1961.

I. Vasileva, *V. Rozhdestvenskii, ocherk zhizni i tvorchestva* [V. Rozhdestvensky, A Brief Account of His Life and Work], Leningrad, 1983.

Vestnik kommunisticheskoi akademii [Herald of the Communist Academy], Moscow 1928. (Biography of M.A. Reisner.)

F. Volkov, *Secrets From Whitehall and Downing Street* (trans. D. Hagen and K. Judelson), Moscow, 1986.

A. Voronskii, *Literaturnye Zapisi* [Literary Memoirs], Moscow, 1926.

G. Yakubovskii, 'Sochineniya L. Seifullinoi i ee kritiki' [The Works of L. Seifullina And Her Critics], *Novy Mir*, 1925, no. 10.

S. Zhitomirskaya, in 'Muzyka revolyutsii; po stranitsam rukopisei Larisy Reisner' [The Music of the Revolution: From the Pages of Larissa Reisner's Manuscripts], *Literaturnaya gazeta* [Literary Gazette], 21 May 1975.

INDEX

The series VIRAGO PIONEERS was launched in April 1986 to considerable acclaim:

'New assessments, useful to students and writers . . . each author setting her own idiosyncratic pace and tone'
– Victoria Glendinning, *Guardian*

'Virago should be applauded for setting such a high standard'
– Ann Roper, *Irish Times*

GEORGE ELIOT
Jennifer Uglow

One of the most brilliant writers of her day, George Eliot (1819–1880) was also one of the most talked about. Born Mary Ann Evans in the Midlands, she lost her faith and her family in a lonely struggle for learning. She lived – unmarried – with George Lewes from 1854 until his death in 1878: intellectual and independent, she had the strength of spirit to defy polite society with her highly unorthodox private life. So why did she apparently deny her fictional heroines the same opportunities? In this detailed and thought-provoking appraisal of her life and work, Jennifer Uglow explores George Eliot's ambivalent attitude to choice and change, especially for women, and illustrates how Eliot confronts the inner tensions of central images of Victorian life, such as class allegiance and the woman's role, to create a vision of a more generous way of life inspired by the imagination and the power of feeling.

JULIA MARGARET CAMERON
Amanda Hopkinson

Julia Margaret Cameron (1815–79) was in her late forties
when she was given a camera by her daughter. Within two
years she had developed her hobby into a fine art and had
begun to establish for herself a style and reputation all her
own. Mocked and patronised by the press and photographic
societies, she nevertheless prided herself on her deliberate
opposition to the prevailing conventions of her fellow
professionals. She experimented continually in order to obtain
unique and often intensely dramatic effects, specialising in
portraits and posed groups of allegorical, romantic and
Shakespearean subjects. Friends were what interested her
most, and they inspired some of the finest portraits ever taken
– of the writers Tennyson, Carlyle and Longfellow; the actress
Ellen Terry; artists Holman Hunt and G.F. Watts; scientists
John Herschel and Charles Darwin. Although Julia Margaret
Cameron and her work are regularly mentioned in books on
the history of photography, Amanda Hopkinson is the first
writer to set her work within the context of her time and circle,
and to give her the artistic and feminist appraisal she deserves.

EMILY DICKINSON
Helen McNeil

Today Emily Dickinson (1830–86) is gaining her deserved place alongside Walt Whitman as one of the two great American poets of the nineteenth century. From 1854 until her death, she lived almost exclusively in the small New England town of Amherst, a recluse who saw only ten of her 1,700 or so poems published in her lifetime. She remained largely unacknowledged until the publication of her *Complete Poems* in 1955. Now, in the centenary year of her death, Helen McNeil brilliantly assesses the grounds for and the meaning of her belated recognition. She argues that not only was Dickinson's reclusiveness a strategy for asking forbidden questions, but that the absence of a readership during her lifetime gave her poetry its unique freedom and stature. In an era when women were encouraged to write only so long as they wrote badly or sentimentally, Dickinson's isolation permitted her to decide for herself what poetry could be about and what kind of language it could use. In this impressive study of her life and work, Helen McNeil both celebrates her individuality and shows how the English poetic tradition is altered by an understanding of Dickinson's accomplishment.